Purposeful
PARENTING

ENDORSEMENTS

There are plenty of parenting books that will tell you to love your children even in the tough times but in *Purposeful Parenting*, Jean Barnes tells us how to love them and how to transform the challenges into life-changing events for our children. She goes beyond the "what to do" to the "why to do it" while guiding us to inject purpose and meaning into the life of each child. This is so rich, and you will be such a better parent for integrating the principles into how you are raising your kids.

—Stephen Arterburn
Founder and Chairman of New Life Ministries
Host of the #1 nationally syndicated Christian counseling talk show
New Life Live! and host of *New Life TV* (tv.newlife.com)
Founder of Women of Faith Conferences
Nationally known public speaker
Bestselling author with over 8,000,000 books in print

I wish I had *Purposeful Parenting* when I first became a parent. The wisdom, insight, and practical lessons found within this book will put you light-years ahead in your parenting. Not only will it empower you as a parent, but it will help create a lasting legacy in your kids. If I could read just one book this year on parenting this would be it!

—Pastor Tommy Hilliker
Pastor of Membership at Saddleback Church

Parenting is the highest and best of all roles, and we are all so unprepared for it. Jean Barnes has written a thoughtful and yet practical book to resource you. Not to be missed.

—John Townsend, Ph.D.
New York Times bestselling author of *Boundaries*
Leadership expert and psychologist
Founder, Townsend Institute of Leadership and Counseling

You can be the parent you've always wanted to be—the parent God wants and your kids need, the parent with a purpose. Your life at home with your kids can be calmer, clearer, healthier, and happier today, starting right now.

—Dr. Jill Hubbard
New Life Live Radio

Purposeful PARENTING

Six Steps to Bring Out the Best in Your Kids

JEAN S. BARNES

Love when it's hard to like,

turn chaos to calm,

find sanity in stress,

bring clarity from confusion,

discipline without guilt,

and never give up.

Published in association with the Literary Agency of Dupree Miller & Associates, Dallas, Texas, and New York, New York.

Destiny Image Publishers
P.O. Box 310, Shippensburg, PA 17257-0310
"Promoting Inspired Lives"

This book and all other Destiny Image, Revival Press, MercyPlace, Fresh Bread, Destiny Image Fiction, and Treasure House books are available at Christian bookstores and distributors worldwide.

Cover design by: Prodigy Pixel.

For more information on foreign distributors, call 717-532-3040.

Reach us on the Internet: www.destinyimage.com

ISBN 13 TP: 978-0-7684-0677-1
ISBN 13 Ebook: 978-0-7684-0678-8

For Worldwide Distribution, printed in the U.S.A.

1 2 3 4 5 6 7 8 / 19 18 17 16 15

DEDICATION

For my sons,
Thomas and Michael Van Dyck,
who have grown up to be the men
I dreamed they would be,
men who are pursuing their purpose and passion
to make the world a better place.

SIX GUIDING PRINCIPLES FOR YOU—SIX GUIDING STEPS FOR THEM

1. Love unconditionally because love is the tonic that cures all and covers all.

2. Discipline because you care to get things right.

3. Pursue passion and purpose because finding your mission and message matters.

4. Develop character because tending the heart shapes their souls.

5. Grow in responsibility because owning up is growing up.

6. Persevere to the end because going on keeps you strong.

CONTENTS

Yet I am always with you;
you hold me by the right hand.

Psalm 73:23

WE ALL NEED HELP

Every day, I talk with people who struggle with their jobs, marriages, certain relationships, and creative endeavors and dreams, and I'm reminded life is challenging at best. It's so easy to feel stuck and entrenched in difficulty much of the time.

No wonder so many people want an escape, to get away and be saved from trouble and challenge, especially when it comes to the burdens and vulnerabilities felt in parenting. Raising the next generation is not for the faint of heart. In fact, it's downright daunting in today's world.

Everyone can identify with having been a child and the innocence and smallness that goes with it, especially, as ironic as it seems, when you're the parent. Yet even when adults are overly pressured with life and may have given up hope for themselves, they maintain hope for their children. They hope somehow life will be better for their kids, they hope even while striving and struggling to hang in there, even when weary. Too often, though, the gulf between what one hopes and wishes for their children, and their own resiliency to make it happen, seems to ever widen.

When I was pregnant with my first child, more than eighteen years ago, I became keenly aware of this and how touchy new parents can be. I positioned myself defensively. I wanted to guard against my lack of assuredness in the newly crowned role of Mom, but even this was mixed with an air of proud expectancy. I was like a child trotting off for the first time in Father's oversized shoes, exultant and unsure at the same time. Questions of anticipation swirled through my mind: *What type of parent might I be? How will my child respond? How will my child be regarded and known and someday contribute to the human race? Do I have what it takes to give my children all they need to thrive?*

In the meantime, many of the other new parents I met rattled off the latest child-rearing tactics they'd heard. They beamed about their child sleeping through the night or gaining the appropriate weight. The high expectations I had of my own parenting skills just got higher.

So I listened and worked at learning what it takes to be a parent, and by the start of the school-age years, I'd mastered all the early baby care tasks, the developmental milestones of guiding a child to walk and talk. That gave me a certain confidence, as most parents get at this point.

And then you relax (a little) and marvel at how surely brilliant and clever your child is. You are in the afterglow of getting past all the fundamentals of infancy, and you think, *This is going to be okay. We're walking. We're talking. Parenting is surely a love relationship and a miracle of God.*

Then your children move from moment-by-moment care at home to the larger world of the classroom.

New realities set in, comparison, for one, a big one. Parental fantasies and all those hopes and dreams are now replaced by realities: there are new goals to achieve, there's the treadmill to mount of measuring up—and that treadmill's set at quite a steep incline, moving faster and faster. Any mom or dad who walks the halls of a school or attends an ice cream social with other parents knows the grind. There's constant chatter about how their kids are fitting in or not, doing well or not, getting along. Or not.

All that confidence gained as a new parent suddenly erodes. Now you're not so sure of anything. Are you doing this parenting thing right? Are you really helping your kids or hurting them?

You don't have to question your every move as a parent, or feel lost, stressed, guilty, spent, and unsure. You don't have to stay stuck and crumbling in that place, fallen into that widened gap between what you always hoped for your child and the disappointing realities.

Life does not have to be a defeatist journey.

You can be the parent you always wanted to be, the parent God wants and your kids need, the parent with a purpose. Your life at home with your kids can be calmer, clearer, healthier, and happier today, starting right now.

That is, once you know what things to let go, what things to hold onto, and what steps and principles you need to get past the hard parts, the dry days, the bleak and unbearable. Life can be better beginning at home, in childhood, and in raising children, for that is where most of our troubles begin—in what we got or didn't as we started out in life, how we were enabled or not to go out into a hard and unforgiving world with healing love and forgiveness.

Jean Barnes knows all the right interventions and has a lifetime of experience in helping people find love and forgiveness. She's been one of the parents who at all those school event settings listened to every parent's minute detailed concern for a child. She's lovingly listened as part of her professional servanthood, and lovingly helped both parent and child.

I'm so keenly aware of what a gift this is for parents and children. Now that my youngest eagerly heads for middle school and pre-teen puberty (a topic for another book all unto itself), I'm so grateful for the investment educational psychologists like Jean make, along with fellow parents, and the community to help children thrive. And as Jean will tell you and I see firsthand every day, if we are going to strive and survive, we need this community, help, and encouragement.

The communities Jean Barnes has been part of have been lucky to have her experienced wisdom and championing spirit. I wish she had been part of my team the past twelve to seventeen years! Her optimism, skill, knowledge, and experience seep through the pages of what she empowers children and parents to do. In *Purposeful Parenting*, she gives moms and dads the tools they need for their most important job—helping children grow in love and grace, allowing parents and children alike to thrive.

Jean's heart extends to us single moms as well. Having been a single mom as well, she understands what stops us and gets us stuck, and what makes life hard and dry or challenging. Yet she is unwilling to leave anyone in that no-man's-land between hoping and wishing, and realizing and attaining.

Jean's track record of showing us how life can be better and brighter begins with her philosophy of six essential practices for success. For anything in life, there are things you can do that are positive and good; but for the best results, there are essential things that are more productive and effective, most powerful and healthy and life-giving in every way. I love how Jean observes how it is the same with God and the church; there are things you can do on purpose, with purpose that are good and lawful, as the apostle Paul says in First Corinthians 6:12, but not necessarily helpful.

Jean tunes you in to what's helpful, healthful, productive, effective, powerful, and life-giving. She will help you be a better parent and help you and your children grow in grace and love to thrive as a family and as individuals. She will renew hope in you that life can be good. And she will point you in the direction of what you know to be true but need to have cemented into your heart, so you can live as God created you to—and with him at the helm, everything is better.

Jean understands and unlocks the steps for you too, of all that can be.

DR. JILL HUBBARD
New Life Live! Radio

PARENTING TAKES THREE

…because you're not born a parent

I remember the morning I asked Sammy, a six-year-old in the first grade, how things were going. He was so bright, but couldn't seem to complete a single assignment. I was concerned, and then, at his reply, surprised.

"Awful!" he lamented. "The car won't start, we don't have money to pay the rent, and my mother forgot to take the pill!"

No wonder Sammy couldn't finish anything. He carried to school a bag of worries that belonged to his mother. What he needed instead was a sack lunch for his hungry tummy, guiding principles for his searching mind, and certain assurances for his troubled soul to get through the circumstances of the day. Sammy needed something more too, that something-something that tips the scales. He needed that thing I call can-do power and can-do spirit. He needed to know he was the best he could be, and that was enough because God had a purpose and place for him in this life.

The sense of place in this world is that can-do spirit; it is the determination that says, "I can do this. I will do this. Watch me do this." It's that mindset made up of the key ingredients found in these guiding principles: confidence and capability, responsibility and belief, purpose and passion, love, and perseverance. It's what gets you through the tough times and lets you enjoy the good. It's what brings about the positive and progressive in not only yourself but others too, and not just for school or a job but in life.

Sammy wasn't the only one missing some can-do spirit and sense of purpose. His mom needed it too. She could no more fix a simple sack lunch for Sammy than she could digest her full plate of all that was difficult in her life—divorce, a drug-addicted ex-husband, overwhelming bills, and loneliness. She needed things for her mind, body, and spirit: some rest, good health, clear support, guiding principles, certain assurances.

Every one of us needs these things as people, and even more as parents. Your situation may be much less dramatic than Sammy and his mom's, and yet you may be reeling just as much, in need of rest, health, help, and certitudes. At times, any one of these things can be a challenge to possess. Daily living can wear away these things, and with them our energy to parent, leaving us discouraged and feeling a failure as a mom or dad. We were certain the parenting thing would come to us so naturally. We bought into the myth that we're born parents, that parenting comes to us as a second nature, just like eating or sleeping, breathing in and breathing out, that it should be natural and if not easy, at least not this hard. Too many of us have bought into another myth too—that we can or should be able to do this on our own.

PARENTING TAKES MORE THAN YOU

The truth is not one of us was ever meant to parent on our own. Not one.

I can say that because I started as a mom who was married with two little boys. But things were hard. Being married doesn't mean you automatically have someone to help you parent. It doesn't guarantee parenting will be easy. It got more difficult for me when my dream for raising my family in a traditional way dissolved with my marriage. I went through a divorce I never wanted, and for several years was on my own parenting two young sons, a new kind of hard having to be both mother and father, breadwinner and homemaker.

When I met a wonderful man and remarried, parenting wasn't any easier. You can be married to a good spouse and fellow parent, yet feel alone for whatever reason including travel, detachment (temporary or more constant), distraction, and—when things get off track—infidelity. I dealt with all those things, and they were a different kind of hard because I thought I had a spouse helping me parent, and I did…sometimes, and sometimes not. When "not," the gaps felt wider and deeper. I had learned how much better it is to parent in partnership.

Still, I pushed on to do everything I knew to give my sons the best home and most opportunity possible. I studied and learned how to help raise children right, not only for myself but as a profession, and for others. Still, I heard and saw how hard parenting can be every day. As a teacher in the classroom for more than ten years, and school counselor and psychologist for more than thirty-five years, I heard parenting stories of "harder" every day. I worked with children and parents from all kinds of situations and households, and every child would tell you growing up is hard, and every parent would agree that raising up is hard too, especially when you are alone or feel alone, when you have typical stresses like kids who tattle or fail to clean their room, or more dramatic troubles like a husband with an addiction or a child acting out and at-risk.

What I saw, experienced, and studied was that in every situation, and especially some more than others, parenting is just plain hard, and parenting is never possible to do really, really well, ideally, on your own. Even the best parents, the ones who seem to have it together, the ones whose kids seem well-behaved and happy, would tell you there are times you really need superpowers for the job of raising kids well: x-ray vision and the ability to stretch, deflect barbs, and fly.

You understand. You're probably nodding your head at this point. There are so many demands, there is so much energy required of a parent, that help is needed: Support. Reinforcement. Relief. Collaboration. Cooperation. A co-pilot. And not just that, but all of it in spades, supersized, superpowered. In fact, getting that kind of help is probably why you picked up this book. Intuitively, you already know you can't do this parenting thing in the very best way on your own.

God knows too.

GOD DESIGNED FOR YOU TO HAVE HELP

From the beginning, in the Garden, God gave Adam a helpmate—Eve.[1] That is why through God's story, our story, really, in the Bible, he is always showing us the idyll, a model that involves assistance, support, and a helper. God gave Moses a brother to hold up his arms when they were weary.[2] He had Noah bring the animals two by two into the ark for starting over.[3] He had Jesus leave us the Holy Spirit for comfort and intercession.[4] And Jesus had his disciples go in pairs to do their very best work.[5]

God designed a whole system with helpers to keep us going in this life—in the body, with its many parts, and in the church with its teachers and preachers, song leaders and stewards. It's so interesting to me that in the chapter just before God talks about love in the Bible, he talks about this need for a system of many parts and people (see 1 Corinthians 12:11-25).

> *The body is a unit, though it is made up of many parts; and though all its parts are many, they form one body. ...If the foot should say, "Because I am not a hand, I do not belong to the body," it would not for that reason cease to be part of the body. And if the ear should say, "Because I am not an eye, I do not belong to the body," it would not for that reason cease to be part of the body. If the whole body were an eye, where would the sense of hearing be? If the whole body were an ear, where would the sense of smell be? But in fact God has arranged the parts in the body, every one of them, just as he wanted them to be* (1 Corinthians 12:12,15-18 NIV 1984).

This is where, as a parent and a Christian and someone who has devoted my life to family counseling and psychology, I've been amazed that both God's design and what psychologists call "best practices" say exactly the same thing.

The Ideal Family System

Evidence from a multitude of studies and research shows clearly that children who have a family system of two loving, committed parents thrive.[6] These children have confidence and develop a good sense of self, which frees them to think beyond themselves, succeeding in work and other pursuits. Their home lives may vary, some from the city or suburbs and others the countryside, some rich and some poor, but they have a three-pronged family system in common: a mother and father who are married and love one another, experiencing intimacy and spiritual growth as individuals and a couple and with God. The parents are committed to raising children in unison, as a team, reinforcing one another in the important areas like character, how to love and persevere, live their purpose and passion, and practice discipline and responsibility. The siblings have a strong relationship for learning to negotiate, compromise, and compete with one another—the stage for rehearsing how to relate to others through life.

Some of the reasons for success from such a system are obvious: Two parents in disagreement present confusion to a child. A home split by discord can make for a fractured sense of safety and self. It's difficult for one parent, alone, to earn enough, and have enough time and energy to support others. One parent can sometimes slip and fall, get sick and tired—and where is the relief, the stand-in, the support? One parent cannot always be there. One parent cannot be everything, do all, and go everywhere at all times. Only a true superhero can save the day in some of these situations.

Does that mean if you're a single parent, you're doomed? Or if you're in a marriage where your spouse is difficult or distant, that you can't do this? Or if you're divorced, you can never raise a child who thrives? Am I saying you should feel badly or less-than, inadequate or "not enough," if you're on your own? That you're not ideal and can't be the parent God made just for your child?

Not at all!

This whole book came about because I believe in every parent's can-do. I believe in every parent being the best they can be to bring out the best in their child. I've seen parents in all kinds of situations become successful. A first step is understanding your family system, identifying where you need help and where you may already have it without realizing it.

What Is Your Family System?

Whether you've thought about it before or not, you already have a family system. There's you and your child already forming the system. Now who else is in the picture? Look hard at this and put it on paper. Write down the heading "My Family System." Now answer:

- **Who is in my immediate family?** (List every guardian and every dependent.)

- **Who helps me parent?** (List every person who acts as a support and helps you reinforce rules and discipline or boundaries and values.)

- **Who picks up the slack** when I'm sick or need to be away from my child, or need help getting my kids to and from school or events? (List the people you call on for backup and support.)

- **Who do I include** in celebrations like birthdays or holidays? (List the people included in every intimate gathering.)

- **Who do I call** in trauma or emergency, when I need a listening ear or help? (List anyone who's got your back.)

- **Who has been there** to tend to everyday matters like picking up the mail, mowing the lawn, watching the pets, getting my dry cleaning?

Does what you see on this paper surprise you? There may be people you never thought of before who help you along. You may have a bigger family system than you knew: a friend, relative, someone from church, or teacher who supports you and is there for you. Would you say any of these people are "like family"? Why or why not? Does this encourage you? Or, on the other hand, does the paper you're holding look empty? Are you also feeling that way inside, with too many blanks after some of these questions?

God knows, he never wanted that either.

God Gives Us Himself

Whether you're on your own or surrounded by support, God meant for you to begin life, and parenting, with him by your side.

He is your father and you are his child (2 Corinthians 6:16,18). He is the center of your family system, whatever that may be. Just as the wheel needs a hub upon which its spokes are fixed to roll, God is there in the middle of everything: the mess, the miracles, and the everyday matters. Whatever spokes of support you have, one parent or two or a village, God promises to stay and keep you going.

A STEP TOWARD A BETTER FAMILY SYSTEM
Call on Your Heavenly Superpower

The God who made you knows you, and your child, and cares about every detail of your life. Keep this prayer from Psalm 139:1-18,23-24 on an index card to carry with you, a reminder of how the God who made the heavens and the earth knows you and all that is best for you. He is always with you and will make a way for you through any, every parenting challenge.

You have searched me, Lord, and you know me. You know when I sit and when I rise; you perceive my thoughts from afar. You discern my going out and my lying down; you are familiar with all my ways. Before a word is on my tongue you, Lord, know it completely. You hem me in behind and before, and you lay your hand upon me. Such knowledge is too wonderful for me, too lofty for me to attain.

Where can I go from your Spirit? Where can I flee from your presence? If I go up to the heavens, you are there; if I make my bed in the depths, you are there. If I rise on the wings of the dawn, if I settle on the far side of the sea, even there your hand will guide me, your right hand will hold me fast. If I say, "Surely the darkness will hide me and the light become night around me," even the darkness will not be dark to you; the night will shine like the day, for darkness is as light to you.

For you created my inmost being; you knit me together in my mother's womb. I praise you because I am fearfully and wonderfully made; your works are wonderful, I know that full well. My frame was not hidden from you when I was made in the secret place, when I was woven together in the depths of the earth. Your eyes saw my unformed body; all the days ordained for me were written in your book before one of them came to be. How precious to me are your thoughts, God! How vast is the sum of them! Were I to count them, they would outnumber the grains of sand—when I awake, I am still with you.

Search me, God, and know my heart…and lead me in the way everlasting.

That means you can call on him for whatever you face, whatever family system you've come from or find yourself in right now, because he will fill you with can-do power, the strength you need when you're weary, and the strength he'll exercise for you when you can't seem to summon it on your own (2 Corinthians 12:9-10 and 13:9). He's not just talking about strength to soldier on, either, but to soar (Isaiah 40:29-31). That is his promise to you, his assurance so you can live and parent well. He also gives additional assurances for:

- **daily provision** (Matthew 6:25-30, 2 Corinthians 9:8, Philippians 4:6-7, and 1 Peter 5:6-7);

- **companionship and being there**—he will never abandon nor forsake you (Deuteronomy 31:6 and Hebrews 13:5);

- **purpose** (Jeremiah 29:11);

- **healing** (Matthew 9:22, Acts 3:16, and James 5:14-15); and

- **help to overcome whatever is in your way**—trials, troubles, and temptations right here, right now (John 16:33, 1 John 4:4, and 1 John 5:4-5).

He promises to go with you through every little thing, and every big thing too: the times you're so tired and still need to not only get yourself ready for work and the kids off to school, the times you're discouraged because your son keeps fibbing or your daughter keeps messing with her sister's room. Those are the times it's easy to think, *My kids don't need a mom or dad. They need a superhero.*

That is just what God is, a superhero always at work, always on the job (Psalm 121:4). He gives you ways to tap into his superpowers too:

- **In prayer**, you receive his listening ear and an opportunity to release your cares on him (1 John 5:14-15). At any given moment, he gives his presence (Jeremiah 29:14 and James 4:8). At your request, he provides guidance and answers (Psalm 37:1-4, James 4:2-4, and 1 John 3:22-24).

- **In Bible reading**, he shows his will and ways, gives practical advice, stories, and examples of what works (and doesn't) to resolve conflict and navigate the circumstances of the day. For instance, he doesn't just say "be good," but explains how and how it works: "Do to others as you would have them do to you (Luke 6:31 and Matthew 7:12); and, what some people today call "karma" is actually his ancient wisdom, "Give generously, for your gifts will return to you later" (Ecclesiastes 11:1 TLB).

- **In fellowship** with others who follow him, he gives you encouragement, inspiration, and motivation to be better (Hebrews 10:23-27). You also receive his guidance through wisdom, correction and support, mentoring, or as God puts it, iron sharpening iron (Proverbs 27:17). In fellowship, you get one more thing too—meaningful relationships.

God Gives Us Others

While God designed the ideal model for your family system and wants you to have that, he knew not everyone would get it. We live in a fallen world. Marriages dissolve. Spouses leave or die. Relationships suffer discord. So while God made everything good to begin with (the Bible tells us in Genesis 1:31), he also does the remarkable to remake it (Job 5:9). What's broken or damaged, he rebuilds, renews, restores. Where one family system may seem lacking, where some spokes on the wheel are missing, he fills in himself and gives us other supports.

"See," he tells us in Isaiah 43:19, "I am doing a new thing."

He did that even in how he sent Jesus to earth. He gave baby Jesus to a teenageD, engaged girl, whose fiancé easily could have abandoned her. But by plugging into the superpowers of God, that young girl, Mary, became a mom, and then she and Joseph became parents of the Savior of the world.

I'm sure they started out feeling not enough, less-than, even "bad" by the judgment of many in their community. But they became can-do parents. Despite poor beginnings, able to give Jesus only a manger for a bed, a life on the run from authorities, and the scorn of some neighbors for associating with the lowlife of the day (those transient shepherds), they raised a king.

They provided a loving home with two committed parents who knew the power of God. They understood that when a child is placed in a parent's arms and care, there are things parents need to know about the ideal parenting model: how much to feed the little one's stomach, and what to feed the child's soul, when to lay down the child for rest, and when to call him up for learning, creating, building, and doing what only he can do, following his purpose and passion in this world.

Mary and Joseph may not have known a thing about parenting, but they understood that from the time babies are born until the time they leave home, children learn how relations work at their parents' knees. Children see how people laugh, argue, share, confer, cry, comfort, yell, hug, and love one another and their neighbor and God. Children internalize these images and form a template for how to treat one other, communicate, and interact. They learn what healthy relationships look like and that is, in turn, what they model.

And something else Mary and Joseph discovered—parents can enlist helping hands and hearts.

God Gives Added Support

Since Mary was a virgin, and God the father, Joseph, in a way, was actually a stepparent or an adoptive father. He stepped up and stepped in to fill a role Jesus needed in an earthly father figure. In Jewish culture at that time, most men would have left Mary and been seen as righteous in doing so. But Joseph didn't. He stayed. He loved Mary and the baby she carried so much that he made them his. He looked out for their welfare, even finding that stable for Jesus's birth.

If Joseph could take on such a remarkable role in such a restrictive culture that otherwise would have scorned an unwed mother and her groom, imagine the different ways you can bring in parental support. Turn to your own family first.

- **Enlist grandparents.** More than 2.5 million grandparents have taken on the role of solely raising grandchildren.[7] What if you ask grandparents to help you financially or with lifts for the kids to and from school, or FOR their wisdom and all they've learned from experience. They can be your backup and give your children a bigger picture of the world. While "grandfamilies" may seem new, they're actually an original family system.

- **Become a multigenerational family.** According to the Pew Research Center analysis of the 2012 Census Bureau data, 18% of families in the United States today include parents, grandparents, and aunts and uncles too.[8] That's 28 million assorted family members pooling all their resources to live under the same roof because they otherwise couldn't function on their own. Some say the American economy that began failing in 2008 has brought about this pooling parenting effort. But living and functioning together is historically how many families have lived. Think of pioneers settling the West, immigrants settling America, generations and tribes under the same roofs and estates throughout Europe, Africa, and Asia—everyone in the family unit had a role in helping with daily chores, responsibilities, and needs from financial and passing along traditions and history, to reinforcing the tradition, values, rules, and boundaries.

- **Call upon the church to support you in teaching and training.** As early as possible, Mary and Joseph took Jesus to church and consecrated and dedicated him to the Lord (Luke 2:22-52). They brought him to church so much that once, when he was missing, they found him in a place so familiar to him that he was surprised they hadn't thought to look there first. "Didn't you know I had to be in my Father's house?" he asked his parents, standing in the tabernacle (Luke 2:49). That is where Jesus grew in wisdom and stature, in favor with God and man. How might you call on your faith community to help you, married or not, raise up your child in smarts and respect, in both God and others' favor?

However you choose to fashion it, your family can be made up of a system of supports because God never meant for you to go it alone as a parent, and he never meant for you to automatically know everything yourself to raise your child in the best way.

PARENTING TAKES PRACTICE

Not one of us is born knowing how to parent and how to give our children everything needed to thrive, so it's not lost on me that even Jesus's parents needed help and know-how. Think about it: God gave us a picture

A STEP TOWARD A BETTER FAMILY SYSTEM
Choose a Godparent

Cinderella and Sleeping Beauty had fairy godmothers, and Little Red Riding Hood had a grandmother. Even in fiction, parents have called in extra help.

One mom did something similar. After she and her husband adopted a baby boy, she suddenly found herself single again. She knew she needed help. She lived across the country from her family, so decided to create one with godparents. This mom wasn't Catholic and didn't make the arrangement legal, but called on a couple she loved from church to:

- Pray for her and her son.
- Share their common faith in Jesus. They went to church together and made it typical conversation to talk about where they saw God show up in their lives, and how to live more completely for him in different situations.
- Care for her child's well-being enough to secure his safety, health, peace, and opportunities. Sometimes that meant they kept her son when she had to work weekends. Other times they talked with him about making good choices. When he was applying for college, they helped with admission forms and scholarship applications.

Godparents weren't chosen on the basis of finances, athletic prowess, or glamour. Rather, they were people this mom could rely upon for support and as step-in, backup parents. "For more than twenty years they were the hands and heart of God to me and my son," she said, "offering nonjudgmental acceptance, unconditional love, stability, and role models."

Such practical and powerful help is better than any fairy tale, and can help parents otherwise alone make their own happily ever after.

of the ideal home life with even Jesus, and there he started with an unwed teen and a step-in dad. If ever there were two people who might have gone to a parent-teacher conference and said, "We don't know how to do this!" it might have been those two.

Had you or I been able to listen in on such a conference, you might have heard what I believe—in the beginning, no man or woman knows how to parent!

Not one of us, after all, is born a parent any more than we are born a bicycle rider or a scratch golfer. Having children may be as natural as taking a next breath, but being the parent you're created to be takes some tools and exercise, some experience. Just like learning to ride a bike took some knowledge of how to sit in the seat, balance your legs on the frame, and push the pedals, there are skills needed to parent. Just as practice riding that bike took trial and error, some spills and then sailing down the road, so does parenting—because parenting isn't something you *are*. It's something you *practice*.

I thought of this one day playing golf. I love golf, and took it up as a guilty pleasure and a form of exercise when my children were young. I thought, *I will become a golfer*. But early on I made some awful strokes and played embarrassingly. I didn't become a golfer by simply possessing the sticks or taking to the course. I didn't become a golfer by reading books about the sport either. I did read a lot, sought instruction, mentally rehearsed the ten steps to a perfect golf swing, and showed up to rounds with my friends. But that didn't make me a scratch golfer. It was practice, and practicing some more, and a commitment to keep on practicing.

For more than thirty years, I practiced. Sometimes I hunkered down and really focused on my strokes and my game, but most the time I just got out there and played. I loved the green and the camaraderie. I loved becoming a golfer. I loved thinking, *I can do this. I will do this. Watch me do this!* I loved taking one shot and then the next, and going round the green, taking each hole deliberately, purposefully one at a time.

Recently, I was golfing with a friend and I could feel her eyes studying my assessment of the shot, and then the shot itself. I stood at the tee, swung with confidence and force, and watched my ball sail down the green to land near the hole.

"You have a beautiful golf swing," my friend said. "It's so natural!"

I laughed and thanked her, but thought, *Other than the breath I took before making that swing, nothing about that stroke was natural!* The ease of that shot, the precision of landing the ball near the hole was practice, and experience, and intention and purposeful practice, more and more of it, years of it.

So it is with parenting. When you expect a child, you begin reading about the feeding and development, the needs, and best environment to create. You talk with friends and listen to experts on how to raise healthy, happy kids. You fill up on lots of advice and tips, determined to be the best parent possible, the one God wants and your baby needs.

Then you hold your child in your arms. *A miracle wrapped in skin,* you think. You feel so much love, so much desire to help this little being go into life with every good thing, every opportunity. And then your baby cries, wails, followed by screaming and food slinging, meltdowns and throw-up, pooping and peeing.

This is not what happens for just some parents or some children. It happens to everyone. Every child will stray and rebel at some point, test the limits and yours, devour your energy but refuse the meal you just slaved to fix. Every child can talk back now and then, but when you ask about the day—crickets, not a thing to say. All children can wear you out but refuse to sleep, keeping you from rest too. They can display brilliance and 100 percent concentration to figure out the latest gadget or game, but when it comes to a chore or homework assignment, seem unable to focus or finish. They become the center of your attention and then scatter it. They can give you every delight, but also your deepest agony. They can steal your heart, and then break it too.

Nothing prepares you for this. Nothing can floor you, stop you, and trip you up like the realities of raising a child. There's mess. There's mayhem. There's eventual maelstrom. You find yourself praying for a miracle because you think, *Without one, I can't do this!*

But you can.

With can-do spirit and intention and purpose you can tackle any next thing in your parenting path. That spirit is not something naturally given to some parents, and absent in others. Just like it takes practice and experience to be a cyclist and a scratch golfer, the can-do spirit of a parent comes from applying what psychologists and family counselors would call the best principles for:

- **loving** in ways your child learns to love;
- **disciplining** so that your child can be disciplined;
- **building** your character so that your kids develop theirs;
- **taking responsibility and teaching** it so your children can do for themselves;
- **discovering your passion and living with purpose,** and helping your children do likewise; and
- **continually saying, "I can do this.** I will do this. Watch me do this because I have a God-given purpose and passion and place in this world."

Developing this can-do spirit comes from exercising faith like a muscle, believing that God keeps his promises to stick with you through one challenge, and choosing to believe again that he will help you through the next circumstance too—until your faith and can-do spirit and purpose, like that muscle, can be relied upon again and again.

This muscle isn't something one parent gets and another doesn't. It's a muscle every parent can develop, whether you are a single parent or happily married, living in drama or what seems so ordinary, whether you face odds that seem insurmountable or issues that seem just blips in the road, like Johnny sneaking out to play when you've told him to stay home or Rachel staying up a few nights way past bedtime.

Every kind of parent and child needs can-do spirit and a sense of purpose. I'm reminded of this fact by another bright student of mine who concerned and surprised me. Little Lord Fauntleroy, as I secretly named him, was a cute, curly-headed fourth grader who couldn't have been more different or from more opposite circumstances than Sammy. Where Sammy showed signs of neglect, never having provision for lunch and often coming to school unkempt, Little Lord Fauntleroy (LLF) seemed as doted upon as his fictional namesake, the poor little rich boy in Frances Hodgson Burnett's novel who was spoiled with a never-ending supply of tailored velvet suits, chocolates, and playing cards.

My fourth grader wasn't dressed in expensive clothes or nibbling on candy and equipped with pricey playthings, but he was always clean and neat, his hair always combed, and he knew his manners, even if he didn't always exercise them. For all his signs of receiving lavished attention and guidance, however, my LLF was no different from Sammy in completing his schoolwork. LLF was bright. But at the end of each school day, he would pile all his books into a huge backpack and lug home the assignments he had somehow avoided finishing in class.

The next morning, however, unlike Sammy, LLF returned to school with every assignment completed.

That's a problem? you wonder.

Well, yes, it is. You see, LLF wasn't the one doing the schoolwork and he was learning, all right, but all the wrong things. He had grasped how to get out of any personal responsibility and to manipulate. He wasn't getting the know-how he needed from the assignments, or the adventure of trying and the fulfillment of achievement. He had begun down that slippery slope that was only going to make school tougher, but also "life on his own" a series of failures, discouragements, and downward spirals.

The problem was that neither LLF nor his mom, with all their right appearances, had any more can-do spirit than Sammy and his mother with all their wrong situations. In fact, Little Lord Fauntleroy's family system was as deficient as Sammy's.

In his family, LLF was calling the shots as much as Sammy was burdened with them. LLF had two parents living under the same roof, but neither was engaged with the family in a healthy way. The marriage was distant. LLF's mom sought from her son the attention she needed from her husband. She drew the boy's bath, gave him back rubs, served him breakfast in bed, and completed his homework.

Meanwhile, the boy's father was hard-working and busy with his career as a business executive—too busy, though, to pay attention to the guidance and occasional correction his son needed. For example, when LLF used his father's expensive tools and left them to ruin in the rain, there was plenty of yelling and berating afterward, but no other consequence or making use of what could have been a teachable moment for father and son about the rewards of responsibility.

So those tools weren't the only thing going to ruin. So was Little Lord Fauntleroy's character and drive, his sense of identity and ability to know: *I can do it. I will do this. Watch me do this.* And his mother and father were going to pay the cost of that along with him, becoming stressed and trying to do things for their son that he could do himself, creating a Little Lord Frankenstein who never fully develops and matures or has confidence for life.

Parenting doesn't have to be that way. You can love parenting just like I loved golfing, and you can become good at parenting just as anyone can become good at riding a bike. Your parenting can become natural and your kids can grasp important life lessons and those essential principles that help them work through the challenges and problems. You can steer your child down a good path, through any valley, over any mountain, just like the cyclist who learns how to balance and pedal and builds muscle and stamina and determines to keep the faith that all that forward motion gets you somewhere.

And just like a teenage mom and foster father were able to raise a king, you can raise a child who depends wholly on God and gives to the world out of that. You can possess can-do power and use it purposefully, intentionally so that your kids have the power too. You can be the best parent you can be, and it will bring out the best in them too.

Chapter 1

LOVE: MORE THAN A HUG

…because love is the tonic to cure all and cover all

Last summer, at our large family reunion, we lingered one evening at the dinner table. We'd spent the day swimming and boating, water tubing and water skiing on the lake, and now we'd just enjoyed a summer's feast. We were full of food and happy, and no one quite wanted to let go of that rare moment of everyone together and things being right. We kept nibbling at things, laughing, and telling stories.

Lori, cute, curly-haired, and a very grown-up six-year-old, decided she wanted to stay over at her grandmother's cottage.

"Pleeease," she begged her mom and then dad, who looked to each other, maybe a little surprised at first but then not.

They nodded to each other knowingly and smiled. I could almost read their thoughts, *Lori is becoming more independent with each passing day. Our little girl is growing up.*

"Okay," Mom said to Lori, who, bursting with joy, hopped up and down. "You have the clothes you came in to wear tomorrow morning. They're practically clean. You only had them on a few minutes before changing into your swimsuit and then shorts. Oh, and you have your towel and brush and things from after swimming." She smiled at Grandma, who winked back. "You're set."

"But, Mom, can't you take me to get my nightgown, my blanket, my pink pony—"

"You've got everything you need," Dad said. "Besides, it's a good ten minutes across the lake and ten minutes back but it's your bedtime now."

They went back and forth on this till finally Lori's bottom lip began to quiver. "Oh, pleeease? My toothbrush! My nightgown! My pink pony!"

"All right," her father said. "Go get your shoes and—"

Even as he gave permission, Lori sprinted to the long flight of stairs that lead to the pier, where she'd left her sandals. "Yeah, yeah, yeah," she said, scrambling down.

"Hurry," he called down to her. "Get your brother's swimsuit and come on now. Hurry up!"

Lori stopped on one of the stairs. "Dad!" she yelled, turning back. "Dad, I'm going as fast as I can!"

"Lori!" I could see and hear his frustration, that stern-bordering-on-angry tone every parent gets, feeling pushed by all the demands of getting their kids to bed on time, eating well, doing well—the million little things that feel so important in a day. Dad couldn't help but voice it either. "Don't talk in that tone of voice," he snapped.

Lori picked her way down the rest of the stairs in tears. She was trying to do the right thing and her dad still barked at her.

Later, after everyone drifted to where they were staying for the night, Lori's grandmother and I lounged in the living room to unwind before bedtime. Lori sat between us on the floor, braiding the mane of her pink pony, confiding as much in him, it seemed, as us.

"I don't know why such a happy day had to end with Dad being so angry," she said. "I was hurrying. I was *trying* to get my sandals. I wanted to be responsible like Dad and Mom always tell me." She looked up at us. "Why Mom would want me to stay over without my toothbrush, I will never understand…."

I could hear Lori parroting her mom now, a dental hygienist.

"She always says, 'Go brush your teeth,' and I already have my six-year molars and four permanent teeth—see." Lori grinned like a Cheshire cat at the pony that she planted squarely in front of her. She looked him in the eye as her smile faded. "If I don't brush my teeth, they will rot in my mouth! Besides, I was just doing everything they asked." Her voice trembled, signaling tears just beneath the surface. "I was *trying* to do everything right."

WHAT YOU WANT THEM TO REMEMBER

Trying to do everything right. It's what we're about as purposeful parents, and most of the time what our kids are about too. But all the niggling frustrations of the day get in the way. You want to give your children wisdom and know-how, discipline, character, responsibility, purpose, and perseverance. But in trying to impart these things, there are episodes. Tears! Melt-downs! Like Lori, wanting her pink pony and blanket, your kids may get stuck on some one thing, and then you get stuck on something else, and you clash.

Is that what we want them to remember? The snapping and barking to straighten up and fly right, to get their teeth brushed and get to bed on time? Or is it the love you have for them? The love they can carry into everything they are and do?

It's so important for your kids to have the essential ingredients needed to get them through life, and love is the most important, the tonic that cures all and covers all.

Love, after all, is where parenting begins and ends, right? Love is the glue. As the old standard song says, "The greatest thing you'll ever learn is to love and be loved in return."[1] It's what matters most, and what you want to remember (and what you want your kids to remember) at the end of the day, at the end of their lives. But in everyday life, both parents and kids can get stuck on the things that don't really matter, like how much you brushed your teeth or how fast you hurried. You can get so caught up on these things that you forget to reinforce, and they forget to remember, how much you love them. One of the most poetic passages of the Bible puts this truth beautifully:

> *If I speak in the tongues of men or of angels, but do not have love, I am only a resounding gong or a clanging cymbal. If I...can fathom all mysteries and all knowledge, and if I have a faith that can move mountains, but do not have love, I am nothing. If I give all I possess to the poor and give over my body to hardship that I may boast, but do not have love, I gain nothing* (1 Corinthians 13:1-3).

That is because love is not only the glue that holds things together. Love is the key that can move mountains, or at least your seven-year-old into, well, everything from doing his chores to achieving something like no one before him. Love can drive you to do the astounding, beyond brains and brawn, savvy and style, things that last and are remembered and affecting.

For example, a desire for more love, demonstrated by brotherhood and fellowship, is what drove the completely deaf Ludwig von Beethoven to work for twelve years on what's considered the best-known and greatest musical work in the Western Hemisphere, the "Ode to Joy," or Symphony No. 9.[2] Enduring love for his wife is what compelled the Indian emperor Shah Jahan to build one of the wonders of the world, the Taj Mahal (or "crown jewel" of palaces).[3] It was for love that King Edward VIII gave up the throne, abdicating as king of the United Kingdom in 1931, in order to marry divorceé Wallis Simpson.[4] Love is what drove Eric Liddell to run a race longer than he had trained for, defying the odds, to win the 1924 Olympic gold medal for the United Kingdom in the 400-meter race.[5]

Love does, indeed, change everything.

How Love Is Constant

No one reminds me more of just how transforming love can be than Benny. When we first met, Benny was four years old and crawling along the floor beneath a classroom table. He was in constant motion with minuscule attention span, one of the most extreme cases of attention deficit disorder (ADD) I've ever encountered, compounded by poor motor skills and coordination too. Benny couldn't get through even a short lesson without disrupting not only his education but that of the entire class. Yet his teacher couldn't ignore teaching all the other students just for Benny's constant, particular needs.

So Benny and I became well-acquainted. We began meeting on a regular basis. Quickly I could see that his high energy could drive even the most patient teacher or mom to wit's end. But Benny's mom knew how to keep her wits about her. I discovered how the day I met her in the hallway.

She was on her way to volunteer in Benny's classroom, and he was walking by my side to my office. The moment he saw her, Benny broke from my side to run into her arms, which were open wide. She grabbed him and raised him into a big bear hug.

Every time I saw them together, it was the same: exuberant hugs, lots of love. You couldn't help but notice how she began and ended every interaction with him in loving ways. She always demonstrated her love with not only the hugs, but pats on the arm, rub of the shoulder, a kiss on the top of the head. And she told him outright, "Love you, Benny."

What a blessing, the way she loves him, I thought. It wasn't just the hug. Love is so much more than hugs. It was that even in her frustrated moments and times she needed to discipline Benny and teach him things, she began and ended by showing and stating her love for him.

How Love Is Unconditional

Benny's mom loved him unconditionally, or as Dr. Ross Campbell says, "no matter what. No matter what the child looks like…. No matter what we expect him to be, and, most difficult, no matter how he acts. Unconditional love means we love the child even though at times we may detest the behavior."[6]

This kind of love is the most important thing you can give your child. Dr. Berry Brazelton, a pediatrician and author, explains that's because this kind of love is essential in building a sense of trust and belief in oneself.

When you love unconditionally, your children see that they are treasured and cherished. They develop an internal sense of their own preciousness, or, as the Bible puts it, how they are "fearfully and wonderfully made" (Psalm 139:14) for a purpose and on purpose—sensibilities that are the foundation for self-worth.

For Benny, time confirmed just how much of a blessing this kind of love can be. His issues haven't gone away and probably won't any time soon, maybe never. He's still challenged by extreme hyperactivity and awkwardly so because of those underdeveloped motor skills. When we first met, he couldn't hold a pencil or join other kindergarteners in a relay race because he simply didn't have much strength or coordination. He still struggles with these things—keeping focused enough to use that pencil, and looking like a wobbling newborn giraffe on the verge of toppling to the ground when he runs. For Benny, so many simple things that other children tackle with ease, instead are challenges that set him apart. He's smart and needs help in lots of extra areas, so if he doesn't get it, he checks out and acts out in ways not always good for him or others.

Through all the challenges, though, his mother is there patiently teaching, disciplining, and, most importantly, simply loving him. She can get as exasperated as anyone with his behavior, which has altered even how their family does things. For instance, rarely does she take him to a restaurant where they are seated and served. Instead, like so many families with a

A STEP TOWARD LOVING BETTER
Find Love-able Moments

How do you know the moment your children need to hear "I love you" most? Is it just when you tuck them into bed at night? When they're hurt or sad? What about when they hit a home run, forget their lines in the school play, start a new program or sport or hobby, apply for a scholarship, see a friend move away or make a new friend, lose a pet or bring home a stray, talk about something beautiful to them or funny, take something that doesn't belong to them, help someone, disappoint you, or break your heart?

Every terse and tender moment is when your kids need to hear the words and experience the behavior that says, "I love you." When you're intentional about speaking your love, you'll find that both you and your kids become more lovable because you're more able to love despite circumstance or condition.

To say "I love you" more, think "Even when" and "Especially when". This activates and enables expression: "Even when you don't unload the dishwasher like I asked, I love you. (And you still have to unload the dishwasher!)," and, "Especially when you were able, though it was hard, to forgive that classmate who was mean, I love you."

member who wrestles with ADD, they go to cafeterias where Benny can fix his short attention span on choices for supper, and can practice his motor skills serving his own plate and carrying his tray, things that keep him busy and help him behave.

It's unconditional love that finds alternatives like this, that says, "I am going to love you *in spite of* and *regardless* and even *when*—in spite of this, regardless of that, when you do or are this way." That kind of love, because it is a constant, reassures your children and creates a safe environment for them to try new things, to ask for help when needed, and to grow.

Anything less than that kind of love is conditional, and conveys the message, "I love you *when* you get straight As" and "I love you *if* you do what I say." Conditional love changes with the circumstances, as uncertain and unsafe as a faulty electrical circuit that flickers off and on again, always on the verge of erupting into sparks, igniting a fire, going up in flames, and leaving your relationships in ashes.

Thank goodness Benny's mom showed him a constant love not based on anything he did or didn't do. That kind of loving has made all the difference for him. Though, as a second grader now, Benny doesn't crawl under classroom tables, he can still make you at moments want to do so. He will always be a boy in gangly motion, with a short attention span. But he's learning and succeeding, and it is the safety of a constant, loving environment that is paving the way.

How You Can Love Imperfectly

Loving in that transforming way isn't easy though. How do you love someone when she or he is getting on your last nerve? How can you love the child who, much as you may be reluctant or loathe to admit, disappoints you?

Part of what helps Benny's mom is learning to let go of dreams of the perfect child. You know those dreams. All parents have them, whether our children have come to us naturally, by adoption, or some other way. You imagine tiny arms wrapped around your neck, sweet thank yous, and heartwarming pictures in crayon tacked to the refrigerator, gratefulness at the dinner table or when tucked into bed. You envision your child doing great things, conquering the world, or at least some corner of it—at least the homework.

Then Reality steps in and pulls up the shade letting the light of day filter into Dreamland. Angry at being disciplined, your child yells, "I hate you." Or there is your child bullying the neighbor boy, mean and saying ugly things. You never imagined seeing your daughter give a hard elbow in the chest to the neighbor boy for no reason. You never thought your son could fail so miserably at math, or perform so embarrassingly at the trumpet or on the soccer field. You are shocked to hear your daughter tell her classmate, "You are such a loser," or gloat, "I knew I'd win because I'm better."

Where did that child come from—that can't be my child!? you think.

Getting such a hard look at how your child can be versus how you dreamed they would be is like planning on a wonderful trip to the villas of lush, sunny Italy, then ending up on the isolated tundra of Siberia.

The reality is your child, like every other, is not perfect, just as that Italian villa is filled with not only flowers and sunshine, but lizards and snakes too. Perfection is an illusion. Reality can be unsightly, wounding, and devastating. Reality can also be beautiful because even with all your imperfections you can love your child completely. You can:

- **Let go of how you wish your child could be and may become, and accept your child as he or she is right now.** Your child may have your looks, name, mannerisms, build, and any other number of similarities. But that doesn't mean your child will share your ambitions, personality, or even your values. Your dreams for your child may not be theirs at all. The ancient proverb acknowledges this: "Even small children are known by their actions" (Proverbs 20:11). So this is a head-on, intentional choice to make, a mindset to deliberately nurture again and again, and the essential first step to loving unconditionally.

- **Celebrate the mix of strengths and weaknesses in your child.** This doesn't mean praising or excusing bad behavior or tendencies. It means loving your child, even the flaws, while still wanting the best for them. You can do this like Benny's mom, who can hear all about her son's constant motion, and before tackling what to do about it, says, "Yep, that is so Benny." See how that works? There's not a declaration of how awful he can be or a praising of it, just an acceptance: *That is him.* Another mom I know goes one step further. When she's told her daughter tends to leave her sweater or books and things wherever she wills (dropped to the middle of the floor or right in front of the door), Michelle's mother smiles wanly and says, "That's what we call a Michele-ism." This is neither praise nor a defense for behavior that needs correcting, rather a comment that acknowledges: *Yes, this is my daughter. This is who she is, and I know it, and I accept her.*

- **Honor your child's identity.** Affirm and call out the very best of and in your child, what *is*, reinforcing all that makes your son or daughter special. One mom I know does this for her definitely right-brained daughter by remarking on the doodles on her homework, or her eccentric outfit of a striped shirt with flowery pants, or her inventive combinations of ingredients to make pizza (cheese and veggies with no tomato sauce). The mom proclaims simply: "My little artist." These parents are calling out something deep in their children's identity and loving it, tending it.

And the ironic thing is that loving your children just as they are, flaws and all, helps them transcend those weaknesses or failures, becoming and achieving more.

BECAUSE LOVE CHANGES THE BRAIN

Even science confirms that love gives your children can-do power. An important study published in 2012 from the University of Washington at St. Louis, Missouri, shows that the child who feels loved and is well nurtured early in life grows more brain capacity.[7]

Love actually brings about an anatomical change. The hippocampus, the region of the brain important to learning, short- and long-term memory, spatial navigation, and stress responses, grows 10 percent larger with love and nurture. That means children loved well, especially in those early, formative years, have greater capacity to problem-solve, reason, remember, and handle stress.

In the study, ninety-two children, at age three to ten years, were followed for nearly a decade. Scientists observed live and on video outer behavior: how children were loved and nurtured, and how they reacted to the variety of parenting exhibited, some unconditionally nurturing and others not so. Along the way, researchers also tracked, by brain imaging, what was happening inside each child. Indisputably, the children receiving the most healthy, unconditional love and nurture showed definite growth of the hippocampus region of the brain, and as the brain physically grew, these children displayed more calm and confidence, joy, and ability to think their way through problems; they achieved greater and higher results in all manner of things than children not nurtured well or shown unconditional love.

Whether parents considered themselves loving and nurturing wasn't based on their own self-assessment. It was more than a hug. Instead, love was measured by positive behaviors, spoken words, expressions, body language, and responses. Love was demonstrated by speaking with positive reinforcement, smiles and hugs, and other things—things beyond personality and natural affinity of the parents. In other words, it wasn't just parents naturally inclined to be perky, optimistic, or quick to praise who were considered loving. It was parents of all different kinds of personality types using certain skills, practices, and actions that were loving—and all this dispensed unconditionally, not just when a child behaved or did well, but regardless.

That is encouraging because for years a variety of other studies have suggested that love and nurture can influence a child's *performance*. For instance, one University of Minnesota study, begun in the 1970s and following 267 children of first-time, low-income mothers, suggests that early love and nurture from a parent improve a child's intelligence (the actual

I.Q.).[8] The Washington University in St. Louis study provides the first solid evidence that a parent's love and nurture throughout development changes the actual brain anatomy in children, enabling more *capability*.[9]

All of these studies suggest that the key is in how parents show love and nurture from even the early years of a child's life, and that this healthy parenting can be learned. Parenting education is the key.

This thrills me because the art, science, faith, and psychology on parenting agree: there are identifiable skills and actions for showing love that every parent can learn to exercise. And all these things undergird what God has been telling us all along—that love makes us able because love "bears all things, believes all things, hopes all things, endures all things. Love never fails" (1 Corinthians 13:7-8 NKJV).

SO WHAT'S A MOM OR DAD TO DO?

One of the first identifiable love practices that helps children thrive seems so obvious: spending time together. I'm talking undivided attention time, no television shows or computer games, text messaging, or distractions with Facebook in the background, just one-on-one time together. This may sound simple enough, but isn't focusing on one another increasingly a struggle in these times of multitasking, with calls for our attention from every direction, anyplace, anytime?

Even without the technology, when your children are young, simply delighting in them can be a challenge. When I was a young mother, in my twenties, I was divorced and raising two energetic boys on my own. I sometimes wondered how to possibly give them each the attention they needed, and still have enough reserve left over for all the other demands in my life.

I could start the day with the best intentions, and quickly find myself chasing after all the things that needed to be done instead of simply delighting in my boys. There were breakfasts and lunches to make, and piles of laundry waiting by the washer, that was waiting for a call to the repairman. There was getting us all ready and where we needed to be for the day. And then The Day at work with all its problems to solve. By the time we were all home again, we were tired but there still was homework to do and lesson plans to finish, supper to prepare, more laundry and dishes. Pile on top of that the grocery shopping, bill paying, activities and church, mail and housecleaning, and—whew!—it was all I could do to get us all to bed at a somewhat decent time in order to start all over again the next morning.

That's when I heard something that changed my life.

Practice the Thirty Minutes a Day Rule

I was taking graduate courses during this time, and one of my professors was talking about what causes emotional disturbances in young children. He said if more parents would spend at least thirty minutes a day with their children, so many issues could be alleviated.

Thirty minutes a day? I wondered. Don't we already spend hours more than that together every day?

No, my professor showed. Today, both the two-income families, and single parents alike struggle. Everyone's busy, and even when they are together the rhythms of family life are so complex and fragile. One thing goes wrong and an entire morning routine can be interrupted. The things you mean to do, get lost or neglected or dropped entirely. By the end of the day, you're tired and your kids are too. And still there's the laundry, the dishes, the meals, and the preparation for another day waiting. No wonder moms and dads who work outside the home spend on average less than ten minutes a day on learning activities with each of their children.

Beyond that, my professor said he was talking about spending at least thirty minutes a day of undivided attention with your kids—and that's what made a difference: one-on-one time of simply delighting in one another, listening to one another, connecting. You would be surprised, he added, how many parents and children don't give one another even fifteen minutes a day of undivided attention.

I thought about all the times I'd been in the same room with my boys, folding laundry or reading and going over school papers, while they played or did homework. It was good just to be near one another. But that didn't compare to the times we played a game together, or worked together to fold the laundry and cook dinner, while as things about their day spilled into the conversation. I loved those moments, and as my professor spoke, I knew immediately the power of simply delighting in one another and being there to listen. I knew that the thoughts and feelings shared in such times were sometimes secrets and always treasures, precious and rare, often not unearthed again.

That very day I determined to practice the Thirty Minutes a Day Rule with each of my boys. I knew this was something I could do!

While one of my sons got ready for bed, brushing his teeth and laying things out for the next morning, I could read a bedtime story to my other son and we could chat or play or make something together. Then as that son got ready for bed, I'd flip my focus to my other son for one-on-one time. We did the same thing in the morning, and alternated through the week who got one-on-one time first.

This spilled into other times during our day, and other events too. There would be a meal or special reason to celebrate with each son. Practicing the Thirty Minutes a Day Rule became intentional—and turned into so much more. By intentionally making thirty minutes a day for simply delighting in one another, we learned how to really pay attention to each other in snatches too. The moment one son achieved an A+ in a difficult subject, we celebrated by making a special dinner together; the time my other son completed a task he loathed without having to be nagged into it, we went for ice cream and laughed ourselves silly. Looking for ways to give one another undivided attention became a lifestyle, and it strengthened our relationship just like layer upon layer of glue holds things together, because nothing makes the ones you love feel more cherished than your attention, your constant practice of being there.

In *being there,* I discovered another wonderful practice in how to show the kind of love that's transforming. This practice is about seizing extraordinary moments that might otherwise pass you by as ordinary. It's about seeing the cracks in your child's soul, where values, discoveries, and new ideas can be planted and begin to seep in and take root. It's about moments like the epiphany I had one Christmas.

Practice the Teachable Moment

As my family gathered for our December celebration, I had a candy dish filled with See's chocolates on an end table. I love See's Candy, and it's a special treat, not an everyday thing at my house. No wonder, then, that my granddaughter, then three years old, locked eyes on the chocolates when she came to visit, and couldn't stop staring them down.

After a few times of telling her there was to be no candy before our supper, and even then just one piece, I thought, *Prudence!* I removed the temptations to the third shelf of the kitchen cabinet.

The next morning, upon entering the kitchen, I saw Haley standing on a high stool, chocolate smeared all over her mouth and dress.

"Haley!" I said, eyebrows raised. "What are you doing?"

Her chocolately lips quivered. "Nothing, Grandma! Just looking." She tearfully denied all wrongdoing, even with the evidence of it all over her.

"Haley…," I said in a *you-know-better* tone.

She bent her head. She did indeed know better, and so did I. From all those years raising her dad and his brother, I knew: *Here was a teachable moment. Here was where I could love Haley enough to set the course right here, right now for something life changing.*

The teachable moment, after all, is all about that: finding what can open up a discovery, change the course of how one behaves, bring wisdom and insight and personal growth.

But it's not something you can construct. It is the moment that comes completely unexpected. You can't plan it. Your children won't set it up like a stage on which you can act out a well-rehearsed play. The teachable moment slips in through the cracks and steps up behind you. It surprises you and your child. It's completely random and often tied to something that demands an emotional and moral response. It can be a moment your child has done something wrong or disappointed you or themselves, when you both witness something startling and disconcerting or something that gives you pause. It's that second that something stops you in your tracks or raises a question. When it's because of some wrongdoing or witness of wrongdoing, the temptation is to swoop in with a line like my tone to Haley, "You know better than that!"

But they don't. Not really. They don't fully understand the *why*, or the consequences and effects, the costs and tolls. So here's your opportunity to help them grasp the weight of a matter in an unforgettable way. You have the chance to gently take a circumstance by the shoulders and present it to your child, examine it together for what it is, and what it can be by our choices. You have an open door to punish, admonish, or pontificate for a moment (and there is a place for correction to stop something that can hurt your child or someone else)—or you can choose to impart a lesson for a lifetime, because the teachable moment is just that powerful.

It might be that moment when you and your daughter see a boy being bullied in the park. You can intervene and then talk with your daughter about the horrors and harm of bullying; how any person can stand up to a bully, why they should and how in doing so can give others the courage to follow; and how bullies usually strike out of their own deep wounds because they need help too.

With Haley, it was this moment of being caught in the act of doing something wrong, knowing enough to try and deny it, yet the evidence was all over her clothes, across her face, on her hands. I wanted her soul to be stained as well—with understanding, not just knowledge, of why certain rules are good for us. I wanted her to see how easily she could have fallen from that stool or gotten a tummy ache or even sugar shock from all those rich chocolates. I wanted her to have something sweeter than candy, the wisdom for a lifetime that breaking the rules can not only hurt us but others. I wanted her to taste the disappointment of the rest of the family who would miss out on our special treat, to know that everything we have and do always costs someone something.

While I could reprimand Haley in order to teach these things, there were other ways I could inspire a deeper understanding and create change. These are the things any of us can do when the teachable moment presents itself:

- **Use the emotions running.** Tap into what your children are thinking or feeling, and ask about his hopes or her fears in a situation. What do they wish? What do they regret? What do they dream for and want more than anything? This gives you a window into their souls, and opens the way for you to bare and share your own soul. Emotions can help you connect with your child.

- **Guide your children into discovery with questions.** This means getting your children to think deeply and exploringly. It means asking questions, but not just any that lead only to knowledge. You want questions that lead to understanding, the ones that don't seek one acceptable answer—a *yes* or *no* or parroting of what your child has already heard from you ("don't do that") and thinks you want him or her to repeat. Rather, the best questions help your children explore a situation and their own part in it, the context and values attached. For instance, I could have asked Haley, "You know what you're doing is wrong, don't you?" Or I could ask, "Why do you think we needed to wait for that special candy, and to share it?" The first question demands a *yes* or *no* answer; the second causes her to consider her own conscience and mine and others'. *Why* and *how* and *what do you think* questions will always get you closer to understanding than questions that seek only a *yes* or *no*.

- **Listen with all your heart.** This may be the most important thing you can do, since the teachable moment is as much for you as your child. In listening, you will discover your children's insight and beliefs, and probably something from them about life, and they will receive wisdom from you about values and conscience. So there is some give and take, and it may not be clear who is doing what as they open up and you lean in. But as they spill their thoughts, look them in the eye. Don't interrupt. Perhaps repeat things they say as a question to make sure you're hearing what they really mean and to encourage them to explain more. Watch their body language as much as listen to their words: Are they keeping you at a distance with arms crossed? Are they at a loss with hands thrown up in the air? Are they frustrated and angry with tears or fists? Are they looking for escape with darting eyes or an actual moving away from you? When you actively listen, you do some of your most meaningful work as a parent. You show your children that you love them enough to know and understand them. In turn, you also teach them by modeling how to be a good listener.

- **Defer judgment.** There are times that clearly correction is needed. Your willingness to save correction for later allows you time to hear out your children, to truly know and understand why they did what they did, and more thoughtfully consider what correction measures will make the greatest impact. There are times, like the instance with Haley, when you know why your children did what they did—they wanted that treat. But your willingness to allow your children to speak without an immediate stamp of approval or disapproval teaches them how to think for themselves, trust you, and bring their troubles, questions, and struggles to you for help in sorting out. This can so surprise your children, this show of such determination to love them through their good choices and bad, that you give them pause, startle them into thinking deeper, turning them from their own wants into considering others. Isn't this kind of transformative turn the goal?

WHERE LOVE MAKES THE DIFFERENCE

Of course, you can go wrong in how you love your kids or how they love you back, in a dozen little ways. What's worse, you can see the breakdowns and not even realize that it's love that's missing, that love is the antidote you need. I'm talking about when your six-year-old starts fibbing all the time, or when your son and daughter go to war day after day in acts of sibling rivalry, when your fourth grader picks apart everything and everyone, when there are angry outbursts and episodes of conflict.

The root of every single one of these problems is love, or really the lack of it. Children lie out of fear (they don't want to be punished) or to hide something (there is no trust). Sibling rivalry stems from jealousies (there is envy and hurt). Conflict and anger come from wanting but not getting your way, disagreement, and simply no understanding or willingness to understand.

God says there are none of these things in love: no envy or meanness, no arrogance or selfishness, no anger or ill will. Rather, love is patient and kind, doesn't envy or boast, isn't arrogant or self-seeking or easily angered, keeps no record of wrong, delights in truth (1 Corinthians 13:4-8). Love gives your child the roots to grow and the wings to fly, and something to return to when there are troubles or questions. Even John Lennon got this when he sang, "Love is the answer, and you know that for sure."[10]

Take a closer look at where love goes wrong, where there's an absence of it, and how to use love to make things right.

With Critical Spirits, Love Can Turn Hurting Words to Healing

Stephen, a seven-year-old, came to school without one good thing to say about anyone or anything. He called other kids "stupid." He reacted to every new lesson or assignment in class with "Not this!" or "This again?" and "Can't we do something we really need instead of this crap?" He actually used even more coarse language than I will repeat. And he wouldn't be quiet.

Right away we needed to talk, though, honestly, I wished I could talk and Stephen would stop! *How does someone just seven years old get so negative?* I wondered.

Then I met his mother. She came to a meeting I'd requested, complaining about everything, "I couldn't find a stupid parking place. It took me forever just to get to the building. The classroom wasn't easy to find either." She said a few more coarse things too.

Wow. There were a lot of issues Stephen and his mom needed to deal with, because as I've said before, one problem usually does not march alone.

But the immediate issue to tackle had to do with words. Even when you can't control your circumstances, you can control your words, and your words can either build up or tear down.

This mom's words were wrecking balls. They were so critical, negative, and demeaning that no wonder Stephen spoke the same language. Good words and thoughts were foreign to him. He and his mom needed a lot more love in their lives, and especially in their language. They needed to speak encouragement rather than discouragement, blessing instead of curse, and to call out the positive more than reinforce the negative. This was so important because they were on a slippery slope, just a word away from the kind of discouragement and despair that can stop or trip and debilitate. They spewed those things onto others too.

Words have that power. God says a harsh word stirs up anger (Proverbs 15:1), and what you say can mean life and death (Proverbs 18:21). Life and death! The proverb goes on to say that the one who speaks good words will be rewarded. And science and psychology echo the Bible. One study has found that just hearing sentences about the elderly caused participants to walk more slowly. In another, individuals who read words of "loving kindness" showed increases in self-compassion, improved mood, and reduced anxiety.[11]

Words spoken truly and with genuine feeling do, indeed, affect your thinking and behavior, your reactions and beliefs.

What Stephen and his mom needed to do, then, is the same thing you can do when you catch yourself or your child cursing, saying things that are negative, critical, false, mean, and nonproductive. It's not a magic answer or list of steps to take. It's a decision. You stop using words that tear down: *stupid, fool, crazy,* and worse. You do both the simple and hard thing of catching yourself or your child talking negatively and just say, "Stop!"

Then you practice blessing rather than cursing. You speak words that bring life. You say something constructive rather than destructive, positive instead of negative. If you can't do that, say nothing until you can. This is an intention, meaning you determine to do it, you actively look for opportunity, and you choose to build up. Make it a habit in your house to practice blessing in one of these ways:

- **Put praise on paper.** Susan said she and her husband decided before their children started school that they would take turns writing to each of them an encouraging, loving note every morning and tuck it into the lunch sacks. "These aren't letters," she said. "Most of the time they're just scribbles on a Post-It: *You are magnificent. You can do this today. I love you.* But every note reminds the kids that we believe in them, and that they each are special. We wanted the words to be things they would internalize, and I think they have. I've seen them saving the notes. My son stashes them in his top dresser drawer, between the socks and the T-shirts. My daughter keeps hers in a pretty box where she puts her beads and little trinkets. They have the notes as reminders, especially for the times they will need them, that they are valuable and loved."

- **Bless your children around the table** as in the examples from the Bible. This cue is straight from Jewish culture, as families from Abraham's to King David's to Jesus's family would have practiced. Every Friday night, at their special *Shabbat* dinner, Jewish fathers place a hand on each of their children's heads and praise something specific about what each child uniquely brings this world: "God, thank you for Kathy and the way you made her to run fast." Or, "Lord, thank you for Phillip's kind heart." Do this in your own way by praising one thing beautiful about your children in your prayers before meals.

- **Speak a blessing as a prayer straight from the Bible, Numbers 6:24-26:** "May God bless and protect you. May God's face shine toward you and show you favor and grant you peace." Or, upon waking from sleep or tucking in your child at bedtime, pray a personalized version of God's promise in Jeremiah 29:11: For God knows the plans he has for you, my daughter, plans to prosper you and not to harm you, plans to give you hope and a future.

- **Mark the milestones with blessing.** In their book *Lord, Bless My Child*,[12] William and Nancie Carmichael identify in Bible six critical times for blessing to be received from God through parents for their children: upon conception, while in the womb; at birth; in infancy; for puberty or as a rite of passage into adulthood; upon marriage; and in old age. Birthdays, graduations, the start of a new school year or sport and hobby are each opportunities to celebrate with your child, and can be as formal as you like, or not. The key is to make it intentional and dedicated.

- **Speak it on the thresholds.** A single mom, Deb, prays God's promises and blessing over her daughter whenever they cross the threshold of the front door to their house. "Whenever we entered and left our home, we prayed for God to prosper and protect us. The idea came from Psalm 121:8 that says 'the Lord will watch over your coming and going.' I loved that, so that became our prayer. Now saying this prayer is just what we always do, like buckling up when you get in the car. I want my daughter to know she is blessed through the day, every day. I wanted her to hear me say the blessing, and to be able to repeat it to herself and others. Just last week we brought home a couple of Shara's friends from soccer practice, and as we walked in the front door, Shara and I looked at each other, laughed, and she said to her friends, 'Lord, watch over the coming of the soccer team,' and I added, 'because our living room field is only so big!'"

Deb and Shara's practice reminds me of something John Trent and Gary Smalley pointed out in their book *The Blessing:* "In the Bible, Abraham spoke blessing to his son Isaac, who spoke a blessing to his son Jacob, who spoke a blessing to each of his twelve sons and two of his grandchildren. When God blessed us with the gift of his Son, he said his Word 'became flesh and dwelt among us' (John 1:14). God has always been a God of words."[13] And his words are ones of promise, blessing, goodness, and mercy for, as the shepherd-king of the Bible says in Psalm 23, "all the days of our lives."

With Sibling Rivalry, Love Can Turn Competition to Connection

Rick, a handsome fifth grader, transferred to our school in the fall and quickly made friends. He was charming and outgoing, fun and funny. But as fall turned to winter, not just the weather changed. Rick changed too.

He began telling tales about his weekends. "I played baseball with one of the Knicks," he announced one day in class. He teased other students. "You stink," he'd tell the boy sitting next to him, then laugh. "Just kidding." Only he kept on tormenting the boy, who began to cringe the moment Rick entered the room. Before long, fights erupted. Rick, the new boy, the quickly popular boy, was just as fast unpopular, and his turn in behavior had become old. His teacher called me for help.

Rick's father walked into our meeting with obvious weariness and defeat. His shoulders sagged as did his spirit. He admitted what happened at school was going on at home too, only in reverse. Rick's older brother Jon, normally amiable and fun-loving, had begun to tease Rick until they broke into fights.

"It's pretty much non-stop whenever they're in the same room," he admitted. But his wife saw nothing wrong. "They're just boys being boys," she said. Rick's dad felt at a loss.

See what I mean about how when there's one problem, it doesn't march alone?

As much as their boys needed some resolution, Rick's mom and dad needed to support one another's concerns and work together to find peace and create harmony. At the root of each of their needs is what we're talking about throughout this chapter: a whole lot of concentrated, unconditional love.

You see, Rick, the "baby of the family," was getting a free pass to bad behavior from his mom. Without realizing it, she made excuses for him ("C'mon, he's just a kid" and "He's the youngest"). She had "dethroned," as psychologists call it, her firstborn, Jon, from her attention.[14] Dethroning

is when one child is diminished in some way as another, given more attention, is brought into the family.

Rick's mom was horrified when she realized this is what she had been
doing. She didn't love Jon any less or Rick any more, but her personality and Rick's were so complementary that in practice she tended to favor
him. The effects were cyclical: Jon, who butted heads with his mom anyway, became increasingly jealous, enough to lash out at Rick, who in turn
behaved at school as he was learning from his brother Jon. The sibling relationship, after all, is the first social laboratory in which children interact
with their peers, where they learn to cooperate, negotiate, compete, share,
empathize, be self-controlled and play fair, feel encouraged or ridiculed,
valued or rejected. It's with a brother or a sister that a child first learns how
to make friends, save face, and achieve recognition. And Rick had learned
some falsehoods, and experienced some bad behavior that he was enacting
at school.

This cycle isn't so uncommon in families. I've seen variations of it year
after year in the classroom, though few parents would admit to loving one
of their children more than another. (Would you?) Yet a host of studies
show most parents do favor one of their children without even realizing
it, only "favor" doesn't necessarily mean they like or love one child more,
just that there is more natural simpatico or alliance in temperaments.[15]
That's what was happening in Rick's family. Rick and his mom tended to
see and deal with things the same way; and Jon, usually contrary, always
being asked to pick up the slack for his brother, began to feel unappreciated, unheard, and unloved.

Each one of these feelings is a seed of sibling rivalry but combine all
three and you've got big trouble: fights at home, fights at school, and a
growing loathing between brothers and others.

Even though Rick was getting away with a lot at home and that needed
to be addressed, his mom was distressed to learn Jon thought he was loved
less. She never felt that way and never meant for him to either. Yet, as the
old adage goes, perception is reality.[16] Even if one child *thinks* there's favoritism, there *is* for him, or her.

Have you noticed that with your children? Have you ever heard, "Mom, she's wearing my cashmere sweater!" or "Dad, he just rode off on my bike!" Has the clamor for territory, things, and attention erupted in front of you? Does one of your children seem to be the apple of your eye at the expense of making another look bad or even invisible?

These are signs of sibling rivalry, of one child feeling relationship with you is threatened because of the attention you give another, or of one child trying to find his or her place in the family and show how they are special and unique. And these feelings and behaviors can happen naturally at some point in every family, extending outside the family, like with Rick, mimicking at school behavior learned at home.

What can you do? The same thing that worked for Rick's parents:

- **Set up avenues for cooperation.** It may seem counterintuitive when you have children who can't seem to get along, but you want to bring them together more and separate them less. Give your children opportunities to work, not fight, together. For instance give them projects as part of their chores that cause them to seek one another's cooperation. Instead of having them race one another to see who can do their part first to clean the family room just trashed, have them race the clock. Instead of assigning them separate chores, have them complete tasks together, like folding clothes or cooking dinner (and to assure there's no sabotage, make sure they understand they must both eat whatever is fixed). This teaches your children how to appreciate what they each can contribute and do together, and reinforces the Golden Rule of "Do unto others as you'd like done unto you," regardless of age, size, who's got longer or shorter hair, or patience and tempers.[17]

- **Call out rather than compare.** Instead of "Rake the leaves like your sister" or "Why can't you hang up your jacket like your brother?" you can complement with "What a good strategy making this recipe work" and "You are clever to find we had everything for this dish to begin with!" Children really do need to hear what makes each of them special too. I had a conference once with Ashley's mom, who couldn't stop talking of the wonders of her older son, who apparently was handsome, brilliant, artistic, scientific, athletic, and popular. "Wow," I said. Recognizing she'd just bragged, the mom said, "Oh, but I'd never go on like that about either of the kids in front of them." *Why not,* I wondered. *Speak each of their praises.* Ashley was beautiful, with a flair for fashion, and had a wonderful gift for sizing up personalities quickly and accurately. God knows that both Ashley and her brother, who were competing for their mom's attention, needed to hear to their faces what is wonderful about each of them. That's why God tells us, "Before I made you in your mother's womb, I chose you. Before you were born, I set you apart for a special work (Jeremiah 1:5 New Century Version).

- **Let each child bend your ear rather than break your hearts.** Jon needed to be able to tell his mom he felt marginalized, sometimes invisible, often unloved, and constantly pressured to help his younger brother when Rick was entirely capable of taking care of himself. By the same token, Rick needed to tell his parents he was tired of being picked on by Jon, and having a tough time getting along at school too. What this whole family needed—every family dealing with sibling rivalry—is better listening skills. One thing Rick's dad did was to give permission to speak up. When Rick started to tattle on Jon, Dad said, "Don't tell me about your brother— tell me about you." One thing Mom did was what family counselors Adele Faber and Elaine Mazlish recommend as a key listening skill: acknowledging feelings.[18] To help Jon express his pent-up hurt, fears, and jealousies, his mom helped him with the words: "You sound furious [feelings acknowledged]. You wish Rick would ask first before taking your basketball [wishes acknowledged]. You can make a PRIVATE PROPERTY sign for your bedroom door [symbolic activity or creative problem-solving prompted]. You aren't his dumping bag [hurt acknowledged]. Tell him with words, not punches, how this upsets you [coaching for an acceptable expression of feelings]."

- **Encourage responsibility.** After a Time Out, separately ask each child what he or she can do if the problem occurs again. This allows each of your children to open up to you about what happened, perhaps why, and also what role they played in the situation. You'll be surprised at how they can step up and offer smart solutions too. For instance, toddlers and preschoolers who fought over crayons might suggest putting their names on their own boxes of crayons and respecting one another's things. Pre-teen sisters fighting over clothes might agree to each pick one article of clothing they each could share without permission on a weekly basis and specify what is off-limits no matter what.

With sibling rivalry, love really is the answer because the best antidote is also the most preventative measure—catch your kids loving one another well. This practice can be powerful, reinforcing good behavior and celebrating the sibling connection. You'll be surprised, too, that when you look for it, you'll find it.

The moment your children are laughing at the same silly scene in a movie is the moment they're delighting together and even in one another. The time you see your son pick up the jacket your daughter dropped, or squeezes the toothpaste for his brother are the times they are helping one another.

Call attention to those moments, comment on them, call them out, make a to-do over them, say outright that you love how your children love one another. Make them notice that their siblings aren't all bad, that there are wonderful moments, then reward those times. With younger children, put up a monthly calendar for each child where stickers go on the day you observe and note good deeds, kindnesses, and helps. When the charts are hung in a family hub, like on the refrigerator, everyone sees and can praise the goodness even more. With older children, you can write a note or make a card that acknowledges and commemorates good things. Loving one another well becomes a celebration, something imprinted on their minds and in their hearts

With Anger and Conflict, Love Rights All Wrongs

As much as you love your children, you can be angry with them. That's because love and anger are flip sides of same coin: both cost us something, both measure how much we feel, both can be something we hang on to no matter what. But only one—love—is worth treasuring.

That's why the crux of nearly every issue in relationships, psychologist Gary Chapman says, comes down to how to express love and process anger.[19] Chapman, in practice as a marriage and family counselor for more than thirty years at the time he wrote this, said nearly every case he addressed, thousands of cases of people seeking help, centered on resolving conflict and anger in order to love one another better, more, stronger.

I've found that true in my own experience counseling thousands of parents, teaching thousands of their kids, and dealing with my own relationships. No matter how much we love our children and they love us back, conflict and anger are part of the picture, and it's not always pretty.

I learned this at an early age. I grew up in a home where my mother's temper regularly exploded. She could be angry at me, my dad, or any given situation with the slightest provocation. I heard her fight with words both to my face and with my dad in another room, both when I was intended to hear and not. Looking back, it's no wonder that each month when the next issue of her *Ladies Home Journal* arrived in the mailbox, I'd steal away with it and turn the pages fast to read "Can This Marriage Be Saved?" It's also no wonder to me that after nearly sixty years since its beginnings, that column remains one of the most popular in women's magazines today.[20] Whether we're wives or husbands, parents or children, we're eager for solutions to anger and how it separates. We long to know more about how to express love and process anger. We would rather live in and look back upon the picture of a peaceful, safe, loving home.

So we need to know how to deal with anger, because conflict will always be part of relationships, especially between parents and children, who grow up exploring boundaries and pushing them, testing our limits and their independence, trying our patience and their freedoms.

A STEP TOWARD LOVING BETTER
Love Your Self

Where do you turn when as a parent you're the one who needs love? When I was in a difficult marriage and then single again after a divorce, I found encouragement and help…

- knowing Jesus is my bridegroom who cherishes me. He calls me his (Isaiah 54:5 and 1 Thessalonians 1:4); he reminds me that he, too, was alone in this world and left Heaven for me, loving me enough to come looking for me and show me the way Home.

- reading the promises in the Bible reminded me how God would never leave me or forsake me (Hebrews 13:5-6), help me (John 14:26); show me kindness, goodness, and mercy (Psalms 23:6 and 27:13). He would provide for me (Matthew 6:25-27), grant peace (John 14:27), give me hope and a future (Jeremiah 29:11), enable me to do good work (Ephesians 2:10), and love me forever (Jeremiah 31:3 and John 3:16).

- praying. Even science agrees that prayer can help your health, outlook, and even your heart. Prayer is the way to stay connected to God, who is always listening and seeing you through trouble. The beauty of prayer is it can be activated anytime, anywhere because, as David said, God never slumbers, never sleeps (Psalm 121:4).

- staying connected to church provided ritual for our lives, Sunday morning worship services, where we could sing, be encouraged, chat, and pray with others. Church gave us friends, support groups for sharing ideas and solutions to issues, and activities like potluck suppers and game nights where I could nourish my body and spirit.

- calling 211, which is like dialing 911 on your phone, for practical health and human services help in desperate times. Set up by the Federal Communications Commission, the 211 phone number connects people, state by state, to community-based organizations and government services for help with finance (rent and utilities) and clothing needs, medical insurance and programs, job training, transportation, and homemaker and childcare services. You'll find the FCC online at http://www.fcc.gov/guides/dial-211-essential-community-services.

God assures us of this. We're made with tempers. We'll get angry, and maybe for good reason. It's what we do with anger and how we deal with conflict that matters: "In your anger do not sin. Do not let the sun go down while you are still angry" (Ephesians 4:26).

But that's easier said than done at times, right? Like when your first grader, angry at you for being given a Time Out in the corner, scribbles in black permanent marker all over the wall. Or when you find out your preteen, not the best swimmer, has invited friends to sneak over to the vacationing-and-away neighbor's pool for a party. Damage and the fear of it can stay with you a while, making it hard to defuse the anger. But reluctance to let go of anger is what's really damaging.

I overheard two fourth grade boys talking about this once at the most elemental level. Chris was telling how his mom made him go with her to watch his sister play basketball. "The game wasn't even special," he said, "not a playoff or championship or anything, just a regular meet. So I was mad at mom the whole game, mad at my sister after, and then my mom got mad at me for being mad!"

"I know what you mean," Jeff said. "If I ever do something wrong my parents never talk to me about it. My mom just starts yelling and screaming. Then my dad just grounds me. That's it...yelling and screaming and grounding. They don't really care what happened."

"Yeah," Chris said, twisting his limbs around his chair like a pretzel. "They say, 'I love you,' but they just want to be mad."

You say "I love you," but your behavior, and maybe your words too, say you're mad. That's not what you want them to remember, is it?

So how do you referee the fights and manage the anger? There are things you can do that are healthy and can actually strengthen your relationships for having worked through the tensions, frustrations, and separations wrought by conflict:

- **Give yourself a Time Out.** Stop. Before you spout off or stuff your feelings, give yourself a second to calm down and put your emotions under the jurisdiction of your brain. Take three deep breaths. If you still feel roiling inside, take three more deep breaths, maybe this time with your eyes closed and palms open. Move, whether that means taking a step back, walking around the block, or just across the room to shut a door. Anger and frustration can melt away with each step. Also, the more you move, like walking around that block, the more you activate endorphins, chemicals released in your body that trigger a positive feeling ("euphoric," you often hear runners and walkers say) similar to that of morphine. Endorphins actually act as analgesics, which can diminish the perception of pain and offer a slight sedative effect. This means you can think more clearly in a relaxed frame of mind, and, as it turns out, body.[21]

- **Hold your judgment.** You don't need to determine in the moment who's right and who's wrong, who's "good" and who's "bad." Such labels immediately pit people against one another. Besides, no one is wholly good or wholly bad. A certain behavior may be right or wrong, but every person is capable of both. What you want is harmony, resolution, and alliance, not discord, conflict, or separation. So instead of issuing a punishment, or acting in a way so as to punish, defer with something like "Each of you go to your rooms for twenty minutes" or "Let's talk about this in an hour." This gives your child or children and you time to think about, and investigate if needed, what just happened.

- **Attack the problem, not the person.** There's an Aesop's fable of a wasp that settles on the head of a snake.[22] The wasp stings the snake several times until, in pain and desperate to get rid of the creature, the snake lays his head under a moving wagon, where both perish. That's what happens when you say things that sting someone opposed to you. When you attack a person and not the problem, you both end up wounded for the moment, and worse—well beyond it. There's a way to love even when you're angry and even in a fight. Of course in those moments you may feel like the snake, reeling in pain and desperation. So now is the time to prepare. Think of how to address issues and not the people. Identify what you see: "Someone's going to get hurt" or "This is getting ruined," not "Theresa, you're killing him!" or "Kevin, you're destroying everything." Describe what you see with respect: "That's a tough one. Two children, one bicycle." Choose your words wisely: "I" statements can be stronger than "you" accusations ("I am so frustrated" communicates more how you feel, where "You make me so frustrated ascribes more blame). Intervene when needed: "It's not safe to be together. Quick now, you go to your room, and you go to yours."

In the end, there will be times when you need to correct your kids.

"That can be so hard," a mom once told me. "I hate to see my boy hurt when I punish him."

Punishment isn't the goal. Correction that helps, not hurts, is. Correction doesn't wound or bruise. It's not used to inflict suffering. Correction shows that there are consequences for everything we do, and how especially bad behavior and ill will costs everyone something. Correction stops us from damaging or being damaged, gives us pause, and helps us turn toward better living and being. So when you need to correct your child:

- **Think about the best timing**, which is everything. Are you exhausted? Have you just come through a long, hard, trying experience? Give yourself a break, get some rest. If you're going to sleep on the issue, be sure to state you'll deal with things in the morning and restate your love. This assures you're troubled by the problem but still love the person.

- **Pick a place where you can focus** without interruption, distraction, or added stress.

- **Look for the win-win**, where everyone gains something. Your goal is to correct, change, transform, after all. So, for example, if your twelve-year-old son keeps sneaking out to meet with friends, you can ground him from seeing them and isolate him to his room. Or you can require he spend a day on a project at home or helping someone in need. By digging a new flowerbed together or painting a room, raking leaves in the yard of an elderly neighbor, or serving at the food kitchen, you can do something productive that opens his eyes and maybe his heart in sharing what's really going on with him and in this world.

LOVE'S HEALING FORCE—FORGIVENESS

No matter how well you practice loving your children, there will come times you still have to say you're sorry. There will be times, because loving well is a practice, when we need to start over or try again, and forgiveness becomes the most powerful fuel for moving us forward.

Randy, a hard-working, cooperative kindergartener, showed me the power of forgiveness, and his mom too. He was struggling in school. Drawing and learning to print his letters were laborious. He tried hard, but his fine motor development was slow and awkward. While other kids were starting to read, he struggled to make out letters that he couldn't yet write, let alone words to read. He was scoring slightly below grade level expectations in other areas too, which pained his mother. When she asked educators to hold him back from first grade and keep working on the basics, she was advised that retention isn't effective in resolving learning problems. Some targeted and tutoring help could help Randy and keep him moving forward. But his mother insisted on holding him back…only she failed to talk with Randy about this. She had four other children to tend. It wasn't that she was hiding it from him or neglecting him. She just was constantly swirling around what each of her children needed and she thought she might be able to talk with him once everyone was out of school for summer, which was another three months away.

One afternoon at the supermarket, however, Randy and his mom ran into their small town's Boy Scout leader. "I'll be able to join this year,"

Randy said, standing tall, pointing at his chest. "I start first grade next fall!"

"No," Randy's mom said, looking at him sadly, then smiling apologetically to the Scout leader. She knelt down to look Randy in the eye. "Honey, I've been meaning to tell you that we're going to stay in kindergarten another year."

Randy just stared at his mom, then looked down, as the embarrassed Scout leader coughed and said over his shoulder, moving down the aisle, "It will be good when you're ready to join, Randy. We can't wait to have you!"

Randy was subdued as they finished shopping and drove home, but he didn't ask any more questions about the decision, and his mom got swept up in all the to-dos back at the house. They never spoke more about it.

A month later, Randy's mom got a call from his kindergarten teacher: "Could we meet for a conference? Randy's completely changed from a kind and hard-working boy to being sassy and disobedient."

That same thing was going on at home, Randy's mom confessed. It didn't take her long to figure out he was angry and hurt from what was not only a crushing blow of being held back in school, but being humiliated with that news in front of the town's Scout leader. From Randy's perspective, he had worked hard and his mom had declared his effort and ability invalid. His budding sense of competence and identity had been bruised and wounded.

"Ohh," his mother sighed. She was even more pained now, realizing she'd worsened a situation for her son when all she ever wanted to do was make things better, smoothen his way, help him excel.

"We can help him here, now," his teacher insisted, and together they talked about how with some extra tutoring, exercises, and attention. They developed some teaching and learning strategies for the last two months of the school year.

Later that evening, Randy's mom sat down with him and told him the plan. "The goal is to work on some things so you will be ready when you're promoted to first grade."

"Mom!" Randy beamed.

As she went to start dinner, the cooperative, loving Randy returned. "I'll set the table!" he offered. "I'll help clean up!" At bedtime that evening, he admitted, "Mommy, I'm so sorry for thinking that I hated you for doing this to me. I love you."

Randy's mom looked deep into his eyes. *So much going on in that little brain,* she thought. She cupped his face in her hands and kissed him on the forehead. *Big brain, it turns out.* "Randy," she said. "I'm the one who is sorry. I should never have made a decision like that without talking with you. I should never have said anything in front of anyone without talking with you first, either. Can you forgive Mommy?"

"It's okay," Randy said, planting a big wet kiss right back on his mom's forehead. With that, he flopped over and went sound asleep. As she turned out the light, she noticed his older brother's Boy Scout manual back on Randy's nightstand.

"How much we underestimate one another," she admitted later.

Indeed. We can fail to love one another enough to solve the problems, tackle the challenges, and shoulder one another through the valleys *together.* But forgiveness is that solvent, that tackling gear, and shoulder to lean on when love falls short. Forgiveness is what renewed Randy's faith in his mom and himself. Forgiveness is what can transform any situation— you failing your children or them failing you.

"Love forgets mistakes," God says (Proverbs 17:9 The Living Bible). And you can make it a practice in your house, not just something to teach your children but to exercise with them. Here's how:

- **Keep a tender heart and a thick skin.** There's nothing like being around a forgiving spirit, someone not easily offended who can receive what you have to give, and forgive what you can't. One year I was counseling two first graders, Amber and Tiffany, in a program for at-risk children. The girls became close friends during the ongoing sessions, and began socializing after school too. One weekend, at the birthday party of a mutual friend, both Tiffany and Amber's parents were drawn into a huge argument. The following Monday the girls had barely entered my office when they were at each other arguing and insulting one other. Borrowing some techniques from art therapy, I had each girl draw a picture. Amber wrote with big letters on her picture "I hate you!" As we continued to process the problem, Tiffany wrote in tiny letters, "I love you!" That short, small sentence spoke volumes to Amber, whose anger immediately melted. Such is the humble spirit, ready to not only give, but forgive, giving for no reason.

- **Look ahead.** Does the wrong done, the feelings of yours that are hurt really matter? Can you let it go?

- **Exercise empathy, kindness, and compassion.** Put yourself in the other person's shoes.

- **Give gratitude.** Make a list, keep a notebook, post notes in a Gratitude Bowl that you read each night at dinner—do whatever it takes to document and remind one another how much you all have been given, how much there is for which to be thankful.

- **Be quick to make things right.** If, like Randy's mom, you know you've caused hurt or done something wrong, don't wait to make things right or apologize. However you say it—straight, plain, elaborate, or simple—just say it, "I'm sorry." Those two words work wonders, as do these four, "Can you forgive me?"

Sometimes, though, how you act says more, offers more, than any words. I witnessed this with Chris, a high school senior I was counseling with his family. Chris was struggling to overcome drug abuse, and it didn't take much one weekend to slip back into his former ways. We met to try and get him back on track.

Chris came into my office with dark circles under his eyes and looking unkempt and unavailable. He stared blankly at the floor and slumped into a chair like he wanted to disappear into it—into the horror, he confessed, he'd made of their lives.

As the details of that horror came to light, Chris's father became enraged. He jumped from his chair and screamed horrible names at Chris, called him terrible things. Chris, already loathing himself for falling back into his old ways, screamed back. The shouts still echo in my mind—searing, piercing, ugly names and words.

Meanwhile, Chris's mother sat by silently, tears streaming down her cheeks. She was devastated, but looked at her son with such tenderness that he stopped ranting. Tears came to his eyes. Her message was clear: *You are my son. I love you. What you are doing is wrong. You have a choice to make. I have faith in your ability to make the right choice.*

The family left and I silently prayed: *Father, forgive them. Let them forgive one another. Help them love like only they can, and love them like only you can.*

Sometimes, as parents and people who work to help children, praying and forgiving are all we can do. But, God reminds us, praying and forgiving are maybe the most powerful things we can do. You can have confidence, he says, that if you ask anything according to his will he hears you (1 John 5:14-15). He hears whatever you ask. He knows what you say outright and what your heart wishes.

One day, long after that meeting, a new Chris sat in my office, straight in his chair, clear-eyed, cleaned up, even smiling. He was in recovery and doing well. "How could I not try?" he said. "How could I not do this?" The unfailing love of his mother, always evident, even in silence, is what gave him the strength to believe in himself, forgive his father, and overcome.

LOVE LIKE ONLY YOU CAN

That is the power of love, especially when it's practiced beyond one hug, one tender look and forgiving word, and one teachable moment. Receiving one experience of such lavish love, and then another, and then another can make you turn like Chris.

It's not just because I'm a teacher that I can say all these practices of love add up. You can do the math with a week in your life and see the difference practicing love will make for your children and for you. It is practice, after all, that makes perfect. It is because we exercise the things discussed in this chapter that they are called practices! You exercise the teachable moment and show some unconditional love, and then you do it again and again and over again. Transformation is a process. Every destination is reached with one step after another in the journey toward becoming more than you are this minute. Each new road block, delay, or stop asks you to choose how you're going to love because love really is the fuel that will get you and your child to rise and shine.

I was reminded of this when I took in a recent exhibit featuring Princess Diana of Wales. At a time when it seemed everything was falling apart for her, the princess began to embrace the world's problems rather than simply retreat into her own. Her marriage and home life were in shambles, and she was shy and reserved, yet afforded no privacy to work out her most intimate struggles. She could have refused to engage public life. Instead, she stepped into its spotlight to bring the deepest needs of others to public attention and rouse help and support. She distributed food to the hungry in India, walked the minefields of Angola where the poor and impoverished lived and lost limbs or died every day. She hugged AIDs babies in New York, helped fund research that has led to healing treatments for breast cancer, and held abandoned orphans in Pakistan to find them homes.

"Diana used her power just like a magic wand, waving it in all kinds of places where there was hurt," one charity leader said.[23] "And everywhere she used it, there were changes—almost like a fairy tale."

MY PURPOSEFUL PARENT CHECK-IN
How Am I Doing with Love?

I'm seeing my children grow in love, and I'm being my best to bring out their best, by:

- Practicing the Thirty Minutes a Day Rule.
- Finding and using Teachable Moments.
- Loving them unconditionally with words wherever we come and go.
- Righting wrongs with forgiveness and correction.
- Practicing unconditional love in these ways as the tonic to cure all and cover all.

A placard at the exhibit I attended explained what the princess's power was. "I think the biggest disease the world suffers from is the disease of people feeling unloved," Diana was quoted as saying. "I know that I can give love for a minute, for a half-hour, for a day, for a month, but I can give. I am very happy to do that…I want to do that."[24]

Love is the magic wand that Princess Diana waved—magical, healing, powerful. Love is truly the tonic that cures all and covers all—and every teacher and mom and dad have it in their possession to use. It's your most powerful tool, and loving unconditionally is the essential principle that holds all the others together.

Only you can love like no other. Only you are best to give your child love like no one else. Only love will bring your children back to every good thing for them to thrive in life.

Love like that is what brings Lori back to the lake where our family has enjoyed so many summers and family reunions. The lake is where Lori learned some of life's great lessons, where her parents taught her about responsibility and discipline, character, and pursuing her passion and purpose. Most importantly, the lake is where her parents showed her unconditional love, where there were many teachable moments like that summer night she melted into tears for being reprimanded for hurrying.

Enveloped in unconditional love, Lori was able to talk about wanting to do the right things, and her parents were able to wrap her in their arms and tell her they wanted only the best for her because they did indeed see her big heart, her brilliant will to be good. Even now, though busy at work in digital communication in a high-powered job at the White House, Lori will take whatever day off she can to return to that Midwestern lake. It's where she regroups, finds peace, sorts out things, and remembers she is loved and can, in turn, love. She walks the lake, rides the boats, sits on the banks to watch sunrise and sunset, and thinks on how her parents loved her when she hurried and when she didn't, when she brushed her teeth and when she forgot to do so, when she erupted into tears or squealed with laughter.

You may never spend time at a lake. You may have family reunions of two, just you and your child. You may not have boats to ride or banks to sit upon. But you can be there for your children, to love them through sunrise and sunset. Your child's "lake" may be the table in your dining room, or the backyard, or a corner of your office where he or she played and did homework and got in trouble and delighted you. When you love your children unconditionally, when you love them enough to know them in that teachable moment and help them grasp values and wisdom, you give them shores on which to collapse, return, rejoice, and shine.

That's real magic, and the wand you can wave to change the world, the tonic you take and give your children again and again. And again.

Chapter 2

DISCIPLINE: TEACH THE CHILD YOU TREASURE

…because you care to get things right

"Mom, I told you no way," Lilly shrieked and stomped her foot. She was just getting warmed up. She wailed, throwing herself over a chair, screaming and crying, "No, no, no, no, nooooooo!"

Lilly's mom, Shirley, shook her head and put her face in one hand as she described her seven-year-old's fit for the fourth morning in a row. "She simply refuses to ride the school bus because there's a substitute driver she doesn't know. But I can't be late for work one more morning because of having to take her to school myself." Shirley choked back tears of her own. "I've tried everything. I walked her down the street to a friend's house so they could board together. I promised her a reward to just get on the bus with the other kids and go. I sat down with her for a long talk to see if she was afraid, which was a no. She said she doesn't like new people. Really, she finally admitted, she just wants her regular driver back because she likes him. So every morning it's the same. War! Lilly refuses, throws a fit, and demands her way. This isn't working and if it keeps up, I won't be either!" Shirley looked at me pleadingly. "What can I do?"

What can any parent do in such a power struggle with their child? When a child refuses your direction or instruction, when he or she rebels and defies you, fights, melts down, tunes out, turns off, and turns away, you face one of the most challenging aspects of parenthood: discipline. Another word for *battle*, right?

No. Discipline is really another word for *love*, another word for, not *war*, but *ways* to love with care and purpose.

Unfortunately, this is where too many parents buy into the idea that discipline is about making your kids mind and getting them to obey and behave. When you think like this, you go into fight mode, *Me* (authority) against *Them* (the children who should obey) in a battle of wills and for control, yelling and nagging. That's what a power struggle requires, right?

No again. The whole point of correcting bad behavior isn't about engaging in a power struggle at all. Discipline is about teaching, helping your children live with self-control and goals, a sense of direction, doing the right things, not harming and instead helping themselves and others. In fact, the very word *discipline* comes from a Latin noun that means *teaching* and *instruction*. So disciplining your child is a *we* thing. In correcting them, you are on their side, for them, not fighting against them. You invite cooperation rather than demand or coerce compliance. This diffuses the power struggle, where there's no winner or loser of the war for control. Rather, you both win. You teach them something beyond how to behave for a moment, and they learn the means and tools that can carry them through life.

That's the principle of discipline, after all—teaching the child you treasure because self-control leads to wise choices and everyone wants to get wisdom just right.

CHOICES AND CONSEQUENCES

You may have heard the following story before, but its wisdom deserves another telling. An elderly Cherokee, talking with his grandson about life, gives us a clear picture of what this principle looks like.[1] "A fight is going on inside me," he tells the boy. "It is a terrible fight and it is between two wolves. One is angry, envious, regretful, greedy, arrogant, self-pitying, guilt-ridden, resentful, feeling (and wanting others to feel) inferior, full of lies, false pride, superiority, and ego. The other is full of joy, peace, love, hope, serenity, humility, kindness, benevolence, empathy, generosity, truth, compassion, and faith."

The boy stared at the grandfather's chest, which lifted and fell ever so slightly with each breath.

The grandfather followed his grandson's eyes, then put his hand on the boy's heart. "The same fight is going on inside you," he said, "inside every person."

The grandson looked at his own chest. It rose and fell ever so slightly with each breath. He sat quiet, thinking. "Grandfather," he asked, "which one will win?"

The old man looked at the boy and said, "The one you feed."

Constantly through life both you and your children will be faced with choices to do the right thing or wrong thing, exercise self-control or none at all, give or take, work or play, create peace or stir up, unify or divide, love or hate…the list goes on. Knowing how to choose and recognize consequences is essential, for even when a choice isn't made, one of the two wolves inside each of us is fed. Is it the wolf of peace, love, and hope? Or the wolf of anger, envy, and regret? What are you feeding your children and what are they consuming? Mouthfuls of understanding? Cups of reason and insight? Plates of directives, frustration, and punishment?

When you think of discipline in this way, your response to misbehavior, misunderstandings, outright defiance, and power struggles will change. So will your children's. You'll both understand there are outcomes from whatever you chew upon and swallow. For every matter, there are choices and there are consequences. There are two fighting wolves you can feed at any time, and one will always win.

Allowing your children to choose which wolf to feed gives them the chance to:

- **exercise free will.**
- **learn how to make independent and thoughtful decisions.**

- **experience the consequences** that flow from their decisions.

- **realize responsibility and accountability** in an environment of emotional security.

- **separate an action from the person,** which enables one to love and forgive in ways that foster love and forgiveness in others.

- **and focus on the present and future behavior** (punishment focuses primarily on past behavior).

A STEP TOWARD BETTER DISCIPLINE
Find Your Parenting Style in Thirty Questions

Find how you're doing now in terms of discipline style—are you too hard on your kids, too soft, or just right? This quick quiz takes less than ten minutes and can give you an instant clue. Answer if the following statements are true or false from your experience.

1. Often I need to give instructions two or three times before my kids listen. ☐ TRUE ☐ FALSE
2. I am the mom and it is my children's job to do what I say. ☐ TRUE ☐ FALSE
3. The rules I have are based on logic and reasoning. ☐ TRUE ☐ FALSE
4. I establish daily routines. ☐ TRUE ☐ FALSE
5. My kids seldom have chores to do. ☐ TRUE ☐ FALSE
6. When my son disobeys me, I give him a good swat. ☐ TRUE ☐ FALSE
7. I spend time with my child each day. ☐ TRUE ☐ FALSE
8. If my youngster questions a rule, I'll discuss why that rule is important. ☐ TRUE ☐ FALSE
9. Often I'm reluctant to enforce rules. ☐ TRUE ☐ FALSE
10. My child likes me to be right alongside when doing homework. ☐ TRUE ☐ FALSE
11. My kids constantly bicker or fight. ☐ TRUE ☐ FALSE
12. As long as you're in my house, you'll do what I say. ☐ TRUE ☐ FALSEE
13. My husband and I have a few rules that are consistently enforced. ☐ TRUE ☐ FALSE
14. Often it's easier to let the kids do their own thing. ☐ TRUE ☐ FALSE
15. My children are respectful of one another's belongings. ☐ TRUE ☐ FALSE
16. When I come home to find toys lying around all over the place, I hit the roof. ☐ TRUE ☐ FALSE
17. Often I find myself yelling and screaming. ☐ TRUE ☐ FALSE
18. I explain and enforce a few simple rules. ☐ TRUE ☐ FALSE

In the process, discipline becomes something your children internalize and do, not something you must address and bemoan. By teaching and correcting, using choices and consequences, your child learns to feed the better wolf inside. The battles for control and power struggles melt away. The key is in helping your kids see which wolf to feed themselves, which choices are positive, and which consequences lead to more dangerous and snarly issues.

The key is also in how to do the feeding because you can bark directives and expect obedience. But that won't get you where you want to be.

19. I encourage my kids to be responsible and think for themselves. ☐TRUE ☐FALSE
20. Threats and bribes are my main arsenal. ☐TRUE ☐FALSE
21. It's necessary to spank your kids to get them to obey. ☐TRUE ☐FALSE
22. Getting my kids to do chores is too big a struggle. It's easier to do these tasks myself. ☐TRUE ☐FALSE
23. Frequently I find myself doing things for my kids that they could do for themselves. ☐TRUE ☐FALSE
24. I frequently come to my child's defense when corrected by teachers because I don't want the criticism to damage his self-esteem. ☐TRUE ☐FALSE
25. If my child misbehaves in public places, I frequently ignore it. ☐TRUE ☐FALSE
26. I am tuned in to and support my child's feelings and needs. ☐TRUE ☐FALSE
27. I create fun rituals, such as reading to my child every night. ☐TRUE ☐FALSE
28. Teachers complain that my son doesn't follow directions and prefers to do his own thing. ☐TRUE ☐FALSE
29. I would rather give in to my children's desires than argue with them and have them mad at me. ☐TRUE ☐FALSE
30. I think it's very important to praise and encourage my children so they feel loved and appreciated. ☐TRUE ☐FALSE

How do you think you did?

An authoritarian parent would answer true to questions 1, 2, 6, 10, 11, 12, 16, 17, 20, and 21.

The permissive parent who is too lenient would answer true to questions 5, 7, 9, 11, 14, 21, 22, 23, 24, 25, 28, 29, and 30.

Authoritative parents, finding that balance between being firm and corrective while teaching and helping grow, would answer true to questions 3, 4, 7, 8, 13, 15, 18, 19, 26, 27, and 30.

You may find that you lean a couple directions, for instance most of your true answers are split between two categories. Look at how you lean now and keep reading in this chapter for how to find a healthy, authoritative balance.

HOW DO YOU DISCIPLINE?

While it's often easy to see which wolf is winning in children who act up, it may not be clear to you which wolf you're feeding, how the choices you make in correcting and disciplining your children affect their outcome.

Diana Baumrind, PhD, a developmental and clinical psychologist in California, helps us with her groundbreaking, lifelong research on parenting styles. Begun in the 1960s, Baumrind's studies found there are three typical tendencies of parents:

1.   strict and heavy-handed **authoritarian**,

2.   loving and engaged but loose and **permissive**,

3.   balanced and **authoritative**. [2]

Where the first two styles go to extremes in discipline, the last style is more balanced, the target you want to hit. (Later, other researchers added a fourth style—the unengaged parent, but the very fact that you're reading this book makes that one moot for discussion.)

Finding where you are and what you'll want to refine in order to raise delightful children, is a lot like what Goldilocks went through trying to find the best chairs at the Bears' house. Remember how she tried one chair after another and one almost swallowed her and gave no support, and another was so uncomfortable she abandoned it as quickly as she could, but one was just right? Baumrind found that styles of parenting can serve you in the same way. The permissive style can collapse, offering no support for you or your kids. The authoritarian style can be painful and even do damage. But the authoritative style can hold up and help you be the best, most purposeful parent possible. As you think about which way you lean in responding to your kids, take a closer look at the three styles.

Are you Authoritarian? Too Hard?

You've heard the authoritarian parent's typical line, and maybe even said it yourself, "Because I'm your mother/father, that's why!" Or, "Because I said so—now do it!"

Set on shaping and controlling a child's behaviors and attitudes, the authoritarian parent values unquestioned demands and obedience. These parents give directives and orders, discourage verbal give and take, close off and shut down choices and options, and use punishment, threats, criticism, and guilt to curb a child's self-will and enforce their own directives. Like the chair Goldilocks found that was too hard, this style creates discomfort to such an extreme that a child's emerging autonomy is stifled. There's no wiggle room for reasoning or feelings; and no place of comfort or encouragement for children to think for themselves or solve their own problems.

I remember one pretty little girl referred to me by her kindergarten teacher because she was bossy, argumentative, and disrespectful to her teacher and other students. She had a habit of pinching people who didn't do as she demanded, and when her mother came to a conference, I understood why.

Talking about how she disciplined at home, the mom said, "I am the boss. That's it. What I say goes!"

Of course, her daughter was modeling this absolute, authoritarian behavior, which was, "My way, or no way—no matter what." The wolf both mother and daughter fed was the one that needed to be top dog, in control, and obeyed—or else. The environment was one of black and white, complete submission or harsh punishment. Mom and daughter both were living in fear, frustration, anger, and discouragement.

The mom's authoritarian parenting style does real damage because:

- **Control is external to a child and doesn't teach inner control.**
- **There's more focus on obedience than moral development.** The reason behind rules and their impact on others when not obeyed is never discussed.
- **There's an emphasis on power and control** (and clamor for it at all costs) rather than teaching, encouraging, and guiding.
- **The frequent use of physical force**, demeaning, and belittling demonstrates aggression and results in shame, higher levels of aggression and antisocial behavior, even retaliation.[3]

- **dependency is fostered** by the parent's constant directives, leaving little room for flexible thinking.

Are You Permissive? Too Soft?

At the other extreme, the permissive parent is often heard saying, "Okay, one more," or "Oh, all right...." Pretty much whatever the permissive parent's child says or does, goes, because this parenting style is to make few demands and allow kids to exercise as much control as possible over their own activities. Permissive parents tolerate much, rarely take an active role in shaping or altering their child's impulses and actions no matter how incorrect, and use as little punishment as possible, often as a path of least resistance.

This creates some ugly situations that I've dealt with firsthand. In the 1970s, permissive parenting was in vogue and I was working as a school counselor, on the front line of seeing its ineffectiveness. Teachers regularly sent kids to me who would smile in agreement to classroom rules, but return to their own agendas the minute a teacher's attention focused on someone else. These kids were a handful. They didn't get enough attention or limits from their parents, and would run amuck. They never cleaned up their own messes, and expected privileges similar to those of the teacher. They were in constant turmoil and caused division and upset among other children too.

Sandie, a second grader, said so well how these kids of permissive parents affect everyone around them. Her cousin was visiting from another state and even though she was younger, Kelsey got away with so much more, doing what she wanted, when she wanted, and practically with her permissive parents' blessing.

"I really don't like Kelsey," Sandie said. "She refuses to go to bed until her parents do, so last night I went to bed at eight o'clock and Kelsey stayed up until eleven!"

Of course this disrupted the whole family. Sandie wondered why she couldn't stay up late too. In the meantime, Kelsey was a mess, tired and cranky, insistent upon her own way, and willing to have meltdowns or throw a fit to get it. At seven years of age, Kelsey already had a huge sense of entitlement without any self-control or responsibility. What a setup for doom later in life, where this kind of behavior makes a person unlikeable at the very least and avoidable and even shunned much of the time.

Just as Goldilocks found the soft chair couldn't hold her, easy or permissive parenting style won't hold up for you or your kids. Rather, it damages by raising children who:

- **Expect privileges** far beyond their status, and expect others to do for them which interferes with and impacts their academic achievement.

- **Have little sense of responsibility.**

- **Can't find or adapt to structure** to manage their lives, leading to daily chaos and a sense of insecurity.

- **Don't monitor their behavior** and are often inappropriate, causing disruption, upset, and unrest. The constant need for discipline in group situations negatively impacts their relationship with peers and sense of self-worth too.

- **Are immature** and lack impulse control and self-reliance.

- **Lack security** due to insufficient parental guidance, which can result in feelings of anxiety and depression.

A permissive parenting style eventually crashes because it feeds the lesser wolf too, the one that's greedy and arrogant, self-centered, and driven by ego.

Are You Authoritative? Just Right?

But before you think there must not be any style that works when kids misbehave, know there is hope. Just as Goldilocks found the perfect chair by rejecting the extremes of too hard and too soft, you'll find that practicing an authoritative style is the sweet spot on the continuum between authoritarian and permissive styles. The authoritative style gives you a model of how to love with limits, and brings out the best in you and your children. It provides support and is reliable.

When you use an authoritative style, you can set controls and demand high standards of behavior in warm, rational ways that free your child, welcome their expression, and value who they are, if not always their actions. This combination of firm control and positive encouragement helps your children thrive and learn which wolf to feed.

Specifically, as an authoritative parent you:

- **Establish firm, clear, and relatively demanding expectations** for your children—all with moderation so as not to stifle them or hem them in rigidly with no room for self-expression or development.

- **Encourage verbal give and take so there is constant learning.**

- **Value both autonomous self-will** (where your children make their own choices), **and disciplined conformity** (where your kids cooperate and work within rules, parameters, and structure).

- **Share the reasoning** for policies, rules, and direction so your children understand and can apply principles, not just rules, beyond any one situation.

- **solicit objections** when your child refuses to conform (because you don't regard yourself as infallible nor divinely inspired).

- **Set consequences** that enforce the perspective as an adult while recognizing a child's individual interests and special ways.

This style helps your children develop self-discipline, where they gain a strong sense of both social responsibility and independence, and are happier, with greater confidence and self-esteem, according to Stanley Coppersmith in his *The Antecedents of Self-Esteem* book series about behavioral science.[4] You've created an environment where your kids can be more sure of themselves because there's no ambiguity about the rules and limits or who's in charge. This is where kids can thrive and begin to mind, behave well, and grow in grace.

Even babies can sense and respond to an authoritative parent, according to Dr. Everett Waters, a psychology professor at the State of New York at Stony Brook. Researching the response of babies and toddlers to the discipline in a variety of parenting styles, Waters found that the parents practicing love with limits, and setting choices and consequences from the earliest age, got appropriate responses in a timely manner.[5]

Look at the different styles in action: An *authoritarian* parent might yell at or spank a toddler who grabs from the table something curious like a knick-knack or clock, a completely natural thing for a child to do. A *permissive* parent might let the episode go entirely, even if the toddler breaks the object. An *authoritative* parent would take the object from the child, look her in the eye, and say something like, "No touch," while returning it to a place out of reach on the table.

While not happy having the object of desire taken away, the child of the authoritative parent understands not only what happened but why. Within a few more tries, she modifies her behavior, is secure in what she's learned, and can behave similarly in other circumstances according to the choice and consequence shown. The balance between love, encouragement, and firmness is there.

Without those three essentials—love enough to correct and teach, encouragement with the belief your kids can learn and grow, and firmness through the meantime—the toddler of authoritarian and permissive parents is left on shaky ground. Things are out of balance; and as with anything unbalanced, their understanding is wobbly. The toddler of the authoritarian was punished for a natural behavior and may not understand what happened for a long time, and maybe never why. The child of the permissive parent wasn't told or shown in any way the behavior was poor. They need that just-right discipline; without it, no wonder researchers find children grow up with less (and sometimes lacking) impulse control, self-reliance, social responsibility, and independence.[6]

ESTABLISH YOUR AUTHORITY WITHOUT BREAKING THE SPIRIT

So how do you to achieve that authoritative style? How can you be firm but not harsh, hold high standards without pressuring, be ready to correct without waiting to catch them in the act of doing something wrong? How do you become the parent who lovingly teaches and whose children grow delightfully? How do you best feed the best wolf?

Start Now

Both the Bible and child development psychologists agree—it's never too early to start. Because the Lord disciplines those he loves, as a father the son he delights in" (Proverbs 3:12).

More admonition is needed earlier in life and makes a great difference, which is what educational psychologists Michael K. Meyerhoff and Burton White found in researching the children of each parenting style.[7] Authoritative parents who weren't afraid to set realistic but firm limits on behavior before the first birthday had the most self-disciplined, responsible, and well-behaved children—and love with limits was enforced from the moment these children began to crawl. When behavior was either unsafe or unacceptable, toddlers received a clear message to that effect, and the authoritative parents usually didn't have to tell their children more than once not to do something because the admonitions were clear and quick, and disobedience was followed up with immediate action.

The key was the parents' commitment and persistence to put actions behind their words.

Be Mindful of the Love-Discipline Gauge

The child who feels and knows he is loved is the child who will respond more readily to discipline. Before you do a single thing, remind yourself that loving unconditionally gives you more leverage to discipline. Think of what you say and do as having an actual gauge for how much love you give and how much correction. Are your words balanced with both? Are your actions? The measures for this gauge will differ with circumstance, personalities, and the situation, but this is the question to return to before and after the times you're called on to discipline your child: For every correction you give, are you saying and showing your children you love them unconditionally?

Practice the Law of Sowing and Reaping

From fairy tales and fables, to the classroom and conference room, we grow up hearing how we reap what we've sown. A few years ago one of the best-selling business books went so far as to use the idea for both its title and packaging. *The Little Red Book of Selling* by Jeffrey Gitomer[8] taught the principle of sowing and reaping, the consequences of getting sales by your choices, as shown in that old Russian folktale of the little red hen.

Nearly every child hears by third grade, if not well before starting school, the story of *The Little Red Hen*, published by Little Golden Books in the 1940s and popular in the mass market ever since. You know the story. A little red hen finds a grain of wheat and asks for help from all the other farmyard animals to plant it. But no one volunteers for the planting—or the harvest, threshing, milling the wheat into flour, and baking the flour into bread. All the animals refused to help, but then hope to help eat the tasty bread. To their dismay, the little red hen feeds her chicks, and all the other animals lose out. Help out or miss out, the moral of the story goes. If you don't work, you don't get to enjoy the fruits of the labor, other versions say.

Of course, long before the children's story and business book, the Bible gave us the law of sowing and reaping: A few loaves and fish brought to Jesus are turned into basketfuls of food, enough to feed a huge crowd with leftovers too (Matthew 15:35-37, Mark 6:41-44). A widow and her son give to God all they have and are given by God all they need, and then some (1 Kings 17:10-16).

Sowing and reaping is so simple and true, throughout the Bible, as well as in nature, and in disciplining your kids. Apple seeds planted grow into trees that bear apples. Apple trees cut down, die. If you lie, people do not trust you or believe what you say. If you are late arriving at the airport, the plane leaves without you. You do reap what you sow (Galatians 6:7).

There's power here that even a child can understand, whether you're talking about a law of nature, relationships, or the Bible. So when you start applying this principle of choice and consequence, your kids will grasp it, know it, and learn to live by it. They'll understand that every choice reaps a consequence, positive or negative. They'll see how the choices you make determine the quality of your life.

The way they learn this law of life is in how you practice it and reinforce it at home. That is where discipline comes in—not to punish but correct and teach this principle. The goal is not to control your children with such a law, rather to help them make responsible choices to thrive on their own. As they develop self-control, the issues they face belong to them, not you, and that's what you both ultimately want.

Set Choices

However, practicing choice-making doesn't mean setting up a free-for-all where your kids are in charge. You're not giving your children the choice of *what* to do, which can invite a power struggle. You're engaging them in *how* to do it, inviting their participation into developing their own independence. So when you offer choices, it's important to:

- **State the expectation** because some structure is non-negotiable. For instance, eating and sleeping, being hygienic, learning, honesty, and respect for life and places and things are essentials that you as the parent make sure your child gets. So when it's time for school, you don't ask, "Do you want to go to school now?" because getting an education isn't an option. You're responsible for your child to have every opportunity to learn and grow. Where choice comes into the picture is in helping them see their essential needs, understand why certain things are essential, and think and act for themselves on how to get what's needed. So you invite their participation. You say something like, "I expect you to get ready for school in a timely manner. You need to comb your hair and get dressed before breakfast." Then you help them make the right choice. For instance, you help them lay out their clothes the night before so getting ready the next morning goes more smoothly. You make rules for no TV or wandering around the house in pajamas on school mornings, to minimize the temptations that get in the way. For really little ones, five- and six-year-olds, you walk them through the morning: getting dressed, combing hair, eating breakfast and brushing teeth, then grabbing the backpack from a designated place. Your child has a choice then to follow these directions and get ready on time or suffer a consequence such as, "If you don't get to breakfast on time, then you'll have to take your breakfast to school and eat it during snack time." When you always state the expectation, you help your child meet it.

- **Be clear and make sure children understand** both your rules and consequences for breaking them. Say clearly and directly, "You have a choice between this or that way." Give some ideas and instruction on how to go about each way. For example, when you've taught your children the steps involved in cleaning up their rooms, the directive is, "We each need to clean our rooms every Saturday morning." The rule of working before playing applies, so you say, "If you haven't finished cleaning your room by noon, you forfeit going to the movies or playing with your friends." You can be sure your kids understand the consequence by asking them, "What are you going to do?" They should be able to answer, though the real test is in their choice-making itself, where experience becomes the teacher. After one round of choosing wisely or poorly, remind them that they can either learn from mistakes or repeat them and suffer the consequences. They will begin to internalize the truth that they have a choice: *Do the chores and play. Ignore the chores and pay.* Either way, they learn: *I live with the choices I make.*

- **Let age appropriateness be your guide.** So much of children's behavior that annoys adults is developmentally appropriate. Toddlers, for instance, will say "no" a lot because they're developing individuality and increasingly learning to exercise their own will. Few also have little understanding of time. So if you give two-year-olds a choice of either picking out their own clothes in the next hour or you doing it, they may simply respond, "no," and your time option is meaning- less. That hour may as well be a day or forever. For one- to four-year-olds, you're best focusing on rules and choices that regard safety, care of personal possessions, and interpersonal relations, according to Dr. Claire B. Kopp, a professor of psychology at the University of California at Los Angeles, who has studied how to best reach one-to-four-year-olds.[9] Think about rules and choices for toddlers that foster inde- pendence, such as asking your little one to return toys to

A STEP TOWARD BETTER DISCIPLINE
Keep Choices Simple as a Song

Giving parameters with some rhythm, rhyme, and even a song helps your children learn how to behave and act in ways good for them—and everyone around you. These techniques work.

- **When, then:** Teach your kids "When, then" as a principle by talking with them about how certain things are best done before other things, and other things are best enjoyed when those certain things are done first. For ex- ample: "When you've finished your chores, then you may play outside," or, "When you've cleaned up, then we can go to the movies." When, then gives kids a choice and you're not the bad guy when they make a poor choice— there's simply a consequence.

- **Abuse it, lose it.** Teach that taking advantage can take away a privilege be- cause someone loses out when only one person is on the take. A good ex- ample is: just as too much sun can burn your skin, too much of other things can hurt your well-being. That's why you have certain rules like not too much TV (so you don't become a couch potato), not too many video games (so you learn to live in and enjoy a real world, not just a fantasy one), and not too many snacks (so you don't fill up on junk and kill your appetite for nutritious meals, and so you don't gain too much weight).

- **Rap your rules.** The Center for New Discoveries in Learning in Windsor, Cali- fornia, teaches that learning and memory actually increase at least five times the toy chest or bin after playtime. Toddlers especially need ample demonstration, support, and encouragement. Then when you see your five-year-old placing a dirty shirt in the hamper and your six- year-old parking his bike and skateboard in the garage after use, give them big hugs. Praise goes a long way in encouraging them to make those new choices over again: "Look at Gracie being a big girl" or "Ross, you're being so responsible."

■ **To be authoritative, sound authoritative.** Too often parents tell their children to do something and give choices on how, but sound tentative or, worse, pleading. At best, this confuses a child and plants doubt that you know what you mean. At worst, it empowers a child and invites disobedience because it sounds like you don't really mean what you say. Meaning

by using sixty beats per minute in instruction or direction. That's probably why the ancient Greeks sang their dramas rather than recited them. Music does help you remember. So just as singing "The Alphabet Song" helps little ones learn their ABCs, you can use rhyme, rap, and some playfulness to teach your kids your rules. Even a chant or sing-songy approach makes the rules more fun and can get your kids to play along in every way. Here are some good starters:

THE RULE	THE RHYME AND REASON
Put your dirty clothes in the hamper to get washed or they'll stay dirty and stinky.	*Clothes on the floor, clean no more.*
Put your dirty dishes in the dishwasher.	*Dirty dishes left around, no more dishes to be found.*
Anytime you're on wheels, wear a helmet.	*No helmet, no wheels.*
Homework, chores, and assigned reading before play, pleasure, and TV.	*When the work's done, have fun.*
Clean up your own mess because if you don't pick up after yourself, including your toys and things, the privilege or toys are taken away.	*Pick it up or give it up.*
Make your bed every morning before school or you'll practice making it after school.	*Make it in the morning or make it later over and over and over and over and over again.*

what you say is the key. If you mean, "Stop! Now!" then say that firmly, clearly, and with authority. Speak from your gut. Project your voice. That doesn't mean yell at your kids. It means imagine the sound of your voice surrounding your child. Speak with energy in a measured pace with pauses. Fast, eruptive speech usually is perceived as nervousness and uncontrolled. Slowing your pace helps you relax, gives you time to think, and your listener time to take in what you're saying. Practice authoritative responses so they come naturally at the moment needed.

■ **Reward rather than bribe.** Jake's father told me he used bribes to get Jake to follow directions and rules. So many parents resort to this: "If you get an A on the math test, I'll give you a dollar." "If you pick up your toys, you can have an extra cookie." "If you graduate from high school, we'll buy you a car." Giving something to Jake so he would get up and get dressed in time every day for school? "That's worth a dollar to me," Jake's dad said. But, oh, how that's going to cost him and Jake. As popular and commonly practiced as this may be, bribing a child doesn't get the effect you want for long, concluded Daniel H. Pink who researched this for his best-selling book *Drive*.[10] Offering short-term rewards to elicit behavior isn't the same thing as giving your children choices that help them develop and learn self-discipline. In fact, Pink found, the effects are unreliable, ineffective, and can cause long-term damage. Your child works for the reward and when a reward isn't available, the behavior stops. What's been learned? To behave well only when you get something you want? All this teaches is manipulation. It's better for your child to feel the intrinsic benefit of a job well done, says Alan Kazdin, director of the Yale Parenting Center.[11] Incentives focus too much on the end result instead of behavior leading up to the result, Kazdin explains, "You can't throw rewards at behaviors that don't exist and get them."[12] Rather than threats and bribes, consequences for choices made bring lasting results.

- **Talk often about "a better way."** Sometimes you may give your kids a choice and they abide by a rule but still fail to get the point of it. For instance you may tell your fourth grader to come straight home from school because you want him to tackle his homework before supper. He may come straight home from school but play around instead of working on assignments. He followed the rule but missed the point. Get your kids thinking more and more about the point. Reward times they accomplish the greater good by choosing a better way than you even imagined. Apostle Paul said this so well: All things might be lawful or allowed, but not all things are beneficial or constructive or good (see 1 Corinthians 10:23). Just as you're always encouraging your kids to "make good choices," help them to always "look for the better way.".s." You can use teachable moments, like when you witness other kids misbehaving, melting down, or acting out, talk later with your kids about better ways to act. Ask them to identify some better ways of acting in similar situations. Plant ideas of what's better too. Kids can't model what they've never seen nor experienced. Help them know best ways to behave by setting an example and calling out examples in the books you read, movies you watch, and places you go, people you see.

Determine Consequences

To some parents, determining consequences is an easy matter. There's punishment and there's spanking. The trouble is that punishment and corporal or physical punishments are not consequences, and using them creates other problems.

One young mother learned the difference in a powerful way. As she nursed her newborn boy in one arm, she wrapped the other around her toddler daughter. The little girl nestled close with a picture book, but her eyes, green with envy, stayed on her baby brother. A natural jealously sprouted.

She'd once been the center of Mom and Dad's attention. Now the newborn got much of their attention. Mom, drowsy, closed her eyes and the toddler seized her opportunity to slap her brother in the face just as he, too, was drifting to sleep.

The baby shrieked awake as Mom grabbed her girl's hand and said, "Honey, people are not for hitting."

Her bright-eyed moppet teared up and apologized. She sank deeper into her mother's side and watched Mommy comfort and calm the baby, stroking his face, cooing him back to sleep.

Weeks passed and the green-eyed monster struck again. The girl slapped her brother when Mom's back was turned. Patiently, Mom reminded, "People are not for hitting." Again, her little one apologized, sniffling through more tears that fell on a protruding bottom lip.

Soon after, Mom struggled to get the kids ready for her first outing on her own with both little ones in tow. She tucked her sleeping newborn into his car seat and turned to grab her purse and jacket. As soon as her back was to her newborn, she heard a cry. She whirled around as he screamed from being pinched awake by his sister.

Exasperated, Mom grabbed her daughter by the arm and spanked her three times. "I've told you enough times not to do that. You are in big trouble, Missy. Time Out!"

In tears, the toddler ran to her Time Out chair. "But, Mommy," she cried. "You said people are not for hitting."

Preschoolers can try your limits and test your patience with their growing pains, but a pat on the butt (or worse) is coercion, not correction, and even a toddler picks up on the hypocrisy and confusion.

How much better Mom, toddler, and baby brother would be if Mom had not reacted in anger. Parenting on purpose helps you be the parent who thinks through and talks through the situation before it explodes into something hurtful to you and your child. In this situation, Mom could have planned a distracting activity for her daughter from the start. Of course her daughter was going to be jealous after being the sole center of all love and affection in the family then suddenly, overnight, having to share it. Even without the activity, Mom could help her daughter express her feelings and reassure her that Mom and Dad have more than enough love for everyone in the family ("And that's not going away!"). Mom could also engage her daughter in something special, just for Mom and daughter ("Since you're my big girl now, let's you and I make cookies in a minute for Daddy."). After all this, Mom could give a consequence: "If you hit your brother, you'll have to go to the Time Out chair" (one minute for every year of age, so five minutes for a five-year-old, six minutes for a six-year-old, and so on). Time Out chairs work, even if you have to hold your child there and explain the time doesn't start till he or she sits in the chair—so dallying and rebelling to go there doesn't work either. The consequence will be waiting.

And consequences do work.

While you'll find plenty of people in favor of corporal punishment, I'm not one of them. These folks believe a spanking or strike to stop certain behavior teaches a lesson. It does—that an aggressive response in anger is okay. Most parents who spank admit what they intend to be a pat on the fanny turns out to be something much more forceful delivered in rage. I do not believe that tactic teaches a child anything productive.

Neither are child development experts. Research shows why. Nearly half of moms (42 percent) in a survey conducted by Rebecca R. Socolar, a clinical assistant professor at the University of North Carolina, admitted they spank their children—and more for dangerous behavior like getting too close to a hot iron than annoying behavior such as splashing water all over the floor from a bathtub or tracking in mud from outside all over the carpet.[13] Every single one of their children was found to be more aggressive, angry, and developmentally behind in moral reasoning and in self-esteem (some even clinically anxious and depressed) than the children of moms who used an authoritative style of choices and consequences to discipline.

Socolar's study is just one in a deep sea of research with the same conclusions. Spanking as a means of punishment lowers a child's self-esteem, develops anger and resentment toward parents, and can plant seeds of aggression, even juvenile delinquency. "It's an epidemic in America that people readily accept that hitting is an appropriate way of changing behavior," said Dr. Irwin A. Hyman, director of the National Center for the Study of Corporal Punishment and Alternatives in the Schools, which he founded at Temple University School of Psychology in Philadelphia. "But we have fifty years of research showing that rewards and building self-esteem are a much more effective means of changing a child's behavior."[14]

It's not just research that's so convincing to me.

I've seen the faces and behavior of little ones from families where spanking is the punishment for misbehavior. Their lives match the findings of research, and their lack of learning and self-discipline troubles me deeply. These children struggle to grasp the consequences of their choices and often wrestle with a deep sense of shame, that they are inherently bad, because they're used to coercion rather than correction. They're often angry and frustrated, and when faced with any challenge, lash out at others, alienating themselves because that's what they've learned. While I work with them, I'm reminded of the Bible's wisdom: "Fathers, do not provoke your children to anger, but bring them up in the discipline and instruction of the Lord" (Ephesians 6:4 ESV).

And yet encouragement to spank and use corporal punishment comes from many church pulpits and Christian leaders who quote Proverbs 13:24 (NKJV): "He who spares the rod hates his son, but he who loves him disciplines him promptly."

How sad that one verse is pulled out to justify hitting, and so many other passages and examples in the Bible of God's tender care to correct and teach, are ignored. Jesus always taught us to bear fruits, or evidences, of a godly spirit: act and think in love, kindness, self-control, gentleness, and faithfulness (Galatians 5:22-23). Such teaching goes back to his great (and twenty-eight generations-great) grandfather, David, the shepherd-king. David used a rod and staff to ward off wolves and protect and guide his sheep. He wrote in the Twenty-third Psalm what so many of us learn as children, "Thy rod and thy staff, they comfort me."

How does this picture fit with the leader of one Bible study I attended, who shared how his son made him so angry that he hit him with a belt, forgetting he'd ever read the Bible? Right. It doesn't.

Thank goodness more Christian leaders are taking a 180-degree turn on their support of corporal punishment, agreeing it's not congruent with the teachings of Christ.

Truly, the wise parent establishes authority without using physical punishment. Based on a simple rule of always treating one another with respect, there's no hitting, spanking, or physical violence. The rule of respect and wisdom is: "People are not for hitting. I'll never hit you, and I expect you to never hit your brother, sister, other children or adults." Once that's clear, the teaching opportunity is there for you to seize. When your child misbehaves, you have that open door to confront choices or suffer consequences—and you set the consequences by knowing:

- **Consequences are the control.** This is key. Control is at the crux of so many discipline issues, but the "sowing and reaping" or "choices and consequences" model breaks down the wall of you against them. You're not the meanie or bully against your kids, as those punished would feel. There's simply a consequence for every choice. For instance, many battles concerning control are fought around the dinner table. Your child refuses to eat. You easily can go into action by begging, pleading, scolding, and demanding them to eat because you want to make sure they get proper nutrition and grow. That motivation isn't the problem but your responses are when you play into the power struggle. Led by your fear of malnutrition, you've joined the ranks of short-order cooks trying to please the little generals. I know of one mother of a kindergarten-age child who literally became so desperate, she spoon-fed her five-year-old son like a baby. He was victorious in his ability to get his mother to do his bidding; and while he won the battle by deciding what to eat, she lost a bigger war of maintaining authority and teaching him something good way beyond one meal. He'd learned the first time she gave in and fixed something else that he was in control of his mother instead of himself. The sad thing—their interaction made reality a lie. She was treating a five-year-old like a baby and he, a five-year-old, had control of an adult! Eating problems always tell us there are blurred boundaries and a fight for control. On the other hand, giving choices and consequences reestablishes the boundary and solves the battle of wills. So when your children refuse to eat what you serve, they miss out on snacks. They may even go hungry until they will follow the healthful pattern. Hunger will work pretty fast to motivate a child to eat better. The rule you set is this: "Eating a balanced meal is important for your health. If you make the choice not to eat healthy food, then snacks and sweets will be forfeited" or "This is it until breakfast."

- **A few rules consistently enforced are better than lots of rules enforced sporadically.** Before making a rule, ask yourself: Is this rule really necessary? Does it protect my child's health or safety? Does it teach my child how to play and get along with others? Does it teach my child to clean up her own mess? If not, maybe it's not a rule to keep. Too many rules can overwhelm and suffocate a young child's budding identity, and can also give your kids the feeling that you expect them to be perfect, rather than that you're helping them learn how to be self-controlled.

- **Logical or natural consequences make the most sense—and difference.** Rudolf Dreikurs, a medical doctor and author of Children: *The Challenge: The Classic Work on Improving Parent-Child Relations*, explains that allowing natural consequences to follow a natural social order creates the greatest impact on your child. For example, if your daughter plays ball too close to the house and breaks a window, the natural consequence is to repair the window. If the family rule is to place soiled clothes in the hamper, the natural consequence for your son dropping dirty jeans on the floor is they don't get washed. "The order of things is pretty straightforward," Dreikurs says. "Children can understand and accept this flow of things."[15] So when bikes or skateboards are left lying around, they're consequentially put out of use for one day. If non-compliance continues, increase the time of not using these vehicles for two to three days or maybe a week. For school-age kids, homework, books, and materials needed for assignments should be brought home daily, and if Mom or Dad have to drive them back to school to get forgotten things, then the kids owe you the time that it took, doing something for your benefit. With consequences like these, kids (and adults) can grasp the principle of choices and start making better ones pretty fast.

- **Consistency is the glue.** You have no authority if you don't mean what you say and do something about rules unheeded or broken. Don't give a direction if you're not prepared to follow through. Too many parents issue commands too many times. Children quickly learn to ignore the first two commands, like one cute first grader sent to my office for habitually not following his teacher's directions. The boy admitted his response record was to become "parent deaf" at will. With a smirk, he said, "I wait until Mom says something three times, or until she gets mad, whichever comes first, to do what she says!" As expected, the behavior learned at home to not worry, because a direction doesn't mean act now, carried over to school—and Mom's style of issuing commands didn't work. "Children who come from environments that are reasonably consistent and predictable generally have higher self-esteem and more self-confidence," said Dr. Darwin Dorr, a consulting professor of medical psychology at Duke University and editor of *The Psychology of Discipline*.[16]

- **Parents stick together no matter what.** If you argue, disagree, and lose control with your spouse or any other authority figure in front of your children, you sow confusion and anxiousness. You also, unwittingly, teach your kids the art of manipulation and how to pit one parent or authority figure against another. This doesn't mean you'll always think exactly like your spouse or another authority figure. A certain amount of disagreement actually helps you see alternatives, enlarge your repertoire of effective parenting strategies, and temper what to do when you're at extreme ends. But you don't do that tempering in front of your kids. You talk through differences of opinion in private or in a way

A STEP TOWARD BETTER DISCIPLINE
Keep Your Cool When They Melt Down

It's distressing to me that yelling has become the new spanking when it comes to discipline. At the grocery store, in the park, even during church, you hear parents yell at their kids to "Come here," "Stop that right now," "Straighten up." But yelling and nagging don't work, even though every parent has resorted to it at some point.

In yelling with frustration, you may have let off your own steam, but you haven't solved a thing. You might shock your child into stopping for a moment. But after the shock wears off, they haven't learned why to stop, and you may have actually caused additional issues: hurt feelings, frustration, resentment, anger—and all because they don't understand that it's their behavior, not them, that drove you over the edge. Some children yelled at by their parents think there's something wrong with them, or their parents. They wonder, *Why is Mom having a temper tantrum?* Face it, you are having a tantrum when you yell and throw a fit, because your child is throwing a fit. That's Crazy Mother Syndrome.

But you can get a grip. When you feel the frustration rising so much that you want to yell or scream:

- **Withdraw and stop.** "Just one minute," you can say. Or, "Go to your room. I'll come to talk with you in fifteen minutes." Now step away. Do something to break the emotions. Splash water on your face. Sweep the floor. Walk the dog around the backyard. Literally regain your footing. The break gives you and your child time to think and prepare for the discussion. Also, during the break, you can decide what you're going to do if your child starts to argue.

- **Go to Plan B.** Always have a Plan B in your pocket. Determine ahead of time what kind of situations make you and your child melt down. Be intentional, purposeful, and list them: the grocery store, in a restaurant, driving to church or in a service. Decide what you can do. Write out your options to reinforce the ideas and keep somewhere as a reminder for only you. It's easier when you're calm in your kitchen than in the middle of church, a busy street, or that shows respect and how you're going to stand together on the course to follow. You never say, "Do as your mother said," or "See what your father says." Instead, you use "we" in giving direction, and avoid one parent being solely in charge. Otherwise, the other parent's authority is undermined. I saw this mistake while working with a group of mothers whose kids were in a special class to correct behavior problems. Every mother was in full conflict with the child's father, or in a distant or broken relationship with him. None of

Aisle 2 at the grocer's. At the store, for instance, you can tell your child you'll give one warning, then you will both leave if he misbehaves or melts down for not getting something he sees and wants. Plan to go to your car if he begins to lose it and you do too. The very act of leaving the site of the meltdown can help you both calm down until you're ready to try again. In the car, you can talk about what to do differently. Another option is to go home for that talk. Your child will learn how to handle these situations away from them, when not overstimulated or distracted. Parents who are mentally prepared for how they're going to act when children react have a much greater chance of not losing their temper.

- **Self-soothe with self-talk.** If you're thinking, *This behavior isn't fair, everybody thinks I'm a failed parent, other parents don't go through this,* or are repeating some other self-defeating self-talk, things are sure to escalate. But when you're thinking, *I can handle this, this is simply a child misbehaving and not a reflection of my parenting skills, other parents go through this, there are things I can do safely about this now,* there's a much better chance you'll keep your cool.

- **Don't take it personally.** When you feel disrespected, unappreciated, ignored, or put down, you can get mad or hurt. Remind yourself that often what your kids do really isn't about you. They're thinking of themselves. They're hungry, tired, overstimulated, or curious. Remind yourself to look at the bigger picture, that they're thinking of their own wants and desires, not trying to walk all over yours.

At the end of the day, don't beat yourself up emotionally for losing your cool now and then. If you do lose your temper, acknowledge that to your children, not necessarily in a teary confession, but in a matter-of-fact and sincere way. "Mommy lost her temper," or, "Daddy didn't mean to get mad...and he was mad about what you did, not who you are." In so doing, you model good behavior. You show that no one is perfect, not them, not you, but no one has to be controlled by emotions either. You can talk about what you, and they, would be better doing.

these couples were working as a team in disciplining their kids. One parent often gave in to the other's rules, or said *no* when the other said *yes*. Many parents kept secrets from their spouses about giving in; some spouses were just plain absent and uninvolved. The result was exactly what Dr. Everett Waters, psychology professor at the State University of New York at Stony Brook, found in a study of 200 families where parents disagreed over child rearing practices: The children learned to manipulate their folks; and ended up with no respect for authority, and saw their parents as weak and dysfunctional.[17]

- **Staying engaged and working together** is the antidote to raising kids who respect authority in healthy ways single with supportive friends and family, learn how to be united in the way you discipline your kids. This is especially important to remember in an age when, according to one study by the University of Michigan, two in three moms (as opposed to one in three dads) are the sole disciplinarians in the family, setting limits on television watching and computer games.[18]

- **Routine helps reinforce.** Too many caring parents end up sleep deprived for years because their two- or three-year olds rule the roost. It's common, after all, for preschoolers to develop a second wind just when parents say it's time for bed. No sooner is a little tyke tucked in for the night than out he or she pops again, heading to Mom and Dad's room, asking for water or kisses, or playing on sympathies with tales of monsters or nightmares. The ploy is to get snuggles and more time awake. But let this behavior go unchecked and the cycle will continue until you simply give up and allow your kids to stay up, or slip into bed with you. That's when the true monster appears—right next to you with a triumphant grin. But routines help put monsters in their place. A repertoire of soothing activities leading up to bedtime can make kids forget to disobey until they're so relaxed and sleepy that they drift into Dreamland without misbehavior. What works—the progression of a warm bath each night, followed by a story, and saying prayers together. Once you establish a routine for bedtime, you'll see how a little routine helps in other areas too, returning backpacks or bikes not in use to a designated place, for instance, or taking off your shoes at the door, or eating dinner at a set time. Once you've established the rules, you can always break them now and then for some spontaneity or special occasions, but you've got to have the structure first of all to break it. Routines like eating at a set time around the dinner table, teach your kids important things for others areas of life, punctuality and the importance of gathering to feed not just the stomach but the soul. Prayers before bed teach the good of daily giving God time and thanks, praise and even the troubles of the day.

- **Harshness is not the same thing as firmness.** Harshness springs from anger and frustration, while firmness is delivered in a sense of calm strength. Where harshness attacks the person, firmness addresses the problem giving steps to resolve the issue. Nicole, a lawyer at a prestigious New York law firm and mom to five-year-old Sarah, discovered this within weeks of the start of a new school year. She was used to being in control, from the kitchen to the courtroom, but mornings became chaotic and stressful as she struggled to get Sarah ready for school and herself to the commuter train on time. This particular morning had been horrendous. Nicole found Sarah playing with her action figures in the sink instead of brushing her teeth, and getting socks and shoes on. Time was up, and so was Nicole's temper. She grabbed the action figures and flushed them down the toilet, yelling, "You're making us late when you know we can't be, so these have to go." Sarah sobbed, "You couldn't wait to do that, could you?" Mornings had become their battleground, where a cycle of revenge exploded. Like a hammer, Nicole's angry words smashed Sarah's budding sense of self-worth. Nicole needed to master firmness in place of harshness. She needed to take a strong stand toward a Sarah's dawdling, and deliver that stand in a calm, controlled voice. Instead of trashing her daughter's toys, she could say, "Now is time for brushing your teeth, not playing with toys, so I'll take these action figures so you can concentrate on getting dressed for school."

- **Care as much about how you say something as what you say.** Most power struggles could be eliminated if parents' directives to their children were delivered in a calm, respectful manner that doesn't aim to control. Unfortunately, too many time parents bark at their children to do this or stop that, and an offensive tone automatically puts kids on the defense. How you deliver a message truly does invite compliance or instigate rebellion. That means avoid using words like *should, must,* or *have to,* each of which conveys the idea that your words are the be-all, end-all, with no give and take or room or care for what a child thinks and feels. Such authoritarian language only sets you against your children and instigates a power struggle. Instead, offer two appropriate choices versus dictating a command. For example, you might say, "Would you rather have your snack right after school as you do your homework, and then play until dinner time? Or would you rather have your snack and play outside for one hour before finishing your homework before dinner?" See how homework and dinnertime aren't debatable choices but the order of things can be, based on preference and style? This approach engages your kids in what needs to be done or met, and sets them up to receive and engage in how to do it. Tact and tone do go together; even unpleasant things spoken in love can be received well. Think of how Jesus disciplined the adulterous women at the well.

His manner was inquisitive, loving, caring, and compassionate. He didn't shame her. Instead, in a firm gentle voice, he asked her questions while making it clear, "Go now and leave your life of sin" (John 8:11).

PART OF THE SOWING: DIG UP YOUR ROOTS

As you move toward being the parent just right in disciplining your kids, you may need a Time Out yourself. By that I mean take time and space to reflect on whether or not you're parenting in knee-jerk reactions. It's so easy to parent this way, as if on autopilot according to how your parents disciplined you. Either you automatically do what they did because you think it worked, or you do the exact opposite because you're at odds with what you experienced. Either way, this isn't the best, most mindful way to parent and could be hurting you and your kids.

This was the case with Jeff's dad.

Jeff, a large, gawky first grader, was getting into fight after fight with classmates at school, and his dad wasn't doing a thing about it. I learned Mom was the disciplinarian and Dad disagreed with most every attempt she made to correct Jeff. Dad had grown up with an alcoholic mom who was abusive and had disciplined him by spankings that turned into beatings. So discipline to Dad meant something horrible and painful. His mother never established rules and expectations, or taught him how to achieve those on his own. Instead, she berated him, called even innocent and expected behavior *wrong* and *bad*. Her son never felt understood, heard, or helped as a boy. Instead, he was broken. His sense of shame grew with every beating. As a man and then a dad himself, he determined never to correct or punish (and, therefore, hurt) his son.

The result: everyone was walking wounded. Jeff had no self-control or respect for his parents, himself, or anyone else, and was getting away with whatever he wanted. Mom was frustrated because every time she tried to correct and help Jeff, Dad shot down her authority. And Dad could see Jeff created and faced growing problems, but felt clueless about what to do and was contributing to the bad behavior by allowing it.

Jeff's dad needed help to rethink discipline, where it was good and how it could go awry. He needed to know what he experienced as a boy was abuse and not to be confused as a discipline style. He needed assurance that true love for a child is correcting and teaching him, not coercing or abdicating guidance altogether.

But how could he change the thinking and attitudes about discipline that ran so deep in his own soul? How could he make the move toward being authoritative from completely permissive? How could he learn to work together with his wife to be a unified front for Jeff?

How can any parent do these things?

Thinking purposefully, intentionally, and reflectively is the start. No matter what your family background, you learned its patterns. Digging into those roots will help you grow into being the best parent you can be, the one God wants, who sows wisdom into your children's hearts and minds.

Glean from Reflection

Begin by writing down some of the most formative incidents where you were disciplined, addressing for each one what you remember of what happened: What did you do? How did your parents learn of your actions? How did they react? What did they do and require of you? What did you understand of their response, and why or why not? How did it make you feel? How did it change you?

There's power in writing down these things. You acknowledge what happened and you begin to peel back the layers, like that of an onion, revealing how and why you discipline (or not) now.

One of the layers to look at is an outer one—the outcomes. What was helpful, corrective, instructive, or guiding, and why? Make a list of these positives, and any negatives, like what felt hurtful, harmful, spirit-crushing, frustrating, and why.

Now, from the list (another layer to look into, this one interior), identify your emotional vulnerabilities and strengths. For example, maybe a parent's harsh and authoritarian discipline has left you, like Jeff's dad, struggling to trust or forgive, and full of so much shame that you fear failing and even succeeding. Or maybe your strengths are that you're quick to correct things, follow through, don't repeat mistakes, and you're consistent.

Think how each quality leads you to respond with discipline of your children. You'll quickly see how you can attach what you've felt as a child to how you react now. Once you know where you want to be more mindful in correcting your kids, you can begin to take powerful steps forward that will help you and your kids. Knowing is the first step toward change, toward being the parent on purpose that you want and God designed.

Have Faith in All that's Planted

Don't expect change overnight. You may still react, or want to, on autopilot when your kids misbehave. But be encouraged that doing better starts in your head, and now that you know better, you can do better. God promises this. You will be transformed by a renewing of your mind, he says (Romans 12:2). That's where change begins. The Spirit of truth helps you learn and is at work within you to enable you.

Jesus said it plainly too, "The Holy Spirit, whom the Father will send in my name, will teach you all things and will remind you of everything I have said to you" (John 14:26). So, "Ask, and it will be given to you; seek, and you will find; knock, and the door will be opened to you" (Matthew 7:7). The way to do this is so very practical, too. As in any relationship, you:

- **Spend time together.** Tell God your concerns. Ask him questions. Plan to meet with him every day in prayer, praising, and worshipping him. The Bible says when you give God your concerns and every thought, he supplies you with all you need, even guarding your heart (Philippians 4:6-7).

- **Get to know his mind, wisdom, and will.** You can know what God thinks by reading and listening to his Word. There are free phone apps with almost every version of the Bible in audio to hear as you drink your coffee, fix a meal, drive to work, or walk and work out. In the process, God will give you the wisdom (2 Timothy 3:16-17), power (Hebrews 4:12), and hope (Romans 15:4) you need to become the parent he wants and your kids need.

- **Draw near to him and he will draw near to you and help.** God is just a call away and waits to help you (Psalm 145:18 and James 4:8). Look for how he will work in you, through you, and around you. He promises not only his presence to be alongside you through whatever is ahead, but also his strength (Isaiah 33:2 and Philippians 4:13).

Keep Practicing and Sowing

The bottom line is practice. Your actions need to speak louder than words, your sowing the seeds of wisdom needs to happen over and over again. When you keep sowing, disciplining, and feeding the right things as a way of life, you will see change.

Counselors give the same advice. "Whatever you practice, you become," says H. Norman Wright, a psychology professor, the author of more than seventy books, and a marriage, family, and child therapist with a private practice in California.[19] He continues, "If you argue regularly, you become an argumentative person. If you criticize often, you become a critical person." But if you praise, encourage, and keep looking to do the right things, you become someone who is a joy to be around, full of encouragement and goodness.

REAPING DISCIPLINE'S REWARD: GROWTH

That's what you want, after all, to be the authoritative parent who encourages and imparts wisdom in your children. It's the whole point of discipline, teaching your kids to make right choices, or, as the Bible says, disciplining them so they are a delight (Proverbs 29:17).

More delight and less drama was exactly what Shirley was ready for after we talked about discipline as a way of correction and teaching. She knew the battle over riding the bus was going to turn into bigger things unless Lilly learned to make better choices on her own. So Shirley determined to stop engaging in the power struggles, cease growling at her daughter to mind, and stop Lilly's howls of "Noooooo." Shirley determined to start sowing wisdom.

"You have to ride the bus to school in the morning," she told Lilly in a talk before bed that night. "So tomorrow you can get on the school bus on time or you can give up coloring."

Lilly, whose all-time favorite activity was coloring, looked surprised, then troubled, but nodded that she understood. In fact, she didn't yet, not entirely anyway because consequences were all new to her.

So the next morning there was another morning meltdown.

"Fine," Shirley said, calming Lilly instead of reacting to her. "I'll take you to school and I'll also take your crayons since that's your choice."

When Lilly handed over the crayons but walked triumphant to the car, Shirley wondered in a call to me later, if she'd failed.

"No," I reassured. "You've only just begun."
That's the way sowing goes. You plant choices. You give consequences. But there's still tending to do, still teaching for understanding and wisdom.

That evening, Shirley upped the consequences. She was on purpose about discipline. Her goal wasn't just to get Lilly to mind, to perform because Mom said so. Her goal was to teach Lilly that morning needed to go smoothly so they both could go about their day and not get stuck in unnecessary drama.

MY PURPOSEFUL PARENTING CHECK-IN
How Am I Doing with Discipline?

I'm seeing my children grow in discipline, and being my best to bring out their best, by:

- Finding the balance toward being just right as authoritative, not authoritarian or permissive, in my parenting style.
- Teaching the idea of choices and consequences, of sowing and reaping.
- Reinforcing the idea that while there's usually a good way to act and behave, there's always a best way—and pointing my child toward choosing the better way like feeding the better wolf inside.
- Watching the gauge on the love-discipline, making sure I'm balancing the correction I give my child with both a show and words of unconditional love.

"Today didn't go so well, did it?" she asked Lilly that night. She was smiling but firm. "Let's try again tomorrow. You have to ride the bus to school or you'll miss out on the fun things at school and Mommy will get in trouble at work. So tomorrow you're going to get on the bus on time or you'll give up coloring again *and* spend time alone in your room think-ing about it *and* go to bed early so we can get up early to try again. Do you understand?" Shirley could see the recognition in Lilly's eyes that she did understand and was beginning to fully comprehend what consequences meant. Mom wasn't engaging in a fight here. There was just a choice to make.

But choices were all new to Lilly. So the next morning, when the two wolves inside her went to war, Lilly gave in to the howling. "I don't want to get on the bus," she yelled at the door. "Noooooo."

"Fine," Shirley said calmly. "You're choosing to give up coloring *and* to spend time alone after school in your room *and* to go to bed early. Let's get in the car and I'll drive you to school." Shirley was matter-of-fact, and there was no yelling, no battling out what to do at the door. A choice was made. A consequence was coming. This wasn't about her winning or Lilly. It was about Lilly learning.

At home that afternoon the student faced her consequences. She went to her room, without crayons or paper or anyone to talk to—and she didn't last an hour. Within thirty minutes, Lilly burst from her room, promising to be ready on time for the school bus.

Standing her ground wasn't easy, Shirley said, because Lilly didn't make the right choices overnight. But teaching the better way wasn't entirely hard either. In less than a week Lilly had learned the better way of behaving, and both she and Shirley were delighting in their day again.

When you care enough to plant wisdom in your children, you will reap a harvest. It's true that some children will test you. They may rebel. All that you plant may take root but droop for a time. Your child may one day choose to feed the lesser wolf inside. This is one of the most trying parts of parenting. Raising a living, growing being who chooses his or her own way is indeed holy ground. Sowing and disciplining is truly a picture of the divine, what God does with us, spreading grace, nurturing wisdom, allowing us choices and consequences. But his promise is in the harvest. You are establishing the roots of a glorious harvest.

"Start children off on the way they should go," Proverbs 22:6 says, "and even when they are old they will not turn from it." What's sown is rooted deeply in the soul, and the soul is where God lives. Deep calls to deep (Psalm 42:7), and all you are planting will never be in vain, no matter what choices your children ultimately make. God will always call with his ways and his wisdom.

Chapter 3

PURPOSE AND PASSION: GIVE THEM THE WORLD

…because finding your mission and message matters

I was so proud when my oldest son, Tom, began his studies at Duke University as a pre-med student. I delighted at his choice to pursue medicine and heal people. He was always good in science, and would make such a difference in this world, not only giving life to people but helping them live in better, healthier ways. The choice of career was so right for him.

Then, during Tom's junior year, he called with news. "Mom, I've changed my major to foreign affairs and public policy."

What? I thought, as he excitedly described the political science courses he would be taking. *You're too honest to be a politician!* I was careful to listen and not express my instant dismay, but later, the idea of Tom going into politics bothered me even more. I thought of so many families destroyed by public life, the Kennedys especially. *Could our family bear the constant scrutiny, judgment, and testing?*

I couldn't summon any enthusiasm for Tom's choice. I was sad and troubled. I worried he made a terrible decision. I fretted over what to do or say. He was a young man and certainly could make his own choices, but wasn't his true calling to help people heal? Would going astray from what seemed his true gift and purpose lead to years of frustration and misery?

A few weeks later, while cleaning the attic, I came upon a box from Tom's room when he left for college. Inside, were some old newspaper clippings he'd collected about the Civil Rights movement. Beneath the clippings were old cassette tapes labeled "Rev. Martin Luther King Speech" and "President John F. Kennedy Speech." I sifted through the contents, remembering when Tom tuned in to speeches on the television and radio news and recorded them on a cassette recorder. I thought about all the times he'd sit on the family room floor, several newspapers and *Time* magazine laid before him, clipping the articles and talking about them. He asked so many questions about what was happening in our country and even our town at the time. He was so concerned about anyone being marginalized, shut out, put down, or denied the same freedoms and privileges as others.

I set down the box feeling its sudden gravity. While other seven-year-olds were interested in justice on the playground, Tom was drawn to the justice of Civil Rights. Public policy and civil service had, indeed, been some of his natural interests. I thought of all the causes he had championed: defending civil rights on the playground and in the news, working to clean up the environment, and demonstrating to close a nuclear plant. Tom always had a cause.

How could I, his mother, the child psychology major and school counselor helping other children find their true calling, have missed seeing such obvious strengths in my own Tom? Clearly, his gifts for diplomacy, clear judgment, and leadership would aid any career in public policy and service.

I suddenly realized I'd wished the life of a doctor for him because *I* loved that, not Tom.

As he worked in his new major, his natural talents for work in public life became more and more evident. He was strongly committed to using the power of the markets to foster social change and environmental preservation. Today, he flourishes in his career in socially responsible investments. I realize his good and honest heart is doing what I always felt he was called to do, be a healer in this world. He just doesn't do it in the doctor's office or at a hospital. The medicine he dispenses is in working for justice and public discourse and policies that heal social rifts—and his gifts for these things were there all along. I'd just missed them for a time.

Thank goodness, I thought, *I'd not voiced all my reservations about his change of major and career path.* How dangerously close I'd come to doing what's so easy to do: steering a child into the things we want, or wish we had done, or even truly believe he or she will do well in and will give financial security or corporate success and a community's admiration. I'd nearly done just what my own pastor wisely cautions parents against.

UNFOLD, NOT MOLD, THEM

"Your kids are not things to be molded," says Rick Warren, founder and senior pastor of Saddleback Church in Lake Forest, California, and author of the best-selling book *The Purpose Driven Life.* "Your kids are people to be unfolded. God did not bring [them] into the world to satisfy your ego. He brought them into the world to accomplish his purposes."[1]

It's so easy to begin molding when you bring your children into the world and want to give them the moon, to pave a way for them. You have so many hopes and dreams for them that at every juncture you point them in the way you think they should go. You arrange their activities and your own around what you think will help. But these things are more a hindrance. We go astray in thinking that guiding our children means setting their path for them. How can they experience life and find their place in it if we're trying to do it for them?

Our job as parents is to give our children the world, not the moon, and rather than pave a way for them, to let them blaze their own trails.

Discovery can't happen under an iron fist, firm thumb, or in a strong hold, insists Ken Robinson, PhD and author of *The New York Times* best seller *The Element: How Finding Your Passion Changes Everything.* He says, "You can't do this if you're trapped in a compulsion to conform. You can't be yourself in a swarm or under a shadow."[2]

Helping your kids unfold, rather than molding them, is tricky. You don't stand back passively or abandon your children, but you don't hover and push or force either. You navigate this territory delicately, purposefully, like a trail guide leading the way to an adventure of wonders, through uncertain territory. You bring your children to new experiences and horizons and you don't stop there. You don't set them in a wilderness and say, "Okay, there's the world," then walk away. But you don't lift them out of it and try to carry them the whole way either.

Your role isn't an either-or matter at all, being completely involved or not at all. A good parent, like a good trail guide, helps in equipping and navigating. You balance giving your children the world, while instilling a secure sense of belonging, and helping them grow up and develop independence and autonomy to search out their life of purpose and passion for themselves. Psychologists call this differentiation, and it's essential to healthy human development.

Practicing how to help your children differentiate themselves from you begins with planting two important sensibilities in their souls.

Only You Can Be You

First you help your children know they're made on purpose, for a purpose. I love how Ken Robinson, the international advisor on education in the arts, describes this. He says you realize you're made for a purpose when "you're in your element," when your natural talent meets your personal passion and you're doing exactly what you were born to do.[3]

God tells each of us this from the very beginning in the Bible. I have paraphrased and personalized the following important Scripture passages for you to consider:

> *I've made you in my own image and I've made a job just for you to do* (Genesis 1:26-27).

> *You're my handiwork, my one-of-a-kind masterpiece, made to do good works I've planned long ago just for you* (Ephesians 2:10).

> *You're made to do something in your own way and during your own time* (Acts 17:26).

Oh my, do I have plans for you—good things to give you hope and a bright future (Jeremiah 29:11).

Before I even formed you in your mother's womb, I knew you and set you apart to do something special (Jeremiah 1:5).

In grace, I've given you different gifts for doing certain things well, so if your gift is serving others, serve well. If you're a teacher, then teach well. If your gift is to encourage others, be encouraging. If it's giving, then generously give. If you're an able leader, then take that responsibility seriously, and if you have a gift for showing kindness to others, do it gladly (Romans 12:6-8).

Knowing only you can be you is what gives your children both a reason and inspiration to find their own purpose and passion and live it.

You are Wonderfully Made

Second, you instill confidence in your child about how uniquely and specially made they are. Youu cultivate his or her understanding and belief that "I'm amazing just as I am, God delights in me, I am lovable."

God tells us this over and over again in the Bible too:

You are wonderfully made from the inside out (see Psalm 139:13-16).

Your very soul and even your body is so precious to me, holy—you're my dwelling place (see 1 Corinthians 3:16-17).

You're designed by me and for me and this world that I made just for you (see Ephesians 2:10).

I know and love every little detail about you, down to the very number of hairs on your head and every tear you ever shed which I put in my bottle (see Matthew 10:30 and Psalm 56:8).

I chose you from the beginning and will choose you over and over again (see 1 Peter 2:9).

I would die for you—and did (see John 3:16).

Helping your children know their worth, believe in how valuable they are, and how much they have to offer the world, gives them the footing to find their way.

It helps you relax too. Every child will face challenges, disappointments, and may go through fits of starts and stops in pursuing a purpose and passion. But you don't have to have fits in figuring out all the answers for them. They can search and maybe falter and you can reassure without having to pave their way. As they find their own answers and blaze their own trails, your job is to be there, to remind them that while they may not have things figured out, God does. He has a plan. We each have a purpose. There is a way through this life that only they can travel in their own style, in their own time.

SIGNS FOR UNFOLDING AND UNCOVERING

So how to do all that reminding in powerful ways? To truly help without hovering, you use what any trail guide would in new territory: your senses and experience, imagination and intuition. You watch and listen with not only eyes and ears, but with your heart.

Ezra Meeker, one of the first pioneers in the early 1850s to make his way west in an ox-drawn wagon, reassured many a companion traveler of this. Watching and listening will see you through, he wrote in his memoirs. He used these primary skills well to cross 2,200 miles of unsettled territory, through unforgiving wilderness, through disease, and beyond piles of possessions abandoned by other emigrants traveling just ahead of his wagon train—and then their broken-down wagons and gravesites and bodies. Only one in ten of some of the trains ahead of him made it all the way west, many people dying or turning back.

"Do you really think we can get through?" Meeker recalled one father in particular asking at the base of a rugged mountain range.[4]

"Yes," Meeker replied, "I know we can if every man will put his shoulder to the wheel, pay attention, and do his duty without flinching."

What perfect advice for the parent wanting to purposefully, lovingly raise children who find happiness, health, and their own way to make a difference in this world. And who better to receive it from than a trail guide standing on the edge of uncharted territory—isn't that what parenthood feels like so often?

Meeker was just twenty-two years old, with only about six months total formal education when he helped forge the Oregon Trail in 1852. He must have felt about what was ahead just as you do now: *Where are the how-tos and the manuals and the map to raising your child, seeing you both through these growing-up-together years?*

What Meeker learned is what can help you: that the greatest navigation tools are not things that can be bought, but something you already possess—the ability to pay attention. That single tool of paying attention helped Meeker emigrate safely and from more memory than a map when he crossed the country once, then retraced the way again in 1854 to meet his extended family's wagon train, and a third time in 1906-1908 to mark and memorialize the Oregon Trail. Watching and listening helped him know what to look for, the landmarks and signposts.

Difficult as that journey was, doesn't it seem enviable that Oregon Trail pioneers had such evident markers showing them the way? How are you supposed to see the signs of your children on their way to their destiny when you're looking and listening to the hidden places of their heads and hearts?

Watch the Four Signposts

Just as distinguishing landmarks such as Chimney Rock, Fort Laramie, and Soda Springs helped Ezra Meeker and other Oregon Trail guides pick their way west toward their Manifest Destiny, there are four signposts to help you and your children find their way toward theirs. Take a look:

1. **Abilities.** A person typically has 500 to 10,000 skills and abilities, everything from being able to speak and eat, clean and calculate, question and answer, to being a friend and keeping a confidence, playing and working. The problem, sociologists and researchers agree, is that many of these abilities are never developed; most human beings use just 20 percent of their mental ability, let alone capacity.[5] Do you know

your children's most pronounced abilities and skills? Start thinking on what they've displayed so far, and in what areas they seem to pick up new abilities and skills every day. You'll find in the back of this book (see Appendix) lists of skills and abilities that you might not have considered as such because we take them for granted, things like being punctual, devoted, loyal, and confident. There are some people more able in these areas than others, and each of these abilities are highly valued in the workplace. So one way to think on this is to consider the three types of abilities that work centers, educational institutions and colleges, and job force groups especially value, and which of these you see pronounced in your child: 1) job-specific skills (ability to sew, edit, repair electronics, analyze data, coach people, etc.), 2) self-managing abilities (calm, fair, positive, supportive, etc.), and 3) transferable skills and abilities (ability to create or illustrate, formulate or map, etc.).

2. **Talents.** These are the things you're naturally good at doing or being. There are different opinions on whether a talent is born or made, but both sociologists and people who study the psyche are in agreement with the Bible that a talent comes from within. Reverend Martin Luther King Jr. called talent your personal power. "Some [people] are endowed with more than others," he said, "but God has left none of us without talent. Potential powers of creativity are within us, and we have a duty to work assiduously to discover these powers."[6] The apostle Paul saw how these powers are not only inside us but part of the very fabric of our design, our gifts from God, gifts that we each must fan into flame (2 Timothy 1:6-7). The gift is in you, he said, part of you, like embers that burn and just need stirring to come to life. What natural powers or God-given gifts do you see flickering in your child? What things do they excel at or do remarkably that come easily to them or flow from them?

3. **Personality.** Some people are introverts and gain their energy and ideas from time alone or in quiet. Extroverts draw their energy from engaging with others, especially in groups. Which way does your child lean? Is your son an early bird or night owl? Is your daughter critical or ever-optimistic? Cautious or a daredevil? Factual or emotional? Slow to warm up or impulsive? These are all parts of a personality and there can be, many traits in every person. So what are the most pronounced traits in your child? Write them down for the fun of it. If you're unsure of what exactly is a trait, a variety of personality tests abound from employers, sports coaches, schools, counselors, psychologists, churches, and ministries. I'm not suggesting you have your child take an actual personality test since most are geared for adults anyway. But look at some to get a better idea on how to identify traits and tendencies. You can find online the test based on psychologists Carl Jung and Isabella Briggs Myers's widely accepted approach to describing personalities. One online test (the HumanMetrics Jung Typology Test™) involves seventy-two questions that take five to ten minutes to answer with an instant scoring result offered.[7]

4. **Passions.** These are the things your children love most and become completely absorbed in, single-minded about, you might say. Passions run deeper than interests or fleeting fascination. Where an interest rouses curiosity, a passion taps more deeply into something soulful: yearning, desire, a dream or goal. Psychology professor Mihaly Csikszentmihalyi, renowned for his work on creativity, calls a passion that place where intense feeling (almost obsession, as he describes it) and personal happiness intersect, the place where a person is driven toward something because of the joy it gives, even when at great personal cost. When someone enters passion they are in a state of flow, he says—in the zone, in the

groove. [8] Have you seen your children in this place, so caught up in what they are doing that they are completely absorbed in it? Do they have a passion for not just listening to music but making it? Are they in a groove when painting, or digging and planting in the garden, or maybe running? Eric Liddell, "The Flying Scotsman" who achieved the 1924 Olympic gold medal of the men's 400-meter race, described flow this way before Csikszentmihalyi was writing about it: "God made me fast. And when I run, I feel His pleasure." [9] Running was Liddell's joy. When he ran, he was in the flow, the groove, that zone of knowing he was doing exactly what he was made to do for God's glory. This is what you are on the lookout for in your child.

A STEP TOWARD CLEARER PURPOSE & PASSION
Know Your Child in Thirty Questions

You can live with someone and hardly know them. You may know they are an early bird and don't like tomatoes, but what about their greatest hopes, biggest dreams, and deepest fears? See how well you know your children. For each prompt, write out what you know. For the questions, answer with or at least one example.

- Best friend
- Favorite color
- Greatest hero
- Person outside your family who's been most influential
- Biggest fear
- Favorite teacher and why
- Favorite subject or interest and why
- Least favorite subject or interest and why
- Favorite music
- Accomplishment most proud of
- Favorite TV show, movie, and book
- Favorite after-school activity
- Favorite family activity
- Most prized possession
- Biggest complaint about the family
- Greatest disappointment
- Greatest change in the past year or two
- Role typically taken at school, on the playground, in the neighborhood, and with groups of friends: leader, follower, server, loner/independent, peacemaker, mover and shaker?
- Person your child goes to when having a problem
- What embarrasses your son or daughter most?

Three Ways to Listen with Your Heart

Now that you know what to look for, what can you expect to hear from your children about their discoveries?

It's not uncommon for toddlers to say things like "I want to be a doctor when I grow up" or "I want to be a firefighter." Many children do know at such an early age what they're meant to be and do. Then again, kids try on identities when they play. So maybe they're in a phase, trying out something new. Or possibly they're in a stage of mimicking someone they love. How can you be sure?

This is where listening comes into play, and not just listening to what comes from your children's mouths, but to things that speak louder than words: their squeals of joy every time they build with Legos, the newfound energy and creativity whenever in the kitchen concocting their own recipes,

- What triggers anger?
- What makes your son or daughter laugh?
- How popular is your child with peers?
- What common interests do you share with your child?
- Preferred pet: dog, cat, fish, bird, or something else?
- What would your child like to be when grown up?
- What would your child say when asked to identify his or her strengths and weakness?
- What would your child say when asked to identify strengths and weaknesses of siblings?
- Does your child feel liked at school? Why or why not?
- When and where does your child prefer to do homework?

Now check in with your child and ask these questions outright. Compare their answers with what you've written down. If you get:

- 25-30 things correct, you're an excellent observer and listener.
- 15-25 things correct, you're going in the right direction, but could do better.
- 0-14 things correct, you and your children need more time together, sharing and communicating.

No matter how you fare, remember it's never too late to know your child even better. By asking these questions you're already started. Now go further and practice the Thirty Minutes a Day rule (see the Love chapter). In your time together, be intentional to watch, listen, and pray. Within even a week, you'll be surprised at how easy the habit becomes of listening to, sharing with, and more deeply knowing your child.

the peace and calm when sitting with pets and animals. These are signs that can mark the abilities, talents, personality traits, and passions that point the way toward a purpose. They're signs not always read with just your eyes or heard with just your ears, but with the heart, with your intuition and soul.

I've heard it said God gave us two ears and one mouth so we would listen more and speak less. This is so true when it comes to listening with the heart. So often our children are trying to tell us, and the world, things they don't yet have the vocabulary to articulate but feel and know deeply, strongly within.

Bart, a fourth grader, loved science and won the top prize at a science fair but scored below average in science classes at school. How could that be? In the classroom, science lessons involved a lot of chemistry and math, which Bart struggled to learn. But his project for the science fair focused on behavioral science and whether age affects memory. This was interesting to him because of what was going on at home. His grandmother, who lived with their family, began to show signs of a mild form of dementia. Bart wanted to help her, so needed to better understand memory. His project work showed incredible insight, creativity, and drive. He tested memory by flashcards and with tasks, involving dozens of people in exercises over two months, at least ten people for each of five different age groups. His notes were meticulous and thorough, and his conclusions posed as many questions as factual answers.

All of this said volumes about a passionate, insightful, brilliant behavioral scientist in the making. Bart couldn't tell you this was what he knew he would pursue the rest of his life. His school marks in science might have said otherwise too. But what Dr. Martin Luther King Jr. would call his personal power, or the apostle Paul would say was the gift burning inside, was indeed now on fire in Bart—he had found his passion and purpose. He just didn't have the words for these things yet. He didn't know what to call the pursuit, and science classes at school weren't touching it.

A perceptive teacher and Bart's parents were listening with the heart, though, and they practiced this kind of listening that opens doors for your children to unfold:

- **Seek not just to hear but to understand.** What's beneath the words your child says? Think how the feelings and needs that come through change the very meaning of words. You feel threatened if a man brandishing a weapon jumps out at you in a mostly empty, dark parking lot and says, "I'm going to kill you!" But if your grade schooler says this, laughing and cracking jokes during a fun-spirited and lively game of cards, the phrase is more of a euphemism. Listen to the needs and feelings more than anything. Psychologists call this exercising emotional intelligence, not just using cognitive skills of thinking, but tapping in to feelings and desires. The Bible calls this understanding and wisdom, as Jesus said in his first public sermon. There's a danger, he warned, in "hearing but never understanding, seeing but never perceiving" (Mark 4:12). Better understand your children's feelings and needs by asking open-ended questions: "What makes you say that?" or "Why do you wish this?" and "How does that make you feel?" Remember to make this a practice and not a one-time deal.

- **Observe body language.** Think how your children can tell you something without a word and simply a glance, slouch, and a leaning in or away. Now think on when you see them relaxed rather than tensed up or falling apart. When do they throw themselves into an activity rather than hold back? When do they seem driven with joy rather than obligation? What makes them engaged and free to take risks, as opposed to protective, shut off, and defensive? Body language both as they speak and engage in activities can speak volumes about what inspires and ignites passion in your children, and what bores or deflates and deadens them.

- **Consider things without judgment or criticism.** In our busy culture, there's pressure to interpret information and draw conclusions quickly. News comes to us live even as events unfold, and analysts jump in to interpret what it all means even before investigators can gather the facts. We do this with our children. Cody says, "I don't want to play Little League anymore because no one likes me," and his mom immediately gives the feel-good response: "I know Billy likes you—and so will the other kids if you give them a chance to know you." It's easy to rush to conclusions or think we already understand the situation. In so doing, we ignore and brush off what our kids are trying to tell us. Worse, we contradict their feelings. Children repeatedly silenced will eventually shut down. They'll believe what they say or think isn't important and doesn't matter. They can become indifferent and give up. The antidote: watch, ask questions, wait, and pay attention to all that's going on in addition to what they say. Cody's mom saw at her son's next Little League practice how the coach yelled at the kids to win at all costs. He shamed players who made mistakes or did poorly, and created an environment where everyone blamed someone. No one on the team really liked anyone else because there was so much unhealthy competition and a focus on individual weaknesses. Considering a situation fully, over time, even a short time, helped Cody's mom find a new team for him—because he really did love Little League and team sports as they should be—where every player's strengths and the game itself is valued as much as results.

PURPOSEFUL STEPS IN UNFOLDING

All this watching and listening with the heart is something you can do right now. Like Ezra Meeker, leading pioneers across uncharted lands, you are a guide for your children to a great adventure, and you're armed with the best tools for the journey: your eyes, ears, and heart. You know the signposts, so here's what you do when you arrive at them.

Be on the Lookout Early

The Christmas my grandson Jonathan was three years of age, he unwrapped the gift of a keyboard. He squealed with delight and then, all smiles and concentration, plunked away on it as the rest of us continued unwrapping gifts. The adults drifted into conversation, with the buzz in the background of the kids playing with their toys.

Suddenly Jonathan's father hushed us, "Listen!"

The carol played on the stereo earlier sounded again, this time slow note by long, slow note. We looked to a corner of the room where Jonathan sat hunched over the keyboard, tapping out the melody of "Silent Night" on his own. He had never been shown the notes or watched someone else play it on the keyboard, but it was obvious—at three years of age, he could play music by ear.

We were amazed. Today we're used to this. Jonathan's always creating new music, though now mostly with a guitar (which is a lot lighter to tote around than a piano!).

If you're watching and listening with the heart, you'll see hints of such extraordinary gifts and abilities in your children, all the things planted in them even as they were knitted in the womb (Psalm 139:13). Countless studies show those gifts, abilities, and talents do indeed blossom and emerge early in life as they did with Jonathan.[10]

I've seen this in the classroom. Over the thirty years I observed children in kindergarten, I could always spot the ones with a gift for teaching. I'll never forget one class, where an energetic boy marched to the beat of his own drummer no matter what the teacher asked and directed. When it was time to listen to music, he drew pictures on his tablet. When time to exercise, he wanted to work a puzzle at his desk. When time to practice writing letters of the alphabet, he went to the back of the room to count the blocks used for addition and subtraction lessons. His teacher struggled to get him to focus and follow directions, until one adorable little girl swooped in and took the boy by the hand. She led him back to his desk.

"How do you hold your pencil?" she asked him. "I hold mine like this." She showed him, gave him the pencil, and grabbed another from her desk.

Leaning over his tablet with utter concentration, she began to write a letter. "This is how I make a 'G.' See? It's like a 'C' with a handle inside? How do you make a 'G'?"

The boy was mesmerized and started practicing his letters of the alphabet too.

A STEP TOWARD CLEARER PURPOSE AND PASSION
Avoid the Identity Thief Traps

As you're learning how to unfold your children, check yourself on not molding them by falling into these the traps that can turn you into an *Identity Thief*—someone who robs your kids of their sense of self and what they're meant to be and do.

- **Stop owning your children's successes and failures:** When Natalie aced an accelerated math class, her mother said, "That academic ability comes from me—I always scored highest in my class at that age." When Marc won another medal at the science fair, his dad said, "I'm so glad I read him all those science books and took him to science museums last summer. It's all beginning to show." Whenever you take credit for your kids' successes like Natalie's mom and Marc's dad, whenever control, direction, motivation, and reward come from the outside, children never have opportunity to craft an inside. Instead, let them own their achievements and disappointments to discover their authentic selves.

- **Don't over-direct and correct.** Trent's mom couldn't understand why he didn't want to take swimming lessons. He loved the water. But Trent didn't want to be scrutinized, criticized, and micro-sized in the pool. Who does? But that's what happened when he started piano lessons. It was like playing in a fishbowl. "I used to love the piano," he said. "Now if I don't practice, I get yelled at; if I practice the wrong way, I get yelled at more. When I started lessons, my parents started yelling all the time." Forcing your kids to perfect something they love because you want them to excel is the quickest way to deflate their burning passion for it. What if Louis Armstrong, one of the most inventive trumpet players of all time, who shifted the focus of music from collective playing to improvisation and solos, had been forced to stick to a score? What if after being self-taught from age eight, his first official teacher at thirteen forced him to improve his armature, no more puffed out cheeks when he played the cornet? Would we have heard the same musical power, seen the same joy, or received the same ebullience in "What a Wonderful World" in 1967? Setting up lessons isn't a bad thing, but expectation for achievement is. Too much pressure can psychologically damage a child's developing identity. Instead, give your children opportunities and follow their lead. Listen to what they love or don't, where they struggle and why. Help them find the joy in the learning, and when there is no joy, move on to other pursuits.

A natural-born teacher, I thought as I watched this five-year-old girl continue to show what was needed, then encourage the boy to try it for himself.

Natural-born gifts are often seen by both those around a child, and by children themselves.

- **Quit comparing and competing.** Ever told your son to get tips for the game from his older brother, the basketball star? Or suggest your daughter try her cousin's fashion style? Even if well-meaning, these forms of comparison and competition can smother and suffocate your child's uniqueness and dreams. The 2009 documentary A Race to Nowhere: Transforming Education from the Ground Up (see online at www.racetonowhere.com) showed the deadly consequences of unrelenting pressure to measure up, be better, and get ahead. One heartbreaking semester, at a high school where parents demanded their children get straight As for admission to the most prestigious universities, two students committed suicide. They took their lives because of low scores on a test and not being able to bear being less-than or worse than their peers. How sad when we value grades, winning a game, and being the best more than life itself. The Bible gives us a better guiding principle to help us each discover our purpose: "Make a careful exploration of who you are and the work you have been given, and then sink yourself into that. Don't be impressed with yourself. Don't compare yourself with others. Each of you must take responsibility for doing the creative best you can with your own life" (Galatians 6:4-5 The Message).

- **Cease the attention addiction.** I met Michele, a darling first grader, when her teacher said she needed help for academic difficulties. Right away I was charmed. A pretty girl with large brown eyes and short bobbed hair, she could charm anyone—and did. Her entire extended family doted on her. At a family wedding, I was told, she received more attention than the bride. This was Michele's ruin. When challenged, she quickly became frustrated and gave up. When asked to perform developmentally appropriate tasks, she batted those big brown, deer eyes to distract. In the meantime, she never learned basic problem-solving and faltered in finding her place in the classroom. I didn't want that to happen to her in life. She needed recovery from attention addiction, and it was going to be a challenge. By the time a child is five years of age, most child development experts agree, their primary social orientation is established and difficult to change. Help needed to come from outside. Michele's parents needed to stop singing her praises too generally, too much, and for accomplishments that required little effort or for little reason. Teachers needed to stop doling out extra praise. On the playground, Michele needed to see winning wasn't the most important thing, especially if it meant cheating or changing the rules to do so.

Allison Williams, the daughter of NBC News anchor Brian Williams and television producer Jane Gillan Stoddard, knew she too wanted to be on television, as an actress, even before she performed in her first official play or started school. She displayed gifts for these things early. She's now in her fourth season of the HBO television series *Girls*, a comedy-drama following the lives of twenty-somethings. "Even before I knew what acting was, I told my parents I wanted to do what they did," she says. "In *The Wizard of Oz*...one person plays two people and can put on different costumes. That's how I articulated it the first time. I was about four. It was dress up."[11]

Drew Rosenhaus, the NFL's most prestigious football agent, tagged himself at eight years of age a football geek who watched the games intensely, rooting for his favorite teams. (You may know Rosenhaus as the character Bob Sugar in the film *Jerry McGuire*, inspiring Tom Cruise's character.) Rosenhaus knew, even before he was in junior high school, that he wanted to be and would one day work as an NFL agent.[12] His outgoing, forceful personality and keen intelligence added to the mix, but what really empowered him was his passion. He lived and breathed football—and, at twenty-two years of age, signed his first client. Rosenhaus applied that passion again and again, and he's negotiated more than $1 billion in contracts doing what he loves, getting players with the right teams on the field.

Business and corporation leaders especially value people finding and knowing their passion and purpose early in life—so much that companies invest in youth in this way all the time. In its ninety-plus years, Disney, for example, has a history of selecting aspiring young artists to feature. With the Los Angeles-based Young Musicians Foundation, Disney sponsors a ten-day summer camp, inviting gifted young musicians to study under some of America's most distinguished artists including, in its early years, the now late conductors and composers Henry Mancini and John Williams.

In 1992, one of the invitees was Benjamin Schwartz, then twelve years of age. Benjamin had been playing the flute for four years. When he got his first flute at eight years of age, he loved it so much that he never let it from his sight, even sleeping with it for two weeks straight.[13] The youth orchestra experience cemented his sense of calling. Today, Schwartz leads the Wroclaw Philharmonic based in Berlin, has been conductor of the San Francisco Symphony, music director of its Youth Orchestra (leading it on a European tour celebrated in Munich, Berlin, and Prague), and is known internationally as an orchestral and opera conductor committed to new music. His own clarity, parents' watchfulness, and investment of others like Disney early on helped unfold Benjamin for exactly what he is made to do.

Encourage, Include, and Show

The summer after my granddaughter Haley finished third grade, our extended family went on a hiking trip through the Grand Canyon. We met two college professors on a trail and they joined us one evening for dinner. We were talking about the beautiful things we'd seen that day and the conversation quickly turned to the environment, how to protect these places, save the redwoods, and champion new energy sources. My son Tom, Haley's father, was passionately engaged in discussion with the college professors. I sat back, smiling at how Tom was always in his element when discussing how to save people and things, and public policy. I marveled too at how Haley, just eight at the time, had leaned in, riveted. Her eyes sparkled as she listened to her dad and the professors solve the problems of the world with ideas and passion.

She looks so much like her mother, I thought, *but is so like Tom.* They both loved ideas and had hearts for the poor, the left out, forgotten, displaced, and marginalized. It may have been no wonder. Tom was forever tuned in to these things (remember the box of his civil rights clippings and tapes from childhood that I found in the attic?). He talked about them and his work in them at home, discussing the things he followed in public policy, civil rights, and human interests. When the television was on, it usually was tuned in to the news, a talk show about politics or public policy, or a documentary about human struggles around the world—and Haley was always right there by his side, engaged in the viewings and conversations with her dad. She gravitated to all the same things Tom was drawn by. He never forced her to sit and listen. She just loved the same things he did. So through the years he always invited and included her when he could in his meetings, events, rallies, lobbying events, and fund-raisers. They were a dynamic duo, Tom and Haley, when it came to ideas and civil service.

It was no surprise then that when Haley went off to college at the University of Wisconsin-Madison to study journalism—and no surprise that she flourished there and today in Washington, DC, working as a senior technical advisor at the White House. She knew early on what she loved and wanted to do, and her dad encouraged her every step of the way.

How do you measure the importance of such encouragement in helping your children find their passion and purpose early in life? There's no precise way, I suppose. But the Development of Talent Research Project, directed by Professor Benjamin S. Bloom at the University of Chicago, tried.

Bloom, an internationally respected educational psychologist, believed every society has a large pool of talent available to either develop or waste. He wanted to know how that talent was discovered and developed. In his groundbreaking 1985 study, he researched what he called mastery learning or giftedness and found a parent can absolutely influence a child's achievement with simple ongoing praise and encouragement. His Development of Talent Research Project identified world-famous people in six different fields (concert pianists, sculptors, research mathematicians, research neurologists, tennis players, and Olympic swimmers), as well as one hundred men and women under the age of thirty-five who were exceptionally successful. All shared a common factor in how they discovered and developed their achievements and success: They each had at least one parent who praised and encouraged development and competence in their field.[14]

I find that so encouraging myself, as both a parent and professional educator and counselor because it means you have what it takes right now to start helping your child on this amazing road of self-discovery to their destiny. Encouragement is something you don't buy. You don't hire it. You don't need an expensive trainer to tell you how to give it. Encouragement is something you have to give every day, in both the little moments and at the milestones.

Encouragement doesn't mean saying "good job" over and again, and it's more than sheer praise. To encourage is to instill how much you believe in your child and show that belief by setting up pathways for them to continue their pursuits and development. Encouragement means you:

- **Celebrate achievements**, no matter how small. Celebrations don't have to big and elaborate, planned in advance, or cost anything but your heart and a moment to rejoice. Of course you can offer special treats and even plan a sleepover with friends or party, but there are other things that can mean just as much and not cost a thing to your pocketbook. Janey comes home with an A on a book report and you grab her by the hands to do a jig round the room. Dane finishes some homework without having to be reminded and you allow him thirty minutes to play his favorite video game.

- **Create openness for opinions, reflections, and feelings to be expressed without judgment**, and where your children can make their own choices in as small of matters as choosing which vegetable from what's in your pantry to have at dinner, to picking which book to read at bedtime or hobby and sport to pursue.

- **Praise where your child shines.** So Gordon didn't do well on the math test, but wrote a beautiful poem in English class. Give him a notebook or journal, introduce him to your favorite poets, or ask him to read some poetry collections and pick his own favorites. There is always some quality in your child to call out and things that are true gifts but never measured on classroom tests or in formal pursuits, things like kindness, compassion, and humor.

Recently I chatted with a mom about her daughter's creative talents. Kristin was a rising star in the fashion industry and I wondered if she'd always had such flair for style. "Did she show an eye for design early on?" I asked.

Her mom laughed and told about walking into the kitchen one day to find Kristin drawing on the wall. "Not just scribbling, not just child's play," she said, eyes twinkling. "No, there was a pattern to it."

Kristin, just three years of age, was methodically creating a flower border. Her mother noticed and thought how methodically Kristin played with her Barbie dolls too. She didn't just change the outfits on her dolls like other girls. Kristin spent hours assembling and gluing together scraps of paper, fabric, and all sorts of other materials to make truly visionary outfits.

Almost immediately Kristin's mom and paternal grandmother, who both loved to sew, started teaching Kristin the basics of sewing and special techniques. Their praise and encouragement came naturally and easily, too, because they were including Kristin in something they loved and were already doing.

That is a key—including is an excellent form of encouragement. Bringing your child alongside in what gives you joy, helps him or her find joy too, maybe not in the very same pursuit you love but possibly a tangent of it and certainly for something of their own because you are modeling how, not what, to live with passion.

No doubt inclusion in her mother and grandmother's love for sewing fostered Kristin's fashion sense and talent. By her junior year in high school, she was designing and constructing her own clothes, even her prom dress, which won an award.

But just as encouragement fostered her passion, discouragement almost put a damper on it. Upon graduation from high school, Kristin earned a scholarship to Parsons School of Design in New York City, widely recognized as one of the most prestigious art and design universities in the world. Her dad was so proud of her achievements, but unenthusiastic and vocal about her moving to New York City. He feared the crime and her ability to make it in the big city more than he believed in her possibilities. At least that's what his reluctance for her to move said.

So Kristin put off Parsons. She attended the nearby community college. Again, her talents shone. She won acclaim for her design work—and lucky for her Parsons kept calling because sometimes there's just a slight opening of a window of opportunity. So while her dad's objections didn't extinguish Kristin's passion, he didn't fan it either. He just delayed her ability to do what she already knew since coloring borders on the kitchen walls and making Barbie couture from scraps—she had the gift and desire to shape the design world.

"Encourage one another and build each other up," the Bible says in First Thessalonians 5:11.

It can take as much energy, effort, and time to encourage and build up as it does to discourage or tear down.

Barbra Streisand said this to Mike Wallace of *Sixty Minutes* in a rare interview in 1991. She knew she wanted to be an actress at seven years of age but when she shared her dream with her mother and stepfather, she was instantly discouraged.

You're too plain, her mother said, too odd, too skinny, not pretty enough to be a movie star. You should learn typing and be a secretary, she was told. Her stepfather echoed that when once he told Barbra she couldn't have ice cream because she was too ugly. There were rash words, always put-downs, never encouragement; otherwise, he ignored Barbra. "He never talked to me," she said. "My mother never said to me, 'You're smart, you're pretty, you're anything, you can do whatever you want.'"[15]

Even today, after all her achievement as one of the best-selling female singer-songwriters of all time, an award-winning actress on stage and in film, author, philanthropist, and award-winning film producer-director, she still struggles with the pain of those childhood memories. She admitted when she was forty-one years of age, upon the release of her first effort as a film director in 1983, how that pain had robbed her of valuing herself, happiness, and peace. She had talent to burn but the meanness, lack of encouragement, and outright discouragement in childhood left her "a furnace of emotions. Sometimes waves of shyness, attacks of dread. Sometimes traits of the petty despot—a need to control, nit-picking perfectionism, incessant suspicion, incessant testing, [with] always a sense that behind the power and possessions hides a lonely and angry little girl."[16]

This is how powerful encouragement, and discouragement, can be, and how simple either are to impart. If you wonder whether you're encouraging enough or in the right way, consider what Rick Warren gives us for reflection: "Jesus affirmed the people he came in contact with. When he looked at them, he saw their potential, what God intended them to be. He brought out the best in others not by labeling them, but by saying, *I believe you can do it. I know you can do it.*"[17]

Those words are always enough: *I believe you can do it. I know you can do it.*

Tap into Your Child's Learning Style

How your children learn can make a huge difference in their ability to find their passions and purpose earlier rather than later in life. For instance, you can show your son how to trim a tree and he can turn around and do it himself. But give him verbal instructions only, then send him to do it, and he'll flounder.

This is because we each learn in different ways and knowing your learning style helps you grasp something—or not. Some of the most brilliant minds in the world were never appreciated or ignited until discovering their learning style.

Dr. John B. Gurdon is a great example. Gurdon was one of two scientists awarded the 2012 Nobel Peace Prize in Physiology or Medicine for work in stem cell research, a complete shock to his high school biology teacher. This teacher marked him one of the lowest-scoring students in a class of 250, and complained in a formal evaluation how Gurdon didn't follow directions and wanted to do his own thing. "I believe Gurdon has ideas about becoming a scientist," he further lamented. "On his present showing, this is quite ridiculous. If he can't learn simple biological facts he would have no chance of doing the work of a specialist, and it would be a sheer waste of time, both on his part and of those who would have to teach him."[18] The schoolmaster removed fifteen-year-old Gurdon from all science courses for the remaining three years of high school and placed him in a class that studied Ancient Greek, Latin, and a modern language—a course intended for those judged unsuited for studying any subject in depth.[19]

The problem, though, wasn't Gurdon's ability to learn, but his teachers' understanding of how he learned. Gurdon began to shine in college at Oxford (where he was almost not accepted because of those damning high school evaluations in science) because he was allowed to finally study his passion, zoology, and do experiments, things hands-on. Following the verbal instructions in high school never ignited his brilliance, rather shut him down. How much sooner he might have arrived at some of his discoveries had he and educators better understood his style of learning by doing and experimentation.

What style best suits your child?

- **See to learn**. Must you draw a picture for your daughter to get it? At least 50 percent of people are visual learners who need imagery to understand something. This means your child comprehends and remembers things by sight. She can picture in her head what she's learning and probably often closes her eyes to remember something. She'll have difficulty with spoken directions and may be easily distracted by sounds. She's probably attracted to color and spoken language, like stories rich in imagery. What can help her learn better is to sit near the front of a classroom to see what's being taught, use flashcards to learn new words and concepts, write down key words and ideas or instructions, color code things, and draw or see pictures to get new concepts.

- **Hear to understand**. Does your son tend to hear and parrot back what's said? He's probably an auditory learner, often found listening intently but not always taking notes. Auditory learners respond best when told what to do, and liked to be listened to as well. They store information by the way it sounds and have an easier time with spoken rather than written instructions. They often learn best by reading aloud because they have to hear or speak something to know it. They may hum or talk to themselves when bored. Often, others think auditory learners aren't paying attention, though they're hearing and understanding everything said. Help the auditory learner sit where hearing is best, read stories or assignments and directions aloud, record themselves spelling words aloud and then listen to the recording, and possibly take oral exams or repeat back things.

- **Do to know.** Like Gurdon, kinesthetic or tactile learners are hands-on. They want to touch something and make and do it physically to learn. They're prone to draw, build, and move when being taught. They do best when activity is involved, taking apart something, building, tinkering. They like to be active and take frequent breaks, and may have trouble sitting or staying still. They exhibit good coordination and athletic ability, and can easily remember things that were done but struggle to remember what was seen or heard in the process. They often communicate by touching, speak with their hands and gestures, and appreciate physical forms of encouragement like a hug, high five, or pat on the back. To help them learn, offer lots of hands-on activities that involve touching, building, moving, or drawing. Take walks and act out stories related to a concept. Tracing words with a finger helps in spelling, as can frequent (but not long) breaks during reading and study periods. Things that used to be frowned upon in learning can help the tactile learner too: chewing gum, walking around, and rocking in a chair while studying, as well as tapping a pencil, shaking a foot, or holding on to something.

While your child may have one more pronounced learning style, you're likely to find most of us use combinations of styles, most commonly seeing and doing in order to learn. That's where computers are a great tool because they activate seeing, hearing, and doing all at once. But technology isn't the only device for this. Comprehensive projects can help.

For instance, Harvard University's Project Zero Summer Institutes help teachers develop courses for kids to create museum exhibits or research the growth and changes of a forest, activating multiple intelligences and learning styles at once.

Closer to home, 4-H clubs, through the Cooperative Extension Offices and the U.S. Department of Agriculture, involve kids in projects, acts or service, and ongoing studies that require a combination of learning styles.

For instance to raise livestock, a child must read literature on care and feeding, actually give the care, plan the diet, and feed their animals; exhibit the animal at fairs and livestock sales, and report or give presentations on the project. All senses and styles of learning are engaged, and children can discover which part of the project interests and excites them most, unfolding into new worlds.

Create a Thinking Environment

You open new worlds at home too when you create an atmosphere where kids can consider, muse, brood upon things, reflect, explore, imagine, compute, analyze, process, experiment, use logic, and think for themselves. This doesn't mean setting up a laboratory or library in your home...but, then again, why not? Whatever encourages thinking, exploration, and discovery helps children learn what they love and why. Focus on three areas to start:

1. **Thoughtful questions and deeper discussions** where you can talk about anything and seek truth, help your children evaluate the accuracy and soundness of things said, better understand peoples' actions and beliefs, and support their own thoughts and position on issues. Talk about social issues, the news, situations at school or home, and what's said on social media. Be intentional to ask questions that prompt your children to open up about what they know or how they feel. Open-ended questions require more thought and engagement, and often start with *what, why,* and *how.* For instance, "What do you believe?" or "Why do you think that's so?" or "How do you think that works?" Closed-ended questions prompt just a *yes* or *no* answer that can lead nowhere, and usually start with *is, are, did,* and *do.* "Is that good? Are you relieved? Did you do your homework? Do you think that's possible?"

2. **Critical thinking** breaks down issues or ideas into parts so they can be analyzed. Teaching your kids *how* to think, not just *what*, will help them all through life. One mom gave her

kids these tools early. She made games of how to categorize, classify, and think about differences and similarities, relationships and connections, and patterns. She asked her two-year-old daughter to separate toys into category bins: dolls in one container, stuffed animals in another, trucks in a third. Then she asked her seven-year-old son to help her with the laundry: sort the colors from the whites, figure out the water levels for the size of the load, measure the soap, decide on the best water temperature. She asked him things like, "What happens when cotton clothes are washed in hot water?" All these matters require reasoning, logic, and discernment. That's one smart mama, getting help on the chores and engaging her children in things that exercise their brains and open worlds to them. You can do this every day too. Grocery stores are wonderful places for parents to practice critical thinking with their kids. Most children find groceries exciting, full of things that tap all their senses and both their reasoning and creative sides of the brain. Your toddler can learn to separate vegetables from fruits as you go down the produce aisle. Your elementary schooler can help you find the best sized dry goods for your pantry and help you plan a dinner menu. Your middle schooler can help find the best bargains: how much quantity and quality for the money. These things teach them to calculate, compute, and exercise conceptual thinking and math and science abilities, as well as imagination. Learning by a parent's' side is the best way too, as you'll open worlds for them and be able to witness which aspects they love most.

3. **Problem-solving,** something we each do every day of our lives, can open or shut worlds for us. To problem-solve, we measure and weigh things, plan, evaluate the cause and effect, and face consequences. You can teach these skills round the clock, and the process helps kids see what they like and don't, where they struggle and why, and what comes easily. Some

opportunities: When all the kids at the park want to swing at the same time but there only so many swings, you can model how to find solutions. Ask: "How can we all take turns? What can we do in the meantime?" Seven-year-old Kregg was fighting over toys with the neighborhood kids at home, when he suddenly stopped, suggested time-sharing them and even inspired his buddies to repurpose some old trucks ("like Transformers!") so everyone had something. He just might be a budding negotiator, diplomat, or entrepreneur, but the experience definitely helped him unfold beyond the situation and the moment. Don't be afraid to let your kids solve their own problems or even to say, "Find something to do," and see what happens. Nine-year-old Caine Monroy came up with his own solution to boredom and how to make money one summer.[20] Spending the summer at his dad's auto parts store in Los Angeles, Caine found no playmates or toys, just some empty cardboard boxes. He loved arcade games but had no access to them or money to play them, so he asked for the boxes. He fashioned his own games from cardboard, then asked his dad for permission to set up an arcade of them at the entrance for his own business. All summer Caine kept adding games, but there were no customers. On the last day of summer, by chance, a filmmaker walked into the auto parts store to buy a door handle. Fascinated with Caine's Arcade, he bought a two dollar Fun Pass, Caine's idea where someone could play one game for a dollar or for two all of them. So impressed with the creativity, ingenuity, business savvy, and passion of young Caine, the filmmaker asked for permission to promote the arcade and make a video about it. People responded to his ads, and one boy's problem-solving of what to do with his summer launched a short film that went viral, a small arcade business for two years, a scholarship through Imagination Foundation, a website to further creativity ("Caine's Arcade"), a Global Cardboard Challenge urging other children to create

something from nothing, and a bright future in entrepreneur-
ship (Colorado State University has since offered Caine a full
scholarship to its School of Business).[21] Problem-solving may
never have been so fun—and profitable—or one boy's path so
clear of what he's meant to be and do.

Keep in mind, there's no one blueprint on how to create a thinking environment. But you can intentionally look at how your children use these
three ways of exercising their logic where it comes to their friends, behavior,
academics, money, play, chores, faith, and service.

Value Diversity

Years ago I heard a story about a group of animals who determined
the Animal Kingdom needed a school with courses in running, climbing, swimming, and flying.[22] It was decided all animals should take all of
the courses.

So the duck started swimming class and was better than his teacher, but
only made passing grades in flying, and was very poor in running. He was
made to drop swimming and stay after school to practice running. This
caused his webbed feet to be badly worn, and his grade to drop to average in swimming, but everybody felt less threatened and more comfortable
with that...except the duck.

The rabbit started at the top of his class in running, but because of so
much makeup work in swimming, he caught pneumonia and had to drop
out of school altogether.

The squirrel showed outstanding ability in climbing, but was extremely
frustrated in flying class because the teacher insisted he start from the
ground up rather than the treetop down. He developed charley horses from
overextension, and only got a "C" in climbing and a "D" in running.

As terrible as the other students were, the eagle was the real problem student, disciplined for being a nonconformist. In climbing class, he beat all
the others to the top of the tree, but insisted on using his own way to get
there. In running, he soared high above the others to nosedive to the finish
line way ahead of them, with no apologies. Finally, because he refused to
participate in swimming, he was expelled.

The animals suddenly realized they weren't going about school the right way, expecting one another to learn, achieve, do, and be exactly the same. God designed each of them to excel in a specific, unique way. He doesn't expect everyone to be and do everything the same.

What a picture of how we sometimes expect things of one another that get us stuck, even stopped, in finding our passion and purpose. Expecting everybody to fit in the same mold will only get us what it got a wrung-out rabbit, debilitated duck, struggling squirrel, and errant eagle—frustration, discouragement, mediocrity, and failure.

As a wise old owl observed: a duck is made to be a duck and not something else. This is not only a good reminder for us as parents, but for our children and their teachers, friends, and all those we encounter—diversity and differences aren't shameful things, but gifts. We're all good at different things, and all ideas are welcome. When we value our differences and what makes us each unique, we begin to fully find our place in how God designed us.

The Bible explains this so perfectly, how we each have a part to play in this world just as different parts enable the body to function. "If the whole body were an eye, where would the sense of hearing be? If the whole body were an ear, where would the sense of smell be?" (1 Corinthians 12:17). The apostle Paul observes:

> *But in fact God has placed the parts in the body, every one of them, just as he wanted them to be. If they were all one part, where would the body be? ...The eye cannot say to the hand, 'I don't need you!' And the head cannot say to the feet, 'I don't need you!' On the contrary, those parts of the body that seem to be weaker are indispensable, and the parts that we think are less honorable we treat with special honor. And the parts that are unpresentable are treated with special modesty, while our presentable parts need no special treatment. But God has put the body together, giving greater honor to the parts that lacked it, so that there should be no division in the body, but that its parts should have equal concern for each other* (1 Corinthians 12:18, 20-25).

It's no wonder, then, that preachers, poets, and psychologists empha-size the benefits of valuing diversity—how important it is to appreciate the unique contributions each of us make to the world and that others uniquely bring too. Psychologists call this "individualization" and hail how it fosters cooperation and harmony, a sense of unity without giving up individual identity.

I've often explained it this way to parents and children: If we all need to shine the same way, we are trying to outshine one other. We'll quickly burn out in the competition and resentment caused. Self-worth will be dimin-ished. Individual, true gifts can never beam when we're all chasing after the same ones, trying to possess the same gift. What a dark world that would be. But if we're each pursuing and living our own unique way, we each shine. The sky can be full of stars.

The poet Walt Whitman puts this beautifully, with lines memorialized in the film *The Dead Poets Society*, where Professor John Keating, played by

A STEP TOWARD CLEARER PURPOSE & PASSION
Write Your Own Powerful Play Book

The powerful play goes on, and you may contribute a verse. What a wonderful thing to pose to your children. How stirring to ask, "What will your verse be?" The very question prompts thoughts on all the possibilities, and sets kids on a course to finding the purpose and passion they each contribute to this life.

Help them. Start a book or box titled "The Powerful Play Goes On" for each of your children. The journal can be special or a one-dollar loose-leaf binder. The box can be something pretty from a craft store or a shoebox that you've decorated. The point is keeping a container where you can tuck recorded thoughts and papers or mementos that chronicle what your children thinks his or her verse in the song of life will be.

On special occasions like a birthday, or at moments of great achievement (acing a test; winning an award; starting a new project, sport, or activity) write down dat-ed thoughts about "this is what I'm passionate about and why" and "this is what I'm made to do today, and here is where I feel God's pleasure in just being me because…." Tuck in mementos. Print photos from your cell phone and save in the box with a note about the moment.

Over time, a Powerful Play book or box can help children see what they're good at and love, and who they're made to be and what they're good at doing. The process of recording, saving, and taking note of these things is a way too of cherishing right now how God made your kids—the things they each bring to this world. And cherishing is one way to identify, nurture, and celebrate a gift. O me! O life!

Robin Williams, instructs his class to rip out the introduction to their poetry textbook. "Excrement," he says of the idea of looking at poetry, people, and life in one systematic, staid way.[23] "We read and write poetry because we are members of the human race, and the human race is filled with passion.... To quote from Whitman...'you are here—that life exists, and identity; That the powerful play goes on, and you will contribute a verse.'"[24]

"What," Keating, asks his students, "will your verse be?"

Enrich with a Variety of Experiences

What your child's verse will be is shaped so much by experience.

"Nothing becomes real till it is experienced," the poet John Keats wrote in an 1819 letter to his brother.[25]

Isn't it true that you always remember the first big trip you took by yourself as a child, the first time you went to the fair or a rock concert or a festival?

The richer and broader your children's experiences, the greater their curiosity can be stoked, and more deeply their interests stirred. Family trips, visits to museums, craft fairs, concerts, historical sites, libraries, nature centers, games—all these things enrich a child's scope of experience. Television and the Internet can be used for good too, when tuned in to historical sites, documentaries, and educational or learning programs on channels like National Geographic. The following three specific areas are great places to start.

- **Get back to nature.** I'm fortunate to live in a community with miles of riding and hiking trails. While walking the other day I came upon two abandoned bikes and a scooter lying at the side of the sidewalk. Three boys' helmets were strewn along a path into the valley and peals of laughter came from the forest. Somewhere in the trees three boys were discovering something wonderful—and it was good for them. "Being outdoors tends to enrich children's perceptual abilities and boost their confidence," says Neal Halfon, a medical doctor and professor of pediatrics and child health policy at UCLA.[26] Unfortunately, fewer of our children spend any time outdoors anymore. The U.S. Centers for Disease Control and Prevention, in just one generation, found that American childhood moved indoors from unstructured outdoor play.[27] The days of creating playgrounds outside with the imagination are gone, and vanished are impromptu baseball games, climbing trees, making outdoor forts, racing through fields, and your call to "be home for dinner." Today, childhood is spent in rooms, watching television, playing video games, and surfing the Internet.[28] The average boy or girl spends less than thirty minutes a day outdoors, and more than seven hours indoors, mostly in front of an electronic screen of some sort. When children do go outside, it's usually for scheduled events like soccer camp or a fishing derby, and under the watch of adults.[29] You can unlock nature and bring back a fascination with unraveling her mysteries. Gardening and nature inspired Emily Dickinson's calling as a poet. Looking

A STEP TOWARD CLEARER PURPOSE & PASSION
Back to Nature: Take a Daily Dose

What might a daily habit of walking around the block or down the road with the dog bring out in your child? Or bike rides, playing catch, following the sound of a tinkling stream, lying on the grass to look up for shapes in the clouds, listening for a rhythm in the song of crickets or frogs, watching how hummingbirds and bees get nectar from flowers, catching the sunrise or sunset? Or what about making a garden, if only in a pot, coffee can, or emptied egg carton? Or picking berries or tomatoes together?

One Mother's Day, when my sons were in elementary school, they surprised me (thanks to help from their father) with a rose garden planted along the side of our screened porch. We spent many moments musing on the wonders of the blooming roses, the beauty and the thorns, and I believe this stirred a sense of wonder in my boys, who each discovered they are lifelong learners, always pursuing something new and educational.

Who knows how nature will stir your child's spirit? The Bible tells us, *"The heavens declare the glory of God; the skies proclaim the work of his hands"* (Psalm 19:1), and "the earth is full of [God's] unfailing love" (Psalm 33:5).

Your child's purpose and passion may lie just ahead in that forest on a camping trip, or just around the corner of that marathon bike course, or just over the hill of a picnic in the park, or maybe even a half hour leaning out the window or sitting on the doorstep noticing the stillness of morning or evening.

up at the stars under the Ohio night skies drew John Glenn, the first American to orbit the earth and fifth person in space, to become an astronaut. Hunting for birds' nests as a child in Scotland spurred a lifelong love affair with the outdoors for John Muir, the "patron saint of American environmental activity," largely responsible for preserving thousands of acres of wilderness, creating national parks, and founding the Sierra Club, one of the most important conservation organizations in the U.S.[30]

- **Dabble in art and music.** From movies and books, to exhibits and art sales or shows, and to church concerts and live performances on radio and television, there are more opportunities than ever for children to get powerful experiences. But don't just take your kids to things. Go a little deeper. Whether they like observing the arts or being a participant and a performer, stoke their curiosity about the artists, where works originate and how they are appreciated. One dad I know nurtures curiosity about the artists by having his kids plan an Exhibit or Performance Night. The kids get to choose the movie or music, art exhibit or event for an evening, and then the family goes all out. One child is responsible for introducing the work, meaning they have to read or listen and investigate a little about it (created by whom, for whom, where, why, any story behind the story). Another is responsible for coming up with a dish for dinner or snack related in some way to the work or the artist behind it. The kids loved it. When the family went to a school performance of *A Christmas Carol*, his kids loved dressing up like Dickens, and figuring out what a figgy pudding was and how to make one. The dad said his daughter, a budding writer, insisted the family read the book together days after the performance, and her next book report at school looked at how many sayings come from the writings of Dickens ("You're a Scrooge!").

- **Encourage team play.** When Maggie, a sixth grader, joined the middle school volleyball team, one of her gifts became even more pronounced: setting up and assisting. In the classroom and other extra-curricular activities, Maggie loved helping and being a support. She delighted in organizing scripts for parts in the school play, and taking minutes as class secretary. On the court, where her friend, Lynnae, loved to shine and spike the ball to score, Maggie's love for assisting and supporting, really became clear. She loved letting others do the flashy stuff and stepping aside to set up the ball for teammates. She preferred being a part of something rather than in the spotlight solo. Playing on a team helps your children find exactly where they shine, the role they each play best, where they're naturally gifted or must work harder, and what they love most. Your son, who loves batting on the baseball team but not running the bases, discovers he thrives when standing up to pressure, but loses interest in chasing a goal. He might love giving the big, high-risk sales pitch or being the entrepreneur establishing a business more than the one who heads and keeps going the day-to-day operations of a business. Whichever way your children go in pursuing a team sport, they can learn great things for their larger pursuits: how good it is to be part of something larger than yourself, and the joys of working with others toward a common goal, both good qualities for making a difference in this world. But beware of the inherent comparison and competition woes that seem to go along with team sports and games. There will always some people who overemphasize winning or being the best over developing skills, working with others, and having fun. Prayerfully, purposely make sure that's not you.

Identify and Focus on Strengths

Calling out your child's strengths goes beyond praising where he or she shines. You're helping your son or daughter name and claim something important within, their God-given gift, that inner power that Dr. Martin Luther King Jr. spoke of, that fire inside, as the apostle Paul called it, to fan into a burning passion and purpose.

Trust your intuition as you go about this. No one knows your child better than you. So without overanalyzing, observe, reinforce, and call out where you see your child shine. As a mom and dad, you're sure to see what others miss.

For instance, Mitch may not have given a very polished oral book report, but maybe he won the class over with his good humor about it and his funny faces because he's a natural comic. Teresa may have done miserably in the footrace, coming in last, but was the first to help an injured runner, which you know her nurturing, serving heart loves more anyway. It's easy to pooh-pooh such things, thinking, *But I'm his mom* or *I'm her dad and am seeing the good because I love my child.* But never underestimate the power of what you see. You are the parent who knows more. Who better to unearth these strengths from your child's soul than you? Now, once you see these strengths:

- **Call out the quirks.** Everyone has some. What are your child's? Does your son demand to only wear certain red socks with his jeans? Maybe he's a budding designer. Does your daughter always try every new condiment on her hamburger? Maybe she's a young chef or a taste tester, or maybe quality control in food service is her thing.

- **Compliment the qualities.** What's special about your child that's rarely measured by a test or on a team? Does your son look for ways of being generous, not just happily putting his coins in the collection plate at church but volunteering toys to give to the less fortunate? Praise his big heart. Is your daughter always trying to save every stray cat and puppy in the neighborhood? Stock up on the pet food, come up with a housing plan, and hug her tightly, telling her how much you love her love for the lost.

- **Help with queries.** Sometimes we think our job as parents is to give our child the answers, but we do a greater service in helping them form the questions, especially when it comes to pinpointing their strength. Ask your kids: What fascinates you? What can you stay fixed on for hours? What makes you curious? Where would you go for a day if anywhere was possible? What do friends compliment you on the most? What kinds of compliments do you get most from adults? What topics do you like to talk about, read about, and think about most? Why?

In each of these areas, be willing to go with the flow. Your children's interests and strengths may shift and change in unexpected but telling ways.

Steve Jobs, the co-founder, chairman, and CEO of Apple, Inc., who pioneered the personal computer revolution, said he was never sorry that he dropped out of Reed College six months into his freshman year. He was freed from course requirements, and for the next eighteen months he lived with friends, recycled Coke cans for cash, and audited, out of sheer curiosity, classes he'd never shown an interest in or affinity for before, including one on calligraphy and typography. That class revolution-ized his thinking—and the world of personal computers. "If I had never dropped in on that single calligraphy course in college," Jobs said years later, "the Mac would have never had multiple typefaces or proportionally spaced fonts."[31]

We often miss it in being fixed on other strengths, but that kind of curiosity to explore, entertain new ideas, and simply enjoy learning can contribute more than anything to finding passion and purpose.

NOW LIVE THE UNFOLDING ADVENTURE

I was thinking about that the day I met Jacob's grandmother for lunch. But she was more interested in things that were all figured out. Jacob was beginning to apply to colleges, and he was so smart, had such a bright future. She and Jacob's father could just see him excelling at Harvard, their pick for him of all the Ivy League schools.

"We just know he'll ace the math and business courses, and he's sure to be a whiz in finance," she said. She already had a life picked out for him, a career, and to get there she even had the perfect plan to help him rise above the fray of other students competing for admission to the Ivy League schools. A zealous educator, she'd written an after-school program for Jacob to teach socialization skills to autistic children. "I'm so excited just thinking of it," she said. "With his grades and this program, he'll get into Harvard for sure."

While her eyes gleamed, my heart sank for Jacob. *Did he really need his grandmother writing a program for him to teach in order to move toward his passion and purpose?* I didn't voice my question but wondered.

A few weeks later, I saw Jacob's grandmother and got my answer. She was bewildered. She and Jacob's father had sat down to help him finish his college admission application.

"No thanks," he said. He didn't want their help. He was filling out everything on his own—and he wasn't going to apply to Harvard or study business or pursue a career in finance either. "And, Grandma," he said, "you know I never liked tutoring others, so I don't know what you were thinking about me teaching kids after school."

His grandmother was crushed. "He wants to go to school here on the West Coast and major in pre-med," she lamented. "And he wants to be a doctor like his dad. We told him what a hard living that is anymore, how you're on call all the time." She shook her head. "But that's what he wants to do. He's insistent. He won't even discuss anything more about it."

MY PURPOSEFUL PARENTING CHECK-IN
How Am I Doing at Unfolding the World?

I'm seeing my children reach toward and find their purpose and passion, and being my best to bring out their best, by:

- Practicing the art of being a trail guide and scout who leads the adventure of a lifetime.
- Celebrating and calling out my child's God-given uniqueness.
- Watching for and helping my child identify and exercise the four signposts of ability, talent, personality, and passion on the way to his or her purpose.
- Enriching our days with experiences.
- Creating a learning environment at home and with one another.

Jacob! I thought, my heart welling for him. *You're like my Tom...only not like my Tom because you* want *to be a doctor and are dead set on it. Good for you.* It wasn't that I was so happy for someone else's son to pursue medicine. I rejoiced because here was a lad with a firm sense of identity. He knew who he was and what he wanted, and he wasn't going to be pressured by his father, grandmother, or anyone else to be anyone otherwise. He was going to be himself.

Though she may not have wanted congratulations that day, that's exactly what I wanted to give Jacob's grandmother, my friend. I wanted to hug her close and celebrate her and her son for raising up a child who knew his place, purpose, and passion so clearly and surely.

This is the goal, after all, what we all want—to give our children the moon and the world so that here and now they are confident and delighting in who they are and what they're meant to do and be.

Chapter 4

CHARACTER: SHAPE THEIR SOULS

…because you can tend the heart to do the right things for the right reasons

In the late 1990s, when President Bill Clinton was in the news every day for accusations of sexual transgressions and misdeeds of conduct, with headlines everywhere accusing him of abuses of power, I observed two third graders fistfighting outside my office window at school.[1]

Playground monitors stopped the fight and the boys were sent separately to me.

The aggressor came on like the worst used-car salesman, quickly selling his story and denying any role in instigating the fight. He quickly changed his tune, however, when he realized that I'd seen everything from my window.

"I was only practicing to be president!" he said, snickering.

We chatted a long while, but nothing I said wiped the smirk from that boy's face. He left my office with no remorse for being caught in his lies, no sense of sorrow for hurting someone, no display of understanding how violence was not the path to resolving differences, and no care for doing the right thing.

His arrogance and ignorance about the worth of character made me so sad. *What an example,* I thought, *of how our children form their values and moral core based on what they see and hear as acceptable.* I especially felt troubled because he responded in a way that marked a sign of our times. Our children are surrounded by pictures of lack of character—in the news, media, entertainment, and social sites. Why would they understand or ascribe to virtue when those in our highest offices don't? Why would integrity, honesty, justice, care, peacemaking, or humility matter to children who see adults break a vow, lie, manipulate, behave selfishly and arrogantly, and resort to violence—plus get away with it, joke about it, and even find celebrity status because of it?

And here is where sadness turns to tragedy.

Kids see such lapses in character, and worse, actual breakdowns that have led to mental and emotional issues and trauma, *every day* in our schools, media, and homes. We're in a crisis of character and our news headlines prove it.

"There is a hole in the moral ozone and it is getting bigger," according to Michael S. Josephson, founder and president of the Josephson Institute of Ethics, said nearly twenty years ago in the 1996 Report Card on American Ethics and Integrity.[2] The Report Card showed that fifteen to thirty-year-olds at that time were more likely to engage in violent, dishonest, and irresponsible conduct than previous generations. The 2012 Report Card was even more gloomy, showing an erosion of character in our youth when it comes to violence, dishonesty, and irresponsibility.[3]

Add to that the headlines you've seen in the past two years of the increased violence witnessed closeup by our kids in schools—more than seventy-five shootings in schools across the country in less than twenty-four months, from 2012 to 2014.[4]

"What happened to us that we now send our children into the world like we send young men to war?" mused a concluding voiceover on a television drama about a school shooting incident.[5] "When did we lose our way, consumed by the shadows, swallowed whole by the darkness?"

When did we lose our way in teaching children character? How have we failed to get to the heart of what makes our children people of integrity with the strength and conviction to make our world, not just their corner of it, a better place? What if you could reach that one child, maybe your own boy or girl, with the things that form moral conscience? What if you could raise a child who never lied; showed respect for all people and life and things; a child who chose to take the high road in a difference of opinion and looked for a way for everyone to win; a child who stood up to injustice and also showed great grace and mercy? Isn't that one of your deepest desires when you think about your job as parent, raising a child with a pure and shining soul?

The thing is, you can build and develop your child's character. In fact, you alone are the greatest influence in the formation of integrity in your child.

Schools can only build on the foundation laid by parents, but more and more teachers are being called upon to teach kids about integrity, when it's parents who must teach the core values like respect and caring.

Your children need you more than ever, more than anyone to teach them to do the right things for the right reasons because our world, our very souls, depend on it.

THE HEART OF CHARACTER

The good news is everyone's born with a conscience, that built-in alarm system, complete with beeper, to alert a thought or action that violates a personal, moral code, signaling what's right from wrong.

Remember Jiminy Cricket telling Pinocchio how he could always find the right way to go? "Always let your conscience be your guide."[6] Well, Pinocchio had a nose that grew longer when he told a lie. But neither you nor your kids need to see a sign as plain as the nose on your face to sense when you're deceitful or doing less than the right thing. You feel it, know it deep down in your heart. Some describe that internal alarm system or sense Jiminy Cricket was talking about as an eye of your soul that looks toward God.

Interestingly, a study with research from both the University of North Carolina, Chapel Hill, and across the country at the University of California, Los Angeles, shows that people are born with that sense of conscience not only in their souls, but their very blood and bones.[7] The researchers in that national study were looking at the genetic effects of happiness and found that eighty volunteers who said they felt satisfaction and fulfillment in their lives attributed that feeling to a sense of doing good things, living out their values for some higher purpose than their own well-being—and the blood tests from these people showed they were healthier, with greater antibodies for fighting inflammation and disease. In contrast, the volunteers whose blood tests showed more markers for increased inflammation throughout the body weren't as fulfilled or happy in life and didn't talk of values or living for reasons beyond their own well-being.

"Our genes can tell the difference between a purpose-driven life and a shallower one even when our conscious minds cannot," concluded Steven Cole, a professor of medicine and the senior author of the study at UCLA.[8]

Although everyone possesses a conscience, the challenge is that everyone's conscience is not the same, depending on the different teachings and examples of different parents and caretakers. And the rub? Sand runs through the hourglass on teaching children the values that will form their conscience and moral integrity. Research shows most kids can become set on their spiritual values by their thirteenth birthday.[9] And then, the events and experiences of life, can chip away at one's conscience.

No matter how old your child is—a baby, toddler, or well into grade school—you probably feel the clock ticking on the time you have to instill good values into their souls. Those few years you have together at home are precious for helping your kids develop integrity, weigh right from wrong, grow in the virtues that both psychologists and the Bible agree are good, healthy, and best:

- Hope and drive, willpower and self-control, purpose and direction, competence and method, fidelity and devotion, love and affiliation, care and production, wisdom and renunciation—as identified by educator Erik H. Erikson's highly regarded work;[10]

- Temperance, prudence, courage, and justice, as described by the Greeks;

- Faith, hope, and love, as the apostle Paul describes in First Corinthians 13:13;

- Joy, peace, longsuffering, kindness, benevolence, faithfulness, gentleness, and self-control—the "fruits of the spirit," as described in Galatians 5:22-23.

At the core of these things is integrity: doing the right things for the right reasons. Or, as psychiatrist Ross Campbell, MD, says, teaching your children to develop their integrity by telling the truth, keeping your promise, and responsibility for your own behavior.[11] So how do you develop that kind of integrity? What practices help, or steps do you take?

A STEP TOWARD CHARACTER
A Year of Character

To be intentional about teaching your children the virtues, choose one from the following list to explore, talk about, and practice each week. Make this a fun pursuit, like calling the virtue of a week your family secret to identify, put into action, and reward whenever seen during the week.

Caring	Humility
Cheerfulness	Integrity
Compassion	Kindness
Cooperation	Mercy
Courage	Patience
Fairness	Perseverance
Forgiveness	Respect
Generosity	Responsibility
Gentleness	Self-control
Helpfulness	Thoughtfulness
Honesty	Tolerance

Nurture the Capacity to Care

The first place to start in nurturing the capacity to care is in teaching children to empathize with others, because without care there's no regard for anything but one's own need and want, there's no reason or *why* for doing the right thing. Caring and empathy are what connect you to the world because you see things from someone else's perspective, you're able to live outside yourself, and walk in someone else's shoes—or as Atticus tells Scout in *To Kill a Mockingbird*, "You never really understand a person until you consider things from [another's] point of view—until you climb into his skin and walk around in it."[12]

Caring is what deepens and grows your very soul and builds your moral code, explains Martin L. Hoffman, a psychologist and professor emeritus of clinical and developmental psychology at New York University.[13] It's the soil in which integrity grows, and every other virtue.

That may be why God made empathy the first moral emotion to develop in human beings. Around two years of age, toddlers begin to realize and recognize the feelings of others, in particular pain. We've all seen a toddler try to comfort an upset sibling or playmate, and developmental psychologists have documented infants displaying sympathetic distress. For example, a child even as young as one year will pull his or her mother across a room to comfort a crying infant.

While children will naturally begin to display empathy, they need you to shape and direct it, researchers found.[14] Direction can be as small a thing as calling your child's attention to how their behavior affects someone else—for instance, letting your two-year-old know if she grabs all the cookies, others will be sad because they won't get one. The effects, however, can be huge because this is how children begin to feel for others and see that their empathy will be met with acceptance and reciprocity. It's a process that creates what psychologists call attunement—the capacity to take another's perspective, understand their interests, and navigate the way between that and your interests too, an essential to developing a moral code.[15]

To nurture empathy in your kids, and practice attunement, the Making Caring Common Project at Harvard University recommends:[16]

- **Help your child become aware of her own emotions and those of others.** One mom did this with her two-year-old Gracie who had a major meltdown while they were at the grocery store. Mom stopped shopping and took Gracie to the car, letting her know this was a consequence of all the crying and carrying on that were disturbing everyone around them. Like flipping a switch to turn on a light, Gracie realized what she'd done. "I acted like a baby," she cried, folding her arms against her chest. "Now Mommy is sad. Daddy is sad. Papa George is sad. Grandma Vickie is sad. Everyone is sad." Even more significant is Gracie owned what she'd done and how it affected others.

- **Connect the dots between mood or feeling and behavior.** Explore what sadness, anger, or disappointment feel like. Ask your child to describe those feelings and when and where they get them. What do those feelings prompt them to do? Maybe give them an example: When you're angry you may want to run away, slam a door, or throw something. Help them identify what difference that behavior makes: Does it change anything? Help or improve the matter? Hurt anything or anyone? Get them to identify on their own how feelings trigger behavior or situations trigger feelings, and how this happens for every person. You do this by asking them questions, and giving them time to think on things. Identifying these things in themselves is a beginning step to identifying them in others.

- **Give them opportunities to practice caring.** Practice is what makes caring and empathy second nature, just as with other skills. The more you take a look, talk about, and reflect upon situations where care and empathy make a difference, the more your child's thoughts automatically go to responding with empathy.

- **Expand their circles of concern.** Teach your kids that they can zoom in and zoom out of a situation. Where trouble erupts, they can zoom in to what they feel or one other person feels, then they can zoom out to see what people around them are experiencing. This helps them identify the greatest needs, where they can be part of a solution instead of the problem.

■ **Make caring a priority.** Repeat (with words and behavior), "The most important thing is to love others and show others we love them." Make caring and love the rule in most every circumstance from issues of fairness to want. When your child throws a fit, for example, because he or she wasn't given as big a piece of cake as someone else, you can say, "The only time we look at someone else's plate isn't to see if they got more than we did, but to see if they have enough." Always come back to "how well are we loving others, how much are we thinking of and taking care of others."

When you teach your children to live outside of themselves, to be quick to serve and help others, you also teach them how to respect, be humble, self-controlled, and kind.

As the Bible says, the greatest of all the virtues is care and empathy—which is love (see 1 Corinthians 13:13).

Show It to Grow It

Part of helping your kids identify how to care for others and to develop that moral code is showing them yourself. It's like in the real estate business, where everyone emphasizes location, location, location for success. The truism for teaching children about character is example, example, example—and it starts with you.

In fact, there's simply no substitute for your example. I like the way Charles Stanley, founder of InTouch Ministries, puts it, "Well-chosen words are important, but a godly example is riveting."[17]

You know just how riveting, don't you—how your kids are always watching, listening, learning, even mimicking all that you say and do. It's scary how prone our kids are to repeat what we say and do. We don't need to be reminded that to them we are almost godlike figures for a while. All good things come from us: food, warmth, care. So do our outlooks, standards, and deep-rooted personal values, psychologists agree.[18]

That's a good thing, actually, and can give you comfort, not make you cower with fear. It means you already possess what your kids need to learn about integrity and conscience and your moral code. It means every time you:

- go through closets for coats and blankets to give to the homeless, you teach your kids compassion.

- apologize after hurting someone, you teach forgiveness.

- repair something you broke, you teach peacemaking.

- respond kindly to a snarky or mean remark, you demonstrate gentleness.

- turn in a lost wallet, or ask the grocery clerk to check your ticket for an item missed, you show honesty.

- let someone ahead of you in line, you show mercy.

In contrast, so many behaviors that have become socially acceptable but are less than honest and true can give our kids a twisted sense of integrity. Every time:

- a dad says a child is ten, not twelve, to get the cheaper theater ticket or free admittance into an event, he shows how to fib.

- a mom tells a neighbor she's busy the day of the community garage sale because she just wants to be home instead, she shows how to be deceitful.

- a young man calls in sick to the office so he can drive to an out-of-town concert, he shows how to steal his time owed the company.

- you say you're going to be traveling a lot but have no such plans because you just don't want to teach Sunday school the next quarter, you display cowardice.

- you find a coupon expired but try it at the checkout anyway, you give an example of entitlement and pride.

To think little eyes and ears don't see and hear these things for what they are, is deceiving. Trust is chipped away each time you bend the truth or your moral standards. It's so important in parenting especially to check yourself first, like putting on your oxygen mask in an emergency to help yourself before helping others.

This doesn't mean you have to be perfect to give your kids a great example. You just have to be yourself and authentic, purposeful and intent on being your best. You just need to be transparent enough that even when you mess up or make a mistake, you let your children see your heart to make things right. You tell them outright, "I did something wrong." You let them see how you care to make things right, do the right thing. Such openness and vulnerability doesn't undermine your authority with your child, rather it strengthens your credibility as your children see you love them enough to trust them with the truth and do the right thing. Letting them see you care about virtue, integrity, and doing the right things for all the right reasons helps them see how to that themselves.

Even the research shows that allowing your children to see you work out your understanding of integrity and morality will shape your children's character more than any new teaching. As psychologist and biologist Jean Piaget says, this is how your children shape their moral values from within [your family system], modifying old or familiar ideas, not accumulating new ones.[19]

Children are paying attention and will absorb even abstract ideas that shape their character, like making things of the soul a higher priority than material things or success, according to a Columbia University study.[20] That means when you choose time with your family over longer hours at work and a higher salary, you send an important message that you value people over pay, personal integrity over corporate success. Not scheduling your kids in too many activities, and instead enrolling them in select activities in order to spend more time together, tells them people matter more than programs.

Your choices and example will speak louder than anything you can say.

Keep Integrity an Ongoing Conversation

That's not to say making integrity part of the conversation with your kids isn't important. It is—essential, actually, in helping them develop what they value and believe, their moral code. In conversation, you share your deepest values and beliefs, and explain why you believe the way you do, and how your behavior according to these values affects others.

When your kids ask questions about these things, they are beginning to sort out what they believe and value. In conversation, they're thinking aloud about what character and integrity mean to them. They're determining their own moral code.

Psychologists call this essential process induction.[21] Research shows the more you carry on these kind of conversations, the more children develop their sense and practice of altruism, moral reasoning, empathy, and integrity.[22] So how do you start such conversations and keep them going? You'll naturally find opportunities in the events of every day. Those teachable moments mentioned in Chapter 1 are always great for talk about values and why we do according to how we believe. Some intentional ways to get talks going are to:

- **Keep a Conversation Jar** near thc kitchen or dining table. Fill the jar with slips of paper on which you've written or printed questions that lead to discussions of your beliefs and values. You can add to these as you go, but some good starters are: *If you had a million dollars, what would you do with it? Your perfect day would include…what? Where did you see God today? What could we share that we have, and with whom? Where could you make a difference for someone tomorrow—and how? What's the meanest thing you've heard or seen lately? What's the kindest thing you've heard or seen? What are you thankful for and why? If you could give a trophy to someone for being good, who would it be and why? If you could be invisible, what would you do at school (or home or church or over the weekend)?* Now after certain meals, say Friday night dinners or Saturday morning breakfast, make it a practice to pull a slip of paper from the jar and take turns asking one question that everyone answers. Younger children will love what seems like a game, and you will not only be able to help teach your values but get an open window into your kids' hearts and souls, what they are thinking and what's important to them.

- **Share a story**, a movie to watch, or book to read that wrestles with deep character questions, which can easily prompt discussions of character and integrity. Most stories include this element of a character's choices and struggles, but if you want some starter ideas, the Family Learning Association (www.familylearning.org) offers several resources including the booklet *Developing Character through Literature* by Evelyn Holt Otten and the Indiana Department of Education.[23] Then perhaps you choose an evening for Family Movie Night or Family Reading Night at your house. You don't have to formally lead discussions of the story. In fact, it's better when you ask your kids what they think and then let conversations naturally go toward the questions that get at character issues: *Would you have done the same thing? Why? What would you have done instead? What might have happened if...?* Don't be afraid to share what you thought of the character's choices, but do hold back a little and give your kids more opportunity to say what they are thinking.

- **Make car talk**. Parents spend more time taking their kids to and from school and activities today than twenty years ago.[24] (That increase made its largest jump, by 11 percent, in 1995 when parents found themselves driving their children somewhere—school, activities, errands, church—forty-three hours more per year.) Make the most of that time with discussions on things you see along your route. This is absolutely organic to your lives. See a place that's rundown or blighted? Ask what could be done to make it better? What could you do, what about others, or all of you together? See a person who appears sad or mean or in need or wealthy? What made them that way? What could change them? How do they affect your lives or not and why? Keep thinking *who, what, where, when,* and *why* or *how*—and then *what if,* and you'll get to the right questions for the best discussions.

Keep Your Connection

One of the great motivators for children to do the right things is a sense of their parents' attention, love, and connection with them. One medical doctor researching this, Dr. Edward M. Hallowell, found that this is because the child who feels connected to someone or others—groups larger than themselves, be it family, class at school, team, or church—wants to do right by others, protect them, see them flourish and happy.[25] "It's almost instinctual, like pack order, to want to do your part, do right, do well, in order to remain a valued and respected member of the group," Dr. Hallowell explained.[26]

That instinctual motivation leads a child to self-control, one of the virtues that's part of every moral code, whether called *temperance* or *self-discipline, forbearance, rationality,* or *civility*—another essential for well-being.[27] This is what forms your children's sense of trust and sensitivity, which in turn determines how trustable and sensitive *they* can be.

Loving your child unconditionally keeps that connection between you strong, but there are purposeful, intentional things you can do to keep your bond strong too:

- **Get in their face and space.** This means make it a practice to get on their level when speaking with them. I don't mean be their buddy. I'm talking about not talking down to your little ones, rather leaning down or squatting to look them in the eye when speaking, getting on the floor to play with them when you can, pull them up to you so you can look one another in the face on especially important matters.

- **Be a character to develop character.** Kids love it when you play with them and they can see you vulnerable with them in this way. Defenses go down. Interest and engagement soar. Laughing together can knit your souls. You don't have to be a comedian to do this, just lighten up and be playful. Pretend you are from another country and speak with an accent or a new language, talk for the dog, grab your kids' hands to dance round the room, make faces without saying a word during some movie at home, sing what you want to say for impact. The more you enjoy one another, the more opportunity there is to impart all the important things about character.

- **Be real.** When you're vulnerable, you give your kids the freedom to be vulnerable too. Having a bad day? Hiding it doesn't help. Your kids probably already know you're feeling cranky, tired, frustrated, mad, or sad. Admitting so out loud piques their compassion for you, makes them think about your character and theirs. You may be surprised at how you can then together work through whatever you're feeling to be the person you each aspire: peaceful, kind, gentle, prudent, and so on. Transparency gives your children an important lesson too—we don't have to be perfect people, but we can always be people who try to be better and nobler. Earnestness and sincerity comprise the cornerstone of character.

TROUBLESHOOTING THE TOUCHSTONES

Halfway through one school year, Meg, one of the brightest fourth graders in her class, began lying about her schoolwork. One day, she said her backpack with all her homework was stolen on the way to school. But I could see her backpack hanging on the pegs by the door to our classroom. Another day, she said she couldn't work on an assignment in class because she didn't have any paper or pencils. We found them covered by school books inside the back of her desk. Yet another day, after giving the students an assignment to do in their math book, Meg reported hers missing.

You know where this was going. Meg said she couldn't do the work in class because of the missing text. Then—surprise! You guessed it. We found the book wrapped in her coat under her chair.

It's not really such a surprise when young children struggle with certain issues of character like lying or respect. Kids are growing and you're helping them, so you'll struggle too. There will be testing ground. You'll get frustrated, like Meg's mom, when your daughter seems to have acquired a new habit of lying, or your son starts repeatedly sneaking toys, or your child begins vandalizing and destroying property, or your daughter becomes a bully. These are common areas where they're figuring out what it means to do the right thing for the right reasons—only kids can easily give in to fear or insecurity, which can cause them to do the worst things for the worst reasons.

So take a closer look at how to troubleshoot these areas where character has gone awry—when your kids lie, show disrespect, and fail to keep their promises.

When Kids Lie: Turn Fear to Trust

When children lie it's often because they fear a consequence. The good news—this shows they understand the right thing to do. The bad news—they didn't do it, and for that there can be as many reasons as there are lies. But the ways to stop the lies is the same: Give your children assurance. Give them reasons to trust. Help them know they can face consequences with courage—if they keep trying, things will work out, either they will change or the circumstance will change.

Here's an example of how assurances work to stop the lies. With Meg, I discovered the same practice of lying at school was going on at home too. One day Meg told her parents that she had no homework, when she did. Another day, she said she finished it already at school, when she had not. Just the evening before I met with her mom for a conference, Meg said I'd said she no longer needed to do homework, but I hadn't.

Mom and I figured out Meg's lies started after she'd begun an advanced math program for the accelerated students. She did poorly on the first assignment, and her father had threatened to take away her new Wii games until she started excelling again. Now Meg, who already feared failing, feared never getting to play again too. She didn't need punishment, rather encouragement that she could learn and solve the math problems one at a time, and still have time for both playing and problem-solving. She also needed the assurance that avoiding what was difficult or challenging doesn't make it go away. That had been her solution—if there was no homework by her decree, then there would be no failure and could be no punishment.

If your child begins a pattern of lying, most likely fears are at the root of why: fear of not being able or failing or of losing something like a privilege or even your love. You can address those fears so your child is courageous and strong in character enough to trust once more. Use these steps:

- **Save the lecture and start with what's obvious.** The second you begin to launch into how bad it is to lie, how hurtful, is the second your kid tunes out. You can get to those things in time. Instead, begin with what you've seen or know. For example, "So homework isn't getting finished." Or, "You snuck out last night." The important thing is to address the lie head-on, lay it out there fast and factual for both you and your child to address, for you to ask why and he or she to open up on the thinking. This gives both of you a chance to talk and listen. You build connection rather than break it.

- **Identify instead of accuse.** This is trickier. It's so easy to accuse, and truly, only practice helps begin to identify issues, rather than ascribe intentions and blame or failures. Here's what I mean. You can say, "Don't tell me you didn't spill that milk all over the counter." Or you can say, "I see there was an accident with the milk." The first sentence accuses and even implies the milk was spilled on purpose or your child is incapable ("a failure") of pouring it. The second example simply identifies the problem and lets both you and your child move on to look at it openly—so there's no need to lie about it—and solve it. A plan of attack for making identifying rather than accusing your practice is to describe what you see, what you feel, and what needs to be done. For instance,

"I see you left your bike on the sidewalk. It bothers me when you tell me you didn't because not only could you get hurt, but someone else could too [what you see]. Your bike could get stolen or block someone's way or cause another cyclist to crash into it [what you feel]. You need to move the bike to the garage" [what needs to be done].

- **Talk about consequences without issuing threats.** When you threaten, you give cause for fear or defensiveness and create an almost instinctive desire in your child to protect or claim what is "mine," whether that *what* is a privilege, right, thing, or relationship. When you talk of consequences, you can stay more factual and keep more reasoned. For example, you can say, "If you don't do your homework tonight, there will be no more Wii for you." Or you can say, "You need to finish your homework so that you will have time to play Wii before bedtime." The first manner is threatening and not really reasoned—your child could say you just don't want her to have fun. The second approach, however, lays out the facts: "Oh, you didn't finish your homework? Well, you have to do that, so there's no time for Wii." You retain control as a parent (there are things we all have to do and homework is one of them), you are not the bully (the responsibility of how to spend the evening becomes your child's), and you establish trust in consequences and not mistrust because of threats.

- **Stay calm, consistent, and constant.** More than anything, these three Cs build trust and keep things open for no more lies, secrets, or hiding. When you make a huge fuss, overreact with raised voices or aggressive gestures, you awaken fear. The same things happen when you change how you react to a given situation each time, or fail to address something once and then make a big deal of it the next. Your child doesn't know what to expect, which creates confusion and keeps one on edge, in a way that's not good. There's more cause for fear and distrust, and to hide things in order not to deal with, in their minds, what seems to be a monster, The Great Unknowns. Things that work to help you stay calm: Breathe deeply. Count to three before answering or responding. Remind yourself that consistency and constancy are like freeways to trust—they will get you there faster when you follow them.

- **Keep communication safe and open.** If your daughter asks, "Why are you angry, Daddy?" don't respond that "Everything is fine." It's clearly not, and better to admit you're upset or disappointed, but that you care more about a solution because you love her. Children need to know that their perception of the world is accurate, and they need to feel safe enough to talk about all things. That means you pave the way when you listen without interrupting ("Tell me…"), answer without arguing ("Why did you think that?"), and share without pretending ("This is bad but let's figure it out together").

When Kids Disrespect: Turn Disregard to Deference

I know a couple married now for fifty-five years. Whenever I run into them, they're clearly happily enjoying the events of the day. They lean in to listen to one another and don't interrupt. They have this awakened sense of delight in one another's company. They don't always share the same point of view but seem to even relish their differences as though they're treasures: "That is so him," "Yes, that is so her."

I asked them once to share the keys to their success of getting along so remarkably.

In unison, they answered, "Respect," and looked at each other, smiling, the husband then nodding to his wife to go ahead and speak first.

"We respect each other and would never say anything disrespectful to one another," she said.

He nodded. "We promised to never hurt one another."

"I couldn't bear it," she said.

I thought how respect really is just another word for *love*. When you respect someone, whether a spouse, friend, colleague, parent, or child, you show them care and concern. You love them and give them deference, submitting to their right for being—being heard, seen, having an opinion and point of view, fears and dreams and purpose. You submit to the idea they are loved by God as much as you are.

In fact, that makes respect one of the most godly, defining virtues of one's moral code. The Bible tells us God shows no favoritism or partiality (Acts 10:34, Romans 2:11). He loves and regards each of us intensely. But, face it, we definitely have feet of clay, meaning we are so molded by circumstance, personalities, sometimes just the way the wind blows. We get a sense of our need being greater than someone else's, our voice needing to be heard more loudly and clearly. We sometimes just don't like someone else and disregard them or what they are saying or how they believe as "less than."

This is not acceptable. Learning to be a respecter of persons as God is a respecter of persons is essential. But how to teach such an important thing when your pre-teen sneaks out to get a piercing that you already forbade? Or your nine-year-old smarts back to his coach? Or your five-year-old won't

A STEP TOWARD CHARACTER
Make the Golden Rule Real

Help your kids make the Golden Rule real by regularly looking for ways to instill it in their:

- **Mind:** Help them know what's good. Point out what good character looks and sounds like. Talk about the qualities. Call out character strengths when displayed. Recognize, encourage, and reward positive character behaviors. Ask your kids questions to promote decision-making skills.

- **Heart:** Help them love what's good. Promote human dignity by telling them and showing them how everyone is someone and worthy of respect. Reinforce the tools of civility to show how a pauper can be treated the same as a president, not one better than the other. Encourage positive role models and peer relations. Teach empathy considering the perspective of others.

- **Hands and Feet:** Help them do good. Find ways you can care for others and love them as a family. Practice cooperation in work and play. Encourage your kids to think of their own charities, acts of service, and projects they can do to help others.

stay out of his older brother's game equipment? You act determinedly and purposefully so your kids know disrespect is not acceptable, not an option, and will not be tolerated:

- **Respond immediately.** Use a special tone of voice that lets them know they are in dangerous territory when they disrespect anyone. Practice an authoritative, this is serious tone. Children will read your tone, posture, and the way you say something as much as they will what you say. They can tell the difference between ambivalence and an intentional directive, between you asking or telling them to watch out. Then be clear with your words: "Stop. You're not allowed to speak in that way. Ever. Even if you are upset."

- **Check emotions.** Help your child calm down. Usually when disrespect rears its ugly head, feelings have been awakened to the point that they're overriding reason. Let them see how overpowering feelings change a conversation just like smoke from a fire pollutes the air—feelings and smoke get in the way. Show them how to calm themselves by taking a deep breath, counting to five, or moving so they speak without anger, frustration, hurt, or disappointment getting in the way.

- **Practice the Golden Rule:** Treat others as you want to be treated. Love others like you want to be loved. Listen as you want to be listened to; see others as you want to be seen. This is the core of our moral code, as Jesus said in his first public sermon (Matthew 7:12). It's where the Bible and the best practices of psychology meet once more. It's a code found in some variation in nearly every major religion and culture of the world because it operates on reciprocity. Confucius put it this way, "What you do not want done to yourself. Do not do to others." Aristotle said, "We should behave to our friends as we wish our friends to behave to us." Hinduism says, "Do nothing to thy neighbor which thou wouldst not have him do to thee." Buddhism says, "Hurt not others with that which pains thyself." The Golden Rule offers the greatest handle on respect that we have. A study of what made certain preschoolers popular and esteemed because of their character showed how this plays out for little ones. The best-liked children were the ones who looked their playmates in the eye when speaking to them, addressed them directly with words, and responded with relevant information to show they were listening.[28] Less esteemed children avoided eye contact, changed the subject, were disruptive, and talked more about themselves. In other words, they displayed little respect for those around them. Practicing the Golden Rule allows every party its rights and obligations—and one's rights are the other obligations. Everyone wins when everyone has a heart to do right by others. Imagine how strong your children's character would be if they practiced what Jesus taught us first: "Love the Lord your God with all your heart and with all your soul and with all your mind and with all your strength. ...[And] love your neighbor as yourself. There is no commandment greater than these" (Mark 12:30-31).

- **Introduce them to the tools of civility.** They don't have to like what someone does or says, but they may have to listen or give that person room to reap the consequences of their own behavior. Remind kids to listen without interrupting, don't say anything if you can't say something productive or positive or that reaches toward some solution, compromise, or agreement. Tell them, "Sometimes you can only agree to disagree and go separate ways." These ideas will be new; they may never have realized you don't have to like everyone and enjoy them, but you do need to tolerate and get along with people or find ways to separate yourself from destructiveness.

- **Ask them to look for ways to practice Philippians 2:3-4:** "...in humility value others above yourselves, not looking to your own interests but each of you to the interests of the others." Memorize that verse till it becomes something you say to yourself automatically. Check one another on how you are doing this, where and when. Being intentional will have its effect, like in the old hymn "Trust and Obey": "There's no other way" to think and act. This is the way, and so when you can't trust, you obey, you do the right thing anyway and trust comcs in time.

When Kids Fail to Keep Promises: Put Ideas into Action

I've counseled many a brokenhearted child of divorce who was promised something by one parent who never followed through: the pledge to be at the next game to cheer them on, make the fishing trip, show up for dinner, call at a certain time. There are times married parents mix up who will be there to pick up a child from school or attend the school conference.

I've carried the pieces of Danny's broken heart in my own for many years. Danny was a third grader who literally beamed with joy and anticipation about the new bicycle his dad promised him for a birthday. I never saw such a broken spirit and countenance than Danny's when the birthday arrived, but neither dad nor bike were anywhere in sight. Danny was crushed and talked little about his home life the rest of the year.

Children repeat what they've experienced, heard, and seen. When you say you'll be there and aren't, can finish a project and don't, or will do something for them and can't, they are first hurt and angry. Soon, they learn this is acceptable when it's not. In part there are issues here of discipline, honesty, respect, and perseverance. At the core is the issue of integrity. Of course there are things that stall and stop us in our commitments. There always will be. But as much as possible make it part of your moral code for both you and your children to:

- **Mean what you say and say what you mean.** Speak the truth, even when it's sure to make someone unhappy. If you can't make an event, explain why. If you can't finish a task, talk through what is possible, how and why. This means be in dialogue and accountability as well as conversation to make words match action.

- **Be realistic.** Err on the side of caution. Don't be afraid to under-promise and over-deliver. It's better to surprise people with more than they expect. Consider the standards and goals, and measure if they're doable so what you think are possible matches with what is actual in the end.

- **Connect a promise to production**, mapping out the steps between the idea and the follow-through. What has to happen first and then next and by when? Marrying the words to action, and mapping the way in between helps children learn to strategize for success.

SET THE STANDARD

One afternoon I sat at my desk, eyes closed, reflecting back on the years when my boys were young and how hard I tried to build their character by teaching them about the nature of God. I thought of the bright moments, when they showed me they got it: when they told the truth about something wrong they did, or reached out to help someone others were treating badly. I thought of a few instances of disappointment too, when I felt I'd really failed to get across some important virtue.

One day, I felt a sudden warmth, as if a heater had been turned on right above me. I looked up. A beam of sunshine burned across the room from the window and around my desk. The light was so bright, so warm, I wanted to stay in its beam to enjoy it. Everything was so clear in the path of that sunbeam. Enveloped in it, I felt comfort and joy.

Then the doorbell rang. I jumped up to see who was calling. As I stepped from my sunny spot and made my way to the door, I felt the cool of the rest of the room, and had to refocus because it seemed so much darker too. This, I realized, is exactly what it's like to teach children about character.

When you are centered on God, it's like you are standing in that beam of sunshine. There is no shade, no cool, no gray. But when you move away from God, it's as though you've stepped out of a clearing and are retreating into a forest. At first, there is some flickering of light through the darkness. You still feel some of the residual warmth. But as you walk farther away from God, that warmth, and light fade. Soon, you no longer sense God's presence. You're on your own. There's no bright spot on which to center yourself.

When you work with your children on their character, you're not just shaping their souls. You're tending their hearts, ushering them into that bright spot where they will find assurances, comfort, and joy because they are aligned with God's ways. The heart softens in that light, in God's glory, to become more like his. Conversely, the heart hardens the farther it gets from God's radiance. The capacity to tell right from wrong diminishes. God fades from importance. You rely on your own sense for what's right and wrong—and in all that murkiness your sense isn't so great.

"…As the Spirit of the Lord works within us, we become more and more like him," the Bible promises in Second Corinthians 3:18 in The Living Bible. "[The Lord] guides the humble in what is right and teaches them his way" (Psalm 25:9). God sets the gold standard that will guide us through life. His ways are higher than ours, the Bible says in Isaiah 55:8-9. We can rely on him and his Word because they are perfect (see Psalm 18:30).

It's not enough to know what good character is and how to pass it along to our children. We must each love the good too. We must have the will, the hunger even, to act in accord with the good. When we practice this centeredness on God, our children are more likely to be infected by the desire

---

MY PURPOSEFUL PARENTING CHECK-IN
How Am I Doing with Shaping Character?

I'm seeing my children build character, and being my best to bring out their best, by:

- Talking constantly about the importance of doing the right things for the right reasons.
- Talking through the touchstones like honesty and respect.
- Putting the Golden Rule into practice.
- Centering on God and his nature by example, in his Word, and through his promises as our standard for living.

to be God-centered too. This, after all, is the way of the heart. Because I'm talking about a practice, I mean that you intentionally:

- **Make Jesus the head of you household.** Commit to his lead in every area of your life. If you are married, that means seeking God in unison with your spouse so you can be the best parents. If you're a single parent that means knitting relationships around your family that keep God at the center.

- **Look for new, personal ways to show your children how loved they are by God and ignite their love for him.** Rather than focus on things about just church and religion, keep your focus on your relationship with Jesus, God, and the Spirit—how you know and experience them personally. Loving God and staying centered on him as the standard is about relationship with him, not just about membership in a church or subscription to a theology.

- **Read the Bible for wisdom, instruction, guidance, comfort, and encouragement** (2 Timothy 3:16). God reveals himself through his Word, and it's alive, as my pastor, Rick Warren at Saddleback Church, says often, "not just writing on a page in an old book."[29] As you know and understand Scripture, you will see it apply to every area of your life. You'll find your own story in the stories of parents and people who have gone before us. You'll find yourself in that sunbeam of knowing and experiencing the fullness of God, the Son, and the Spirit. Your conscience will grow in harmony with God's nature. Your spirit will become increasingly sensitive to his promptings. The difference between right and wrong becomes crystal clear. God adds to your "faith goodness; and to goodness, knowledge; and to knowledge, self-control; and to self-control, perseverance; and to perseverance, godliness; and to godliness, mutual affection; and to mutual affection, love" (2 Peter 1:5-7).

- **Pray as a family.** When families pray together, amazing things happen. You connect at a deeper level. It's hard to stay frustrated or mad at someone when you're praying for them. When parents pray together, your prayers go to an even more amazing height. You are able to be of one mind, in connection with God, in raising your children. You can take your deepest concerns about practical matters like finances and the soul to God together, and look together for how God is answering you. The axiom, "Families who pray together, stay together" is so true. Praying centers your attention on God and his goodness, not the things or people who can fall apart around you. In prayer, you learn to give God your trouble and listen to him with your life, not just with your ears but your eyes and experiences—and he shows up. You'll see his answers, not always maybe what you wanted, the way you wanted. But his will shines like that sunbeam, clear and bright. And when you fail to see it, others in your family can, helping buoy one another's faith. Maybe you prayed for your son to get into a certain program and it didn't happen, but later you learn he spared your son from something there, or there was something more right for your son in God's plan. Make prayer a habit before meals, at bedtime, and perhaps at other key moments for your family too: before leaving the house for the day, or before certain events. Use the following prayers to help you form your own: The Lord's Prayer in Matthew 6:9-13, the prayers in the devotional book *My Utmost for His Highest* by Oswald Chambers (I've used this one every morning for more than thirty years), and *Jesus Calling* by Sarah Young.

Finally, know that these matters of tending your children's heart and soul will tug at your own. You will find moments of joy as they seem to develop beyond what you imagine. But there will be moments of disappointment and grief too. It will feel like moving from that sunbeam into the dark forest. You'll see things, as I did, like fistfights, where character has completely broken down. But you'll also see healing moments, when a child stands up and steps in with love, peace, respect, kindness, the integrity you so want them to possess.

Whatever the case, whatever the day, press on. Stay centered on the presence, Word, and will of God, who promises: "We also glory in our sufferings because we know that suffering produces perseverance, perseverance character, and character hope." (Romans 5:3-4)

Chapter 5

RESPONSIBILITY:
"I'VE GOT THIS"

…because owning up is growing up

Susan loved school. Mostly, she loved chitchatting her way through the school day. She was a talker, bubbly, and full of energy—so much that we met because her teacher sent her to my office for talking non-stop in class.

"Oh, pretty!" Susan said, bursting onto my desk to eye more closely a vase of flowers. She flitted across the room. "Oh, and this is soft." She hugged a small throw pillow on a chair close to her face, then made a bee-line to some learning toys in a corner, prattling away without pause. I could see what Susan's teacher meant. Our bubbly kindergartner couldn't focus, wouldn't listen, and didn't engage in what she needed to be doing. She was more interested in being entertained and boldly pursued anything that smacked of fun or a game. Even as I arranged a meeting with her parents and teacher, she chattered away about little nothings.

"She's unquestionably smart," her teacher lamented the next day, sinking into a chair. "But she's behind in math and reading."

"She gets away with a lot at home," Susan's mom admitted. She slumped slightly, as if saying the words deflated her. "She's always competing with her older sister and then just wants to goof around."

Smart, competitive, fun-loving Susan, I learned, held all the keys to her own troubles. Her family needed to let her start using those keys herself, stop opening all her doors for her, and carrying her through them too. The problem was Susan was the baby of the family and everyone treated her like one. She had no responsibilities, no chores, no accountability. She never took her own dishes from the table to the dishwasher, or hung up her coat. Her mom picked up after her and cleaned her room when it was a mess. Her sister took over even the simplest tasks after Susan competitively fought with her about them then gave in and gave up. Susan's dad talked her through her catch-up assignments in reading and math and did more and more of the work himself. Susan, meanwhile, poured her boundless energy into games and chatting herself into and out of trouble.

"Things can be so different," I encouraged her mom.

Susan's teacher brightened and sat a little straighter.

"Susan can be self-thinking, self-doing, and self-directed," I said, catching her teacher's eye. "She's so bright and full of energy. We just need to teach her how to use those smarts and that energy—to own up to what she can do. Then we need to hold her accountable to doing it. She can learn how taking responsibility will make her life, and the lives of everyone around her, so much better."

Now Susan's mom straightened in her seat. The very word *responsibility* was a boost. I could see she got it. Children who learn to be responsible own up to all they can do and be—and that helps them, you, and all those around you, even people you may never know. That's because responsible beings take care of themselves and others. They get things done. They're capable, reliable, and competent. They bring comfort and joy because they can create order from chaos. They can keep and hold things together. Responsibility raises up and lifts up.

LETTING LOOSE RESPONSIBILITY

If only we could raise our kids to take that kind of responsibility right now, you might think. You're so ready to hear your kids say, "We've got this, Mom," or, "Consider it done, Dad."

Instead, you find yourself asking your daughter for the umpteenth time to put her bike in the garage, or unload the dishwasher. Or you rush back to school several afternoons a week because your son forgets his backpack… or homework assignment…or coat. Or you have to tell each of your kids to turn off the lights when they leave their rooms. Every. Single. Morning.

I see so many parents struggling in this area and know they just need to redefine the role of parenthood. It's not what you do for your children, but what you teach your children to do for themselves that is important. Every time you do something for your kids that they're capable of doing for themselves, you are clipping their wings.

That's not what you want. You're probably longing for just the opposite, in fact. You probably wish responsibility were like a stray cat that you invite into the house once, then to never leave. Wouldn't it be great if that cat, a little responsibility, began to rear its head in your household? What does it take for your kids to start owning up to things?

Begin with Boundaries

For starters you need to know where you end in helping your kids and where they begin—where to teach, show, and involve them, and where to hang back so they can figure out and do for themselves. There's a line between these places, a boundary, and every parent and child needs to know where it is. Do you know the boundaries right now for what you will and won't do because of what they can? Do they?

You've already had a line the first time you started teaching your kids to feed themselves by picking up their food and then using eating utensils; and again when you started potty training. These are things you know your kids need to start doing for themselves. Sometime after they're walking, talking, and eating on their own, when you're not having to change diapers and dress them, the line of where to help and where to hang back gets fuzzier for so many parents. *Can Mary be relied upon to make sure the dog's fed every morning? Can Johnny be sure to load the washer with his dirty soccer uniform that needs laundering before tomorrow's game?*

Yes, the line shifts and moves as your children learn and grow, but you always want it there, and you want it to become more clear and defined as they do more for themselves and you do less.

I remember talking with one young mom about her daughter who needed to learn more about being responsible. Claire was leaving messes for others to clean up, always losing things, and not listening or following through on directions and assignments in class. Mom brought her baby to our meeting. He gurgled and crawled around our feet as we talked. Her eyes stayed glued on her son even as she spoke to me. He'd pulled himself

A STEP TOWARD LIVING RESPONSIBLY
Is Your Child Self-Directed or Directed by You?

Take ten minutes to find out how you're doing right now in teaching responsibility, and how your kids are doing in living it. For each question in this self-quiz, give yourself two points for something you do often, one point for things you do sometimes, and 0 points for something you seldom do.

1. I assign my child age-appropriate chores.
2. I encourage my children to do things on their own.
3. My child observes or obeys the family rules and routines.
4. Any initiative my kid takes in any area (providing it's not destructive), I enthusiastically support.
5. My child has the freedom to make choices, demonstrate judgment, and learn from mistakes.
6. I encourage my child to accept greater levels of responsibility and independence.
7. As my children mature, I expect them to take on increasing responsibility while I also allow them more privileges.
8. I talk with my children frequently about how to plan ahead and anticipate the consequences of their behavior.
9. I provide my children with structure to complete their homework.
10. If my child struggles with a homework assignment, I give enough instruction to clarify or provide guided help and practice on assignments. When it's clear my child understands the assignment, I back off.

How do you think you did? Add up all the points: If you scored 17-20, you're probably doing a good job teaching responsibility. A score of 16-11 means you're probably doing about right. Below 11 points and your child will benefit from more responsibility.

up by gripping a chair leg and wobbled there, just ready to let go and lurch forward a step. Mom lunged in to steady him. She didn't want him to fall and hurt himself. She thought she was saving him from pain.

This was exactly the picture of what was happening with her daughter. Mom was swooping in too much, all with the best intentions to keep her girl from falling or failing. But by always going to quickly retrieve things that Claire forgot at school, or excusing her from finishing things, or cleaning up behind her, Mom wasn't saving Claire from struggle. Mom was stopping Claire from fumbling through things on her own in order to learn and master doing them herself. No one ever learns to walk or ride a bike or drive without doing it for themselves. Toddlers and teens have to take a step, sit in the driver's seat, steer and go forward on their own. Mom and Dad can't do it for them. The coach doesn't suit up and play the game for the players.

This is the rub, says Deborah Gilboa, MD, who founded AskDoctorG .com. Too many parents weigh matters and think, *If I just help, if I'm just involved I can keep my child from failing that class, or missing out on this great experience, or getting into that program, or being hired for that job or....* There's always something. Says Gilboa, "many of the consequences [parents] are trying to prevent—unhappiness, struggle, not excelling, working hard, no guaranteed results—are great teachers, and not actually life-threatening. It just feels that way."[1]

To be the most purposeful parent, deliberate in helping your children do for themselves, think about what prompts you to sometimes do for them.

- **You're anxious they might not succeed or they'll be hurt or disappointed.** Worry often nips at our heels, moving us to try and control things we think that we can. When tempted to do something for your kids because you're worried, stop and consider what you or they can control anyway, because it is nothing. Shift the worry and yearning to control, peace, and learning how to manage—reminding yourself all that counts is you and your child doing your best in each moment.

- **You overcompensate** because of your own feelings, not theirs. Maybe you feel unloved or unsuccessful, or did as a child. Maybe you feel guilty for things like not spending as much time with your kids as you'd like, or making the money to afford more for them. Ask yourself what you're trying to make up for and why.

- **Peer pressure from other parents triggers your competitive spirit.** Seeing other parents doing so much for their kids makes you think you're a bad parent if you're not doing so much too.

Help, Don't Helicopter

Whatever the reasons for wanting to do things for your kids, you may have already fallen into that Doing Too Much Camp without even knowing it. So many parents belong to that camp that there's a name for them: "helicopter parents," a term recently added to the dictionary to define an increasing type of behavior.[2]

If you didn't already know what it means to be a helicopter parent, you surely recognize the definition in action. Helicopter parents finish what their sons and daughters start. Some actually do the start-up work and all that follows too. They're the parents who type their first grader's story and bind printed copies for the teacher. Yes, those parents who monitor their children's performance and outcomes so closely because they have a path in mind that their kids must follow without one slip or even a hint of going astray. They're the parents I can always spot because they talk about "our homework" and know more about an assignment than their children.

For all their efforts, they hinder more than help.

Really? you might wonder. *Does taking care of the little things like making their beds really hurt anything?* Maybe not if your child is three years old, but if he or she is thirteen, yes! Hovering damages kids by:

- **Reducing their motivation** because when you do things for your kids, there's no room or reason for them to build their "I can-do it" muscle.

- **Increasing their dependency** because they expect you to take care of things.

- **Eroding boundaries** because you're intruding on responsibilities that belong to your child.

- **Planting and nurturing the unappealing sense of entitlement** because your child learns to expect the privileges that belong to an adult.

- **Diminishing sense of self** because your children never develop the competencies that help them grow and discover.

Kids don't like being hovered over either. Research in the *Journal of Child and Family Studies* clearly shows, after tracking several students over the years to college, that the more parents hovered and tried to help, the more frustrated and unhappy students felt with their lives.[3]

Keep Your Focus on Competence

To find that line between helping and hovering, you want to think upon competence. Where your child is able is where you step back. You don't have to guess about where those places are either. Just as you use a tape measure to mark your child's physical growth on the wall, you can assess their capability and competency for handling things by looking at:

- **How do your kids reason and use induction?** Do they understand their actions and the effect of their actions on others? Can they connect what they do (or don't) to others? Once they see those connections, how well do they understand them and care? For instance, does your three-year-old son see that when a ball is thrown, it hits something? Does he understand that a hit can cause hurt and damage? Does he care to not break things or hurt people? If yes, yes, and yes, then he can be responsible enough with inductive reasoning to not throw a ball at a glass door or someone's face. As your children grow, you'll always want to look for their greater ability to reason using awareness, understanding, and care.

- **Can they problem-solve?** Do your kids recognize what's tripped them up or stopped them in the midst of difficulty? Children who haven't learned problem-solving skills, tend to repeat their difficulties over and again. Maybe they haven't recognized the problem or sticking point, or they deny it exists, or they can't see how to work through it another way—to try a plan B and push through differently for a different effect.

- **Do they understand choices?** All behavior is a choice, so if your children look for ways to justify what they do (or what they've left undone), they may not fully understand choices. A sign that they don't understand (or maybe don't care—another issue we'll address later) is when they play the blame game. Do they point fingers at others for things they fail to complete? Can they see that some things are within their power to change?

- **Can they control their feelings?** Part of being responsible is learning to recognize feelings and not necessarily act on them. Do your children respond by impulses? Are you seeing increasing improvement in how, when triggered by certain emotions like anger or jealousy, they can quickly calm down, pull it together, and ponder a situation? Do you see any evidence that they're learning they can change the way they feel by the way they think?

- **How are they at making decisions?** Where do you see them looking at a situation, defining it, gathering information, talking about how they feel, looking at obstacles and options, predicting what can happen in different scenarios, and choosing a way to go? These are the steps of making a decision and the more your child moves through each one before making a decision, the more responsibility he or she is probably ready to assume. The other part of determining competency in decision-making is how sound your child's decisions are based on the values you instill. Are your kids asking: Is this something that would be considered wrong or dishonest? Does it go against my conscience? Will it result in negative consequences? Will it cause me to lose self-respect or can I be proud of it?

When you measure your child's competencies in these ways, you'll probably be surprised. Much of the time our kids are actually a bit more ahead in ability than we think.

One chubby fifth grader, underestimated greatly by his parents, put it this way, "I'm smart but sometimes I don't know how to show it."

His latest check-up at the doctor revealed he needed to lose some weight. The doctor gave Mom a list of healthy foods and recommended daily exercise, but she and Dad didn't let their son take on any responsibility for his own health. Mom controlled his diet and Dad wouldn't let the boy go very far or fast riding his bike in the neighborhood—the boy's favorite exercise.

"Sometimes my parents don't *let* me show what I know," the boy said, "so sometimes I think *why try?*"

THE THINGS YOU CAN DO

Why try, indeed. If we don't give increasing responsibilities to our kids as they become competent, as they can reason, control their feelings, and make decisions at five or ten years old, how can we expect them to do so at twenty or thirty?

Like this wise fifth grader, your kids may be eager and know how to take on responsibility in one area or another: their health, at school or home, with relationships, or in caring for something or someone. They may be ready and not know it. But maybe you haven't known it either. That's okay. The great thing is you're thinking on this now. You're a purposeful parent. By the very fact you're reading this book, you're being intentional and deliberate to help your kids grow and thrive. So no matter where you are in teaching responsibility, and where your kids are in learning it, you can go forward and your kids can be more responsible next week than they are today. Remind yourself: start now!

Start Now

It's never too early to begin teaching your kids about responsibility. From the time they're toddlers, you can stretch and challenge them to be responsible. Your two- and three-year-olds can pick up a mess and return toys to their proper place. Your four- and five-year-olds can dress themselves, brush their teeth, and put dirty clothes in a hamper. Kids at six, seven and eight can take out the trash, feed pets, fold and put away laundry, and help fix a meal. Kids at nine, ten, eleven and twelve can prepare simple meals on their own, operate a washer and dryer to do the laundry, clean their room, and walk the dog. Many children love to join Mom and Dad in household repair projects and can learn from instruction and guidance.

Even if your child is older, and you're just now beginning to work on responsibility, it's still not too late. It can be harder teaching older children for the first time to own up to things because they've already learned not to be responsible. But they can learn. Taking things a step at a time and being purposeful will get you to a better place than today. Each bit of growth in being responsible is a milestone.

I remember the morning my four-year-old grandson proudly called me on the phone to announce, "Nana, I got dressed all by myself this morning. I'm wearing my rainbow shirt with blue shorts and blue socks." He wanted me to know he was not only responsible enough to get dressed on his own but coordinate shorts and socks too. It was a proud moment indeed! What step would make you proud of your child right now?

Keep Believing

Children feel capable when their parents think of them as capable and treat them that way. "Kids will try and succeed in things when they feel your faith in them and themselves," agrees educator Michele Borba. "Never underestimate the power of a caring parent who sticks by a child and offers faith and hope."[4] You can tell them you believe in them, but showing them will mean more. To do that…

Get Out of the Way

Give your kids experiences. Break down tasks and activities into small steps or segments, and teach each segment one step at a time. Provide guided practice until they perform the task successfully, then turn your kids loose to do things on their own. You may have heard it said, "Tell me and I forget, teach me and I may remember, involve me and I learn."[5]

Isn't that true? You can be told to do something or watch it, but you're more likely to remember, know, and understand it by doing it yourself. The research backs this up. We remember 80 to 90 percent of what we see and touch, and only 10 to 15 percent of what we hear.[6] So your kids don't learn responsibility by hearing what they must do. They need to be involved, engaged, and enabled. They need you to step back, so they can step in to do on their own.

Provide Structure, Rituals, and Routine

What really helps kids learn responsibility is some structure. Just as a house, with its four walls and a roof, give you a sense of security in the world, so do rules, rituals, and routine give your kids the assurances they need to get through any given day. Order is the framework from which you come and go, what you can count on and expect in a world that otherwise can be chaotic and confused.

By order, I'm not talking about military school regimen. Rather, what routines help your kids be responsible? What rules? What rituals and courses of action does your family follow?

When Debbie and Arnold asked for help teaching their six-year-old, Kurt, to get ready for school in a timely way, it was easy to see they needed a morning routine. They didn't have one and were harried and frazzled every morning, tossing to one another the responsibilities and morning's tasks, depending on who got up first, and it was never their son. Sometimes Debbie was the one to get breakfast and make lunches; other times, Arnold. Yet other mornings, everyone forged for themselves. They were stressed and things got missed. More than one of them missed breakfast or forgot a lunch, and they were all late getting into the day. Kurt wouldn't get up when called, and when he finally did, he dawdled rather than get dressed straight away. Debbie nagged. Arnold yelled.

No wonder. Leaving the everyday needs to fate just wasn't working. How could any of them be sure things got done and who was to do what? They each needed a plan, and when they got one, peace became a bonus.

Arnold, Debbie, and Kurt talked and decided together on a morning schedule. Kurt, truly a night owl, asked if he could set his alarm for 7:30 a.m. but not get up until the final bell at 8. Debbie and Arnold said okay. Respecting and involving Kurt in the plan helped him own what he needed to do—and those thirty minutes to fully wake up made the rest of the day better for him and everyone. Debbie took on making breakfast, and Arnold making their sack lunches. Everyone agreed on the order for their different turns in the bathroom to shower and brush teeth. Arnold made a chart of their morning schedule so they could keep it straight that first week. He promised Kurt a star sticker for each task completed on the chart every morning, and Kurt loved this. Within two weeks they didn't even need the chart anymore. They just went through what was now routine.

"I like the mornings better," Kurt said. "I'm not so crabby and neither is Mom!"

What rules, routines, and rituals would help the crazy places in your family, where you wish your kids would be more responsible? Would your kids' rooms be a neater if you had a rule that beds must be made and toys put away before leaving them each morning? Would the housework get done every week if you had a ritual of cleaning the bathrooms and changing linens every Saturday? Would the evening go smoother if you had dinner at 6:30 p.m. every night? Would the week go better by starting with church every Sunday morning and family lunch that everyone pitches in to fix (someone sets the table, someone else cleans up)?

Foster Independence and Self-Starting

Giving your kids jobs, letting them each own a job, and expecting them to do it is the best way to get them starting and doing things on their own.

I saw this in the classroom when a teacher assigned Ronnie to feed the class fish all week. Ronnie loved being the fish feeder, and went to the task with all his heart. He felt important, and took on even more responsibility, reading about fish, thinking of ways to care for it better. He became not only the fish feeder but the fish keeper, bringing in plants to keep the tank's water purified and a little ceramic ship for the fish to swim around playfully.

When given a responsibility, most children blossom like Ronnie into not only owning their task but thinking of how to do it even better and be the best.

Value Their Contributions

Sometimes it's easy to do something yourself, thinking, *Well, I can do this more thoroughly and faster.* With that thinking, you're right. You can. You probably always will too because you're not giving your kids the chance to get better and faster themselves. This is why it's important to value what your children take on as a responsibility. Let them know what difference they make when they own up to a job or a value. Talk with them about the consequences of action and inaction. What happens when they don't own up to the truth, or fail to finish a chore?

Show them how their choices are a kind of personal power. There are consequences for what they do or don't do, for every choice they make. The Bible teaches that to whom much is given, much is expected (Luke 12:48). Talk with your kids about how this means responsibilities are not burdens but opportunities. Getting ready in the morning or being at the dinner table on time makes the day go smoother. Doing their chores helps the household run more smoothly. Telling the truth and owning up to mistakes allows for forgiveness and things to be mended.

They'll be more motivated to uphold a responsibility when they know their contribution matters, makes a difference, and is important.

Set Standards and Goals

If you expect your kids to do a bad job or not do the job at all, that's probably what will happen. Psychiatrist and sociologist Michael Rutter found in groundbreaking research that what you expect of a child is what you will get.[7] Children will become what you think of them.

The best standard and goal is something both psychologists, like Rutter and his colleagues, and God agree upon—do your very best. I especially love the way this is said throughout the Bible: "Whatever your hand finds to do, do it with all your might" (Ecclesiastes 9:10), "Whatever you do, work at it with all your heart, as working for the Lord" (Colossians 3:23), and "... whatever you do, do it all for the glory of God" (1 Corinthians 10:31).

Asking your children to do their best is the perfect standard because it's both what they're fully capable of and a little more, giving them something to reach toward. "My best" is a personal challenge too because that standard usually increases as your child grows in ability, experience, skill, perseverance, and drive.

Even with a standard of "Do your best," you'll want to show your children what good, better, and best look like—what to expect, what's acceptable and what's not. To do that, break things down into steps, demonstrate things, and offer guided practice. For instance, if you want your toddler to get dressed on her own, don't just leave her to sort through a pile of clothes or open the closet doors and walk away. Show her how things go together and help her by giving her some order, like "It's easier to put on pants before shoes and socks"). Help her make sure her shirt isn't pulled over her head inside out. She won't get all this right away, but by five years old you can expect her to fasten a coat's buttons, zip up her pants, and tie those shoes on her own because standards and goals can be raised as she's more able.

A caveat: Girls tend to develop fine-motor skills faster than boys, so your son may struggle a bit more with tying shoe laces and fastening buttons into his sixth year. A good rule of thumb is to suit the task to the child, whatever the age or stage.

Stay Out of Squabbles

When my sons were in intermediate school and we lived in the Midwest, one of their chores was to share mowing the lawn. Our yard was flat with few trees so it was relatively easy for the boys to determine how much mowing they each needed to do to finish the job.

Then we moved to Weston, Massachusetts, where our yard sloped and was full of trees and rocks. The boys found it more difficult to determine how to divide the task equally. It seemed impossible to measure off exact halves, not that I was going to get talked into doing so. I could have played referee, but I wanted them to exercise responsibility and work it out themselves because stepping in to referee daily squabbles between siblings is a losing game that erodes responsibility. If you're refereeing, they're depending on you.

Part of the goal of teaching responsibility is getting your kids to keep stretching and growing in competency; and problem-solving, you'll remember, is one of the measures.

When you let them, your kids will figure out how to fulfill their responsibilities. It didn't take long for the boys to figure out a great solution of taking turns week to week, Michael one week and Tom the next. The great thing is when children figure out their own solutions, they're more likely to own them too, and that's what you want.

Ban Blaming and Excuses

What do you do when your kids make excuses or blame others for the things they haven't owned up to themselves?

- **Connect the dots between what they do, or fail to do, and the outcomes.** You forget to take out the dog before bedtime? You might wake up with a mess beside your bed. You forget your favorite jacket at the gym? You'll have to wear something else and it might be gone forever if someone takes it home for themselves.

- **Help them shift toward ownership.** Things are often so black and white for a child: good or bad, win or lose, deserving of fault or praise. When kids point a finger to blame ("But she kicked me first" or "He made me stop watching the clock"), ask them, "But what are you responsible for?" This removes the look at anyone or anything else and gets them to start thinking on what they can do regardless. You'll need to be repetitious and consistent in helping children make the shift, but eventually they will.

- **Forget *why* and focus on *how*.** So often when children blame someone or make excuses, it's because they want to move your focus away from them and what they did or didn't do. Keep asking them, "What could you have done?" Look ahead and ask what they will do next time. Point them toward fulfilling responsibility and get them thinking and mapping out ways they'll accomplish what they're able to do.

LETTING THE COMPETENCE CAT OUT OF THE BAG

So let's say you've already introduced to your kids some of these ideas about responsibility. But you're still butting heads with them over things like finishing their homework and helping round the house. If responsibility really were like that cat you welcomed inside to stay, why aren't you seeing it show up more of the time?

There will always be thresholds where you expect your kids to own up to more, but find yourself hollering and they don't seem to be hearing. Don't worry. Every parent crosses these thresholds. The trick is looking at these places as opportunities to really let the cat of competence, of responsibility out of the bag. Take a closer look at how to do that and see your kids fully own up.

Cleaning Up after Themselves

How many times have you asked for them to clean up even this week? From the bedroom to the bathroom, your kids can be responsible to pick up after themselves and others too. Imagine toys tucked away when your kids are finished playing with them, dirty dishes put in the sink or dishwasher, clean clothes returned to closets and dresser drawers instead of stacked on chairs. What if the backpacks, coats, and shoes could be in the same place when not in use, instead of dropped wherever they're taken off any given moment?

It can happen. Get your kids in the habit of picking up after themselves:

- **Make it a rule.** "You put things you've used back in their place, or I do"—and when you do, take the things left out put them out of access for your kids for a designated period of time. For younger children, a day or two without the item in question will do the trick. However, if this remains an issue, increase the time the item is out of commission. Once you start removing things, it doesn't take long for your kids to start missing them and tending to them.

- **Show them it's the grown-up thing to do.** One mom applauded her toddler for picking up a crumbled paper napkin fallen to the floor. "You're doing what a big girl does!" Mom said, showing her daughter how to pop open the lid of the trash bin by pushing a lever. The toddler quickly got the picture and decided being a big girl was so much fun that she began picking up the pieces of cheese she'd thrown on the floor. Most kids love being taken seriously and given the autonomy of a grown-up, and appealing to their increasing maturity works.

- **Let them own it.** One dad got so fed up with his kids never picking up after themselves that he decided to stop picking up after them too. The soiled soccer uniform didn't get put in the dirty clothes hamper, the dirty dishes didn't get washed. His kids wore dirty clothes for a few days and he told them they couldn't eat dinner till the dishes were cleaned. After each incident, his kids made picking up their messes a priority. "Nothing helps them understand the consequences better than living with them," Dad said.

Helping Around the House

More than anything else your children want your attention. By keeping them by your side as you go about many household responsibilities, they'll learn certain competencies. They'll see how you organize a morning, get the house in order, meals made and fed, yourself and everyone groomed. They'll also be there for helping take on certain tasks: bringing in the newspaper, watering plants, feeding pets. They'll see you making sure the car is clean and when it needs fueling, how to maintain things.

Cooking and making meals is especially great for teaching responsibility. Kids learn how to plan, prepare, pull things together, measure and stretch and substitute ingredients, get things made and cooked and served within a certain time. You'll be amazed at how eager many kids are to make meals themselves and take on this task, using not only all their competencies but their creativity too. One dad I know made Saturday morning pancakes for his kids. They helped him so much that soon they were making the pancakes to serve to him breakfast in bed, and were responsible to clean up after themselves too. Isn't that the kind of responsibility of a parent's dreams!

Going with you on the regular task of grocery shopping is a great opportunity for teaching responsibility. Supermarkets are magical, mystifying places for young children especially—all the different sorts of foods presented in so many rows, the many categories of fruits and vegetables and meats, so many kinds of labels on cans and boxes, and all sorts of people shopping who don't look like Mommy and Daddy. Getting in and through all this and out with what you came for, within the time and budget you've allowed, is definitely a lesson in stewardship and responsibility that your kids will learn from every trip you make to the grocery together.

One mother I know made going to the grocery a lesson on all these things and more. She gave her four- and five-year-old jobs of helping find the exact thing she needed from the shelf. One child was responsible for helping find the right produce, the other the right canned goods. Each were responsible to see that the things on their lists were checked off when in the cart. To ensure this task wouldn't turn into a free-for-all where her kids grabbed things for the cart that she didn't want to end up with at the check-out, Mom printed a list of her needed staples. She had her kids match labels and pictures that they cut and pasted from the grocery ads onto the shopping list for better identification once at the store. Each child was responsible for certain items. They loved owning up to this and shopping became a quest for them. The experience was a learning game on multiple other levels too: finding the best buys, learning to assess cost for volume and quality, sticking to the list and getting just what was needed for their meals and not straying to add what looks good while shopping, managing money—not to mention many interesting discussions such as whether a carrot was a fruit or vegetable, where eggs come from, and what foods are a healthy snack. (It's amazing how many children don't know these things because their parents haven't involved them in responsibilities like grocery shopping. I remember a colleague, Dr. Bob, a speech and language therapist, asking a group of first and second graders, "Where do potatoes come from?" and they all quickly answered, "Bags.")

Doing Chores

Owning up to responsibility really does begin at home. So many children who fail to own up to things in school aren't being asked to at home either, and their parents fail to make the connection. I discovered this early on in my education career, when meeting with parents about a child's lack of motivation or inability to work independently. I'd always ask the parents what household chores their child did independently at home.

The answer through the years and across the country was always the same—very few.

The most common response was taking out the trash, something that requires very little skill or investment. One mother of a third grade boy said, "Oh, this year he's getting dressed by himself without prompting."

Sadly, doing something a four-year-old can be relied upon to do without prompting is hardly a chore.

In the span of one generation, the important principle of children taking on responsibilities with regular chores at home has begun to vanish. A forty-year Harvard study shows this is a real problem in America.[8] Started as an effort to understand juvenile delinquency, the study followed the lives of 456 teenage boys from inner-city Boston, many from impoverished and broken homes, through their lives. What happened to them as youths and what were the effects decades later?

"Boys who worked in the home or community gain[ed] competence and came to feel they were worthwhile members of society," discovered Dr. George E. Vaillant, who headed the research. "Because they felt good about themselves, others felt good about them too."[9] But the boys who didn't have any responsibilities at home or the community not only felt poorly about themselves, but fell into trouble or caused it.

Also, when compared at middle age, one factor stood out—regardless of intelligence, family income, ethical background, or amount of education, those who had responsibilities and worked as boys, even at simple household chores, enjoyed happier and more productive lives than those who had not.

Vaillant concluded that children assigned chores and responsibilities are helped in a variety of ways that created happiness and productivity later in life. Just a few of the benefits of chores:

- **Instill self-respect** by nurturing competence.

- **Strengthen family ties** because active participation creates belonging, unity, and acceptance.

- **Develop domestic skills** like cooking, cleaning, and doing laundry that help kids as they grow, function, create order, and maintain health and hygiene.

- **Create a strong work ethic**, essential for success and making contributions to society.

- **Foster self-discipline** by teaching planning and perseverance.

- **Nurture compassion and service** by practicing care for others.

As you think about what chores are needed in your home and best for your kids, ask yourself, *If my children aren't doing chores, what are they doing?* You want them to have time to play and pursue their interests, so how are those things balanced with being part of your home and community? How are they contributing to the functions, well-being, and joy of your family's everyday life? How can you keep chores purposeful and not used or perceived as punishment? Should you pay your children an allowance for doing chores?

To Pay an Allowance or Not

This is a big question that splits the psychology and counseling experts, educators, and parents alike. Some folks argue that paying children an allowance is the best way to teach them financial responsibility—children learn money is not free but earned by work. Others say chores around the house are the duty of everyone in the family, and children shouldn't expect a reward for simply doing their part.

I've found, both personally and professionally, that linking an allowance to chores is effective with these parameters:

* **Clearly spell out the daily and weekly chores assigned.** Who does what when? Does everyone understand the desired result, timing, and method of the chore?

* **The allowance distributed is to be like a salary** for work completed, meaning there may be deductions for work neglected. ("You didn't make your bed one morning so you've earned twenty-five cents less.")

* **More work and responsibility may earn a child more allowance**, especially as he or she is able to take on things you may have once paid others to do—washing the car or yard work, for example.

* **To teach money management with allowances, specify a savings plan.** For example, you can instruct your children that for every three dollars earned, one dollar must go into savings, another dollar to church or a favorite charity, and the remaining dollar is free to spend.

Finishing Homework

This is a common area where both parents and kids wrestle with blurred boundaries and power struggles. If you're over-involved in homework and overbearing, your children never establish their own sense of competency. Yet if they truly don't understand an assignment, they may need additional instruction or help in the way of a partner to read, rehearse, or practice with as they work to improve.

Whatever the case, refuse to let doing homework become a battlefield. Emotional stress hinders thought processes and doesn't help anything. Use these tips to keep the peace and make progress:

* **Designate a regular time and place.** The best time is the one that works. If your kids get home right after school, establish the routine of a half-hour break to unwind and

enjoy a snack, then tackle homework. If your kids have after-school activities, set up a different routine when dinner is the unwind time and homework follows. Either way, a weekly chart can help everyone stay on the same page of what's to happen when. Determining where homework happens is important too. Designate a quiet place conducive to working such as a desk or the kitchen table. In front of the TV in the family room isn't a good idea. In fact, make it a rule for no distractions like video games, toys, television, and cell phones till homework is completed. The goal is to keep a quiet oasis where your kids can concentrate and think.

A STEP TOWARD LIVING RESPONSIBLY
Chores without Wars

Most parents hate having to nag their kids. Twenty-five percent of parents admitted in a poll by Parents.com that they feel like it's a never-ending fight to get their kids to clean up their rooms, pick up their clothes, and return dirty dishes to the sink or dishwasher. What if getting your kids to act responsible wasn't a battle of your will versus theirs? It doesn't have to be with these steps toward chores without wars:

- **Call a Family Board Meeting.** Kids love it when they feel you're giving them respect, and their ideas and opinions count. A family meeting allows you to respect one another and to pray for God's help to go about your tasks as he's instructed in Colossians 3:12: "As God's chosen people, holy and dearly loved, clothe yourselves with compassion, kindness humility, gentleness and patience."

- **Stay on the same page.** You may not think it's a big deal for your kids to make their beds every morning, but if your spouse does, go along with him. Stay unified. Agree what course to take with whoever is caring for your kids so that there's no question. Children are quick to sense any disagreements and will seize an opportunity to play you and your spouse against one another or to make their own decision about a family rule in lieu of yours.

- **Create feelings of belonging and connectedness.** Look for opportunities to tell your children the impact of what they do or fail to do. For instance, if they don't take out the trash, the house will get smelly and might even attract ants or vermin, putting everyone's health at risk and costing you time, trouble, and possible damage. Your kids will be more inspired to do their part when they understand what difference it makes.

- **Show them how to strategize.** Some students like to attack the most difficult assignments first. Others are more encouraged by knocking out the easier parts. Help kids who struggle to maintain focus by having them estimate the time needed on an assignment. Set a kitchen timer, then see if they can beat the clock—the challenge they set for themselves can be riveting and motivating. These kinds of strategizing skills will help them in every area through life.

- **Help them know their limits.** Although attention span varies with age, kindergarteners usually can focus for fifteen to thirty minutes at a time, and older children for forty-five

---

- **Involve them in divvying up the chores.** Don't just direct and order. When appropriate, listen and give your kids a say in the decisions, offer choices. Least desirable tasks can be rotated.

- **Invite them into setting the consequences up front.** Do this together. Talk with your kids about reasonable consequences (you might have to nudge them toward what's reasonable). For example, if you have a family rule for everyone to clean up their rooms Saturday morning, then a consequence might be no playing or time for other activities until the room is clean. When kids help establish the consequences, they're more likely to buy into and abide by them.

- **Establish the standard, then give training and support.** The directive to clean your room can mean different things to different people. Be specific in spelling out what's required and maybe modeling it and working alongside your child the first time or two (this is called guided practice). For example, tell your kids, "Cleaning the room means your toys and clothes go in their proper place, you dust furniture, and you vacuum the carpet."

- **Use a Chore Chart.** List tasks according to frequency of needing to be done. For example, Every Day: make your bed, clean up your own mess, place dirty clothes in hamper, keep book bag and shoes in designated places, place dirty dishes in dishwasher, feed pets. Weekly: clean up room, cut lawn, water plants. Parents and Kids Together: cooking, washing cars, gardening, household repairs.

- **Make it fun!** Snow White and the seven dwarves didn't whistle while they worked, sing, and dance while doing chores for nothing. Finding play in work can not only help get it done but make your life more of a joy.

minutes to an hour and longer periods that increase with age. Since the ability to concentrate is essential through life, teach your kids to focus by establishing a goal, shutting out everything else, and staying in the flow of doing a task. Let them know it's okay to take a quick break between assignments, and to stand up, stretch, or walk around the table for five minutes, to relieve the mental strain. Some kids work better if the surface of the desk is clean with no visual distractions, while others concentrate better if soft classical music plays in the background. A child who is extremely sensitive to sound will need a quiet, isolated area of the house. One father who was a sensitive student himself recalled climbing to the most remote floor of the library to study in silence. So when his son struggled with sensory overload, Dad came up with an idea to help. He removed the sliding doors of a closet, emptied the contents, and carpeted both the floor and walls to create a nearly soundproof study cocoon for his son—and it did indeed help.

■ **Be ready to raise a hand** to let teachers know when your child regularly spends long hours on assignments that clearly ought to take less time, or if your child has trouble concentrating, has learning disabilities, is dealing with troubling personal issues like divorce or a death, or has come away from the classroom not understanding assignments or lessons. There are reasons kids struggle at times, and there are solutions. If a child persistently resists doing homework, but does well in school and on tests, the homework assignment may not be suitable to your child. Children who love to tinker with how things work, experiment with science, and to learn on their own usually do better through exploration rather than pushing a pencil. Some teachers will modify an assignment for particular circumstances, for instance asking a child to complete every third problem instead of all and substituting a project to present instead. Other times you and your child's teacher may find that lessons are too high- or low-level. This happened with Samir, a fifth grader new to our school from India. Samir scored high marks on the homework in a high-level math class, when he completed it. But more assignments failed to be done, a mystery for someone so capable. "Why?" I asked. "I have come to school to learn," Samir said in frustration, throwing his math text to the floor. "But the work is too easy." Testing showed Samir needed to be in an even more accelerated math class. As the assignments became more challenging, he consistently tackled and completed them. Years later, I read in *Time* magazine how Samir awesomely stood out from the crowd with his math prowess at Stanford University. Imagine if he had been allowed to slide and fall under the radar in grade school because of that unfinished homework. In contrast, there are times your kids need more of a coach and cheerleader, not more challenge. One caring, concerned father noticed his son Mark's frustration with math homework and showed him some more efficient ways to do long division. Meanwhile his wife told her husband to stay out of it, "That's the teacher's job." The dad

A STEP TOWARD LIVING RESPONSIBLY
A Checklist for Creating Competence

DO	DON'T
Encourage independence	Do everything for your child
Expect age-appropriate behavior	Exert too much pressure
Instill good work habits	Throw out structure, routine, and ritual
Build confidence	Expect too much or too little
Require chores	Abdicate help around the house
Teach every choice has a consequence	Direct, demand, and control

SOURCE: *Parenting for Character: Five Experts, Five Practices* edited by David Streight (Council for Spiritual and Ethical Education, 2008), 8-9.

mentioned this to his boss, who agreed with Mom. "Struggle teaches kids about real life," the boss said. "Besides, parents don't have time to teach schoolwork too." Mark's mom and Dad's boss were wrong on this one. Leaving a child in the dark on lessons isn't the same thing as turning on all the lights for them. Sometimes kids do need help on homework; and giving them a flashlight, then letting them use it is best.

- **Check in.** You'll know when your kids really need your help when you check in regularly. Of course, how closely you monitor homework depends on your child's age, level of independence, and how well things are going in school. But always ask at the beginning of a school year what the teacher expects, what kind of assignments will be given, and how much time for homework is age appropriate. Ask your kids what they like and don't about assignments, which ones are hardest and take the most time. This will help you know where you can step back more or where your kids may need different tools, approaches, or even some guided help to begin doing more on their own.

RESPONSIBILITY HELPS YOUR CHILD GROW UP

How can you doing less get your children to do more? The question can rattle you. I can only imagine what you've thought, *If I don't pick up after the kids, our house will soon look like a landfill. If I don't cook and clean, everyone's going to go hungry and dirty.* But try giving your kids more responsibility, and I guarantee you'll be amazed. You won't be rattled. You'll all be raised to a higher level of expectation and accomplishment from one another.

Remember bubbly Susan who flitted around my office, couldn't focus, and only wanted to play? Her mom couldn't imagine that doing less for Susan would get her daughter to do more. But we talked about all these things in this chapter and Mom said she'd try practicing them for a few weeks. She was doubtful, she admitted, but hopeful too.

A few weeks later, Susan flitted by my office on the way to class, her usual bubbly, unfocused self. She gave me a hug and ran on her way, and I turned to find her mom. I wondered if anything had changed.

"A lot," Mom said, as if reading my mind. "A lot's different in our house."

She told me how she left our meeting weeks ago ready to try and hand over some responsibility to Susan. When she started dinner that evening, she asked Susan to set the table.

"Ohhh," Susan said. "I'll do it, Mommy."

Mom went about cooking and within a few minutes realized things were ever quiet. She went to check on Susan, who, ever true, had turned a task into a game.

"Look, Mommy, I'm making it pretty."

Susan had pulled some flowers from an arrangement and put one at the top of every plate. The silverware was in the wrong places, but everyone did have a set.

Okay, Mom thought. *It's a start.* "How would you like to make the table pretty every meal?" she asked her daughter as she showed her how to fold napkins and the proper place for the spoon, the knife, the fork.

"Oh, Mommy! Can I?" Can they? That is just what your job is to see as a parent. You can turn more and more over to your child to help themselves

---

MY PURPOSEFUL PARENTING CHECK-IN
How Am I Doing with Responsibility?

I'm seeing my children grow in responsibility; and I'm being my best to bring out their best, by:

- Keeping the eleventh commandment for parents to never do for my kids what they can do for themselves.
- Helping them develop competency by using reason, problem-solving, understanding choices, making decisions, and controlling feelings.
- Refusing to be a helicopter parent who hovers instead of truly helping by hanging back.
- Providing structure, ritual, rules, and routine that turn chaos to order.
- Setting goals and standards so they can live up to the very best of expectations—and even beyond.

and begin helping others. But you have to start. A child's first start at something is usually not flawless. It's awkward. There will be falls, missteps, mistakes. But by letting them start, you're out of the way, you're not stopping your child from owning up; and in practicing responsibility, they are raising up the spirits and situations of others. You're raising a competent, contributing person for this world. You're raising someone no longer interested in just being entertained but entertaining others.

Chapter 6

PERSEVERANCE: NEVER GIVE IN

…because keeping on keeps you strong

When I first met Mickey, a third grader, he'd missed several days of school. His mom would call in and report, "He's sick today."

As the year progressed, Mickey was sick more and more days, but never for any consistent health reason.

I didn't need a doctor's note to give me a clue as to why.

The days Mickey fell sick usually were times when a lot of reading assignments, exercises, or tests were expected in school. Mickey's reading ability was low. He struggled with learning challenges in both language and memory, affecting reading progress and all his other studies. He couldn't keep up in class, and couldn't bear not keeping up either. He wanted to read but was getting further behind, despite extra help in a special education group. He felt more and more terrible, and was getting sick a lot. Sick at heart.

Then, in the second semester, everything changed.

Mickey's reading comprehension surged from a second to fourth grade level. He began doing better in all his other subjects. He went from missing one or more days a week to not missing a single day of class or extra time in the special education group.

I called his parents to congratulate them on Mickey's turn around, celebrate the achievement, and, I admit, discover the secret of such success.

I don't know what exactly I expected after talking to Michael Sr. on the phone, but it wasn't the dad who showed up at my office and took a seat. Michael Sr. wasn't a picture of anyone driven toward achievement, not the stereotypical image anyway. He seemed unexpectant about the meeting and actually as if he might just have crawled out of bed minutes before arrival. He wore a baseball hat, the visor turned sideways, over long unkempt hair. A pack of cigarettes was rolled up in the sleeve of his T-shirt. He was cheerful, but unquestioning and unconcerned about the time.

I welcomed him and congratulated him on Mickey's amazing progress, particularly in reading. "He's caught up to his grade level in achievement," I told him.

Michael Sr. beamed and slapped his knee. "That a way, Mickey!"

I couldn't help but ask, "What are you doing at home to get these wonderful results?"

"Well, we read together a lot," Michael Sr. said.

"Together?" I nudged for more about such a transformation.

Michael Sr. said he too struggled to read in elementary school. He loved stories though, so he kept trying. One day, after years of trying, he realized he'd read nearly half a book in one sitting. Reading became a joy, not a struggle. Having become a reader himself, it pained the father to see his son struggle so to read because of language and memory challenges. Michael Sr. hoped Mickey wouldn't give up reading.

Then one evening Mickey brought home a social studies assignment for a more capable group of readers.

"Dad," Mickey asked. "Could you help me read this?"

Michael Sr.'s heart welled, and then it broke. He looked at the assignment and knew his son wouldn't understand it. Mickey needed to read the preceding four chapters for the assignment to make sense. Then he needed to get through the challenging assignment itself. "That meant he needed to read eight chapters total," Michael Sr. recalled. He shook his head. "How was he going to do that when making it through one was hard enough?"

Father sat down with son and said, "All right. I'll read along with you on these first four chapters together to understand the assignment."

As expected, Mickey started then stopped after a page. He wanted to read on but was quickly discouraged by words he had yet to learn and complex sentences he labored to get through. He didn't think he could do it.

Michael Sr. said, "How about we partner on it?"

Mickey nodded and his dad started reading one section, then nudged Mickey to tackle the next. They struggled through that first chapter, then another, then the third. Along the way, they discussed each chapter as they went and then went back over any passages that weren't clear to Mickey the first time.

"It wasn't easy," Michael Sr. said. He admitted he would have understood if Mickey wanted to give up after the first couple chapters because, he said, "We weren't even to the real assignment yet. This was just the background. There was so much more to go."

But something about his dad's encouragement, belief, and help spurred Mickey onward. Like the little train engine in the story *The Little Engine that Could*,[1] Mickey tackled the assignment chapter by chapter over the course of a semester, from January to June.

Michael Sr. couldn't stop smiling as he described how his son would bring him the textbook so they could read together. "By the fourth chapter, he wasn't coming to me. He was still struggling a bit and would come to me for help pronouncing difficult words or because he didn't understand something. But more and more he was reading by himself. I remember the day I went looking for Mickey and there he was on the couch, nose in the textbook, reading a section on his own."

THE THREE KEYS TO THE FUEL OF PERSEVERANCE

Don't you wish this picture of Mickey and his father was of you and your children with whatever goals they face? Maybe, though, you're struggling with your kids just to get them to finish each regular school assignment, let alone anything advanced or ambitious. Maybe your children do just enough to get by in school or when it comes to chores at home, but never really give their best, or all. Maybe they stop or get stuck whenever challenged or the going gets tough. Maybe you get, "Just a minute" or "Later" as your children's standard response to doing anything—never "Here I go" or "I'm going to do it" or "I'm not giving up yet."

Maybe your son's begged for months to start band class, and now, after going through the process to find the right instrument and rehearse, wants to give up. Or maybe your daughter hounded you to join the soccer team; but now that she's got the uniform, turned out for practice, and played a couple games, she wants to quit.

How do you keep your kids learning, adventuring, advancing, and keeping on to achieve whatever the goal? How do you raise a persistent, persevering soul who won't give in and won't give up? How did Michael Sr., who seemed so far from being driven himself, find the keys to keep reading when he struggled so as a child, and then go on to help his son accomplish so much in reading too?

Daniel H. Pink, the best-selling author of *Drive: The Surprising Truth about What Motivates Us*, used four decades of research in behavioral science to identify those things that Michael Sr. intuitively tapped into as the ingredients of persistence. Pink says perseverance is made up of three main things: autonomy, mastery, and purpose.[2] You have to have each ingredient in that fuel for the drive to carry on.

Autonomy for Willpower

You might think autonomy is an independent spirit, but it's so much more. Autonomy is what propelled Michael Sr. through his own struggles to read, and what drove Mickey to choose a tough assignment. It's that matter of choice and act of determination that creates the power to persist—willpower. It's your child deciding to pursue something rather than being told. Researchers Richard Ryan and Edward Deci say that choosing on one's own is what leads to engagement and develops the endurance needed to persevere.[3]

Pink echoes that idea, pointing to great artists of the past hundred years who persisted through adversity to create masterpieces—Pablo Picasso, Georgia O'Keefe, and Jackson Pollock. "Nobody told them: You must paint this sort of picture. You must begin painting precisely at eight-thirty a.m. You must paint with the people we select to work with you. And you must paint this way. The very idea is ludicrous…. Whether you're fixing sinks, ringing up groceries, selling cars, or writing a lesson, you and I need autonomy just as deeply as a great painter."[4]

A picture of how autonomy fuels persistence (or not) that might hit closer to home comes straight from the pages of Mark Twain's beloved book *The Adventures of Tom Sawyer*. Remember when Tom is assigned the daunting task of whitewashing the 810 square feet of Aunt Polly's fence? He does the job, but begrudgingly…only he has too much pride to let his friend Ben know. Ben found Tom at the task on a perfectly sunny day better suited for fishing, swimming, or playing. So Ben taunts Tom. But Tom, too proud to be mocked and too frustrated to be doing work when he really would rather be playing too, convinces Ben the whitewashing is no chore at all. In fact he's privileged to do it. He's so convincing he not only gets Ben and other boys who come along to do his work, but he talks Ben out of his apple for the privilege. Then Tom quits, watches his friends do his work, and munches Ben's apple! So much for the power of an assignment driving Tom toward a goal.

Assignments don't work in fueling perseverance anymore in literature or theory as in our everyday lives. If Michael Sr. had never chosen on his own to keep reading, our conversation about Mickey would have been much different. Dad might never have valued reading. He might have given up on it long ago and accepted that same kind of choice from Mickey, and Mickey might have made that choice to quit if he'd been commanded to read more challenging assignments.

Commands and control can diminish and burn away one's persistence like an acid.

The great news is creating and encouraging autonomy is a natural thing to do, like awakening your child's inner strivings and self-directedness. You don't have to instill autonomy. You don't order your kids to be autonomous. You call it out. You give your kids enough time and space within boundaries and structure, and their autonomy emerges. This is like taking a walk with two-year-olds. You don't have to command them to check out the path ahead. Children's natural curiosity and self-direction will draw them ahead to explore, investigate, examine, sniff, smell, taste, listen, and see. They'll want to touch the flowers, examine a ladybug, pick up rocks, *and keep on going*. In the same way, give your child some choices about a challenge, meaningful feedback or instruction, and some berth over what to do and how to do it, and they'll carry on.

Behavioral scientists add that autonomy not only fuels your kids' persistence, but helps them develop conceptual understanding, get better

A STEP TOWARD STRONGER PERSEVERANCE
Avoid the Three Sins in Giving Up

1. **Thou shall not interrupt flow.** That sense of purpose and being in the groove or flow of what you're pursuing not only ignites greater creativity but fuels staying power. When you feel you're doing something you were made to do and for a great reason, you're unstoppable. When you feel your contribution doesn't matter, you give up. Support your kids when they're in that groove and flow. If they spend Saturday morning shooting hoops, hang on the sidelines to cheer them on. Remind your kids they are made for God's glory and every bit of personal progress makes him, and them, shine.

2. **Thou shall not solve.** Instead, stir. Don't try to fix your kids' problems or do their work for them. That only allows them to run on your engine, not their own. They'll begin to depend on you and always call for help or call it quits. Jeff, a fifth grader, was in this mode. On an English assignment about the most influential person in his life, he wrote, "My mom is always there when I need her. She can always persuade me to end up liking what I have to do." At first blush that might sound noble. It's not. Mom constantly fluttered to Jeff's side to take care of things he was able, with time and space, to do himself. Of course there will be times your kids are really stuck. What you can do is suggest how they might break a problem into chunks. Then let them do it. This stirs their creativity and persistence to keep trying.

3. **Thou shall not plant perfectionism.** Nothing squelches drive more than the need to be perfect. Exacting, demanding children become compulsive. They torture themselves over every correction and red mark on their papers. If

grades, be more productive in their schoolwork and at home, experience less chance of burn-out and more psychological well-being.[5] What parent wouldn't want those outcomes?

Mastery for Spirit

When Michael Sr. told me how Mickey soon read on his own, I wasn't too surprised. Every time a child learns a new skill, they grow in competence, and competence is cumulative. The more children realize they can try a new task and master it, the more confident they become and the more tenacious and able to solve new problems.

I saw this repeatedly in school, from the earliest age. When kindergarteners played freely, there was always a group hovered over the building blocks. Sometimes these kids worked together and other times on their own to make more and more elaborate structures: castles, freeways, towers.

they're not first, best, or immediately successful, they give up. A bright kindergartener who refused to read baffled me because he'd read traffic signs, cereal boxes, and familiar books since three years of age. Then I met his perfectionist parents, proud of their son's reading efforts and telling him so ad nauseum. When the boy started school and met other kids reading, he stopped. His need to be best overcame him. Fear of failure became a stronger force than love for learning. He needed reminding that reading isn't a race, rather it's fun and opens worlds. He needed parents to check themselves on the perfectionism they modeled and encouraged. Do you struggle with this? If your children's progress doesn't seem fast or far enough, ask, Do I always focus on results? Are my expectations often beyond me and others? Do I believe in all or nothing? Is failure anything less than perfect? If yes, focus on efforts and progress, not results. Rethink expectations by questioning what's reasonable. Recognize ideals are directions, not absolutes. A wise kindergarten teacher tells her students, "You don't want to join The Perfect Club! Its members are unhappy. They stop if they can't do everything best. They don't let themselves learn from mistakes. They quit!" One child asked, "But if it's okay to make mistakes, why is it so important to be right?" Such a great question can start an ongoing discussion about how being right isn't the goal, rather learning, understanding, growing, and progressing. Show your kids examples of how people can ace a test and fail the class, or fail a test and win in life. Look at England's Prime Minister Winston Churchill, United States President Abraham Lincoln, American poet Emily Dickinson, and Dutch artist Vincent van Gogh, who each failed often yet changed history. Let examples of persistence fuel persistence.

In either case, most every child was individually creating, thinking, and problem-solving in new and different ways to fit, stand, turn, and stack the blocks. These kids became so engrossed they totally missed their teacher calling them to gather for story time or some other activity. They were in the flow of what they were learning, that groove that we talked about in the chapter on how to help your kids find their passion and purpose.

That groove or flow, that psychologist Mihaly Csikszentmihalyi said fires up passion, also is part of the fuel of persistence—the mastery part that makes you follow and finish something to its end.[6] It works like this: You're in a sweet spot, engrossed, doing what you *can* do, not necessarily what you *have* to do, so you keep on. You persist and persevere because your spirit is engaged, not just your physical brain or body. You're so absorbed, so much a master of whatever is in the moment that even the sense of time, place, and self melt away.[7]

You've probably already seen this with your kids when they play. They go from one experience of flow to another, whether building with Legos or creating a drama with action figures. They're figuring out things, using creativity, solving the dilemmas (often of their own making), mastering how to move through the activity. They can continue for hours, even missing or ignoring calls to dinner.

So engagement is what you need for mastery, one of the main ingredients in the fuel for persistence. We'll talk more in this chapter about the way to engage your kids enough for them to find mastery, but take note now of how Michael Sr. intuitively did this: he provided enough structure, resources, opportunity, and encouragement to capture Mickey's attention and heart in that ambitious assignment.

Purpose for Direction

That third ingredient in persistence is purpose, the kind that gives a direction. Mickey's purpose to read with the best in his class was sparked by his interest in the topic they were studying, this drove him through all the preliminary material and the assignment. Purpose showed him the way to go.

That's the power of purpose—it helps you act and gives you energy. Daniel Pink explains it this way: When you've got a purpose you're not just

wandering round or trudging after a carrot. You're "active and engaged...,
listening to your own voice, doing something that matters, doing it well,
and doing it in the service of a cause larger than [yourself]." And it keeps
you doing it.[8]

That's why purpose is so important in the mix for what makes you persevere. Purpose gives you the reason, the *why* for keeping on when other
things call you to stop or give up.

SEVEN POWER BOOSTERS

Now that you know how autonomy, mastery, and purpose make up the
fuel for perseverance toward any goal, what do you do? The following seven
power boosters can work to fuel perseverance: motivation; belief, encouragement, freedom to fail, value effort over ability, realistic goals, connect
work to achievement. These are important additives to those three essential
ingredients we just looked at, and they will make the difference in keeping
your kids going.

Motivation

Motivation actually works more like a spark plug. Motivation is
what ignites the engine that perseverance fuels. Babies are born with
motivation—that inherent drive to learn and grow, according to child psychologists Drs. Robert Brooks and Sam Goldstein.[9] But motivation can be
squelched if you're not careful.

In their combined fifty years of clinical practice and studies, Brooks and
Goldstein found that drive develops as motivation when kids inevitably
come to a challenge and their inner "I can" force is stoked. But how to do
that? Two essential ways are to:

- **Provide islands of competence**, places where your children
  experience success. Michael Sr. did this for Mickey by establishing times to sit down together and help him through the
  preliminary reading for the more ambitious assignment. By
  reading the simpler material, Mickey gained the confidence
  and "I can do it" spark. The key for Dad was to help but not
  to do for his son. It would have been a mistake if Michael Sr.

read all the preliminary material to Mickey. That's a temptation for every well-meaning parent. But it's not a help, ever, to do the more challenging things for your children when you want them to learn to do it themselves. Help your kids by connecting with them on the task (even being present and smiling from the sidelines counts), establishing some structure (Michael Sr. did this by setting a place and time), and then giving a wide berth for your kids to try and do on their own.

- **Tap into natural curiosity and interest.** In the earlier chapter on passion, you already learned how important it is to nurture curiosity. That importance is worth repeating here because curiosity can drive your children to stick with something. Left to our own devices, most of us do wonder about things we encounter: *Why does he act that way? What makes this work (or not!)?* You can stoke those musings intentionally, on purpose, when you care more about pouring a sense of marvel, awe, and wonder into your kids than facts, figures, and dos or don'ts. Make your family one that celebrates questions and asking. Every encounter or place is game for this. *What are those little specks that float in a shaft of sunlight—are they there even when the bright light isn't showing them off? What makes a dentist like his job when I don't like him doing it?* Consciously, deliberately pursue an approach of questioning, and you'll find that the more you intentionally look for wonder, the more it will come to you naturally. Leonardo da Vinci did this and his curiosity drove him to keep pursuing achievements all his sixty-seven years of life in nearly every area of genius: art, architecture, science, mathematics, music, literature, physics, kinetics and anatomical studies, and philosophy. One way he practiced *curiosità,* that insatiably curious approach to life and unrelenting quest for continuous learning, was to observe and describe in almost every situation and setting.[10] To observe and describe, da Vinci made it a practice to carry notebooks with him everywhere. But you can practice observing and describing in simpler ways that don't require any work. Look for something of awe every day, over breakfast, on the way somewhere, or at bedtime. Make it a daily exercise, a ritual to marvel, just like brushing your teeth is something you always do after a meal. At appointed times, ask one another to tell about something beautiful that day, or "What's the most curious thing from today?" Points of wonder can be as simple as what caused the patterns in the frost on the window pane, or why the moon changes shape from night to night, what the shape of clouds mean to the weather, or why dogs turn in circles before settling down to sleep. The more curious your kids become about things, the more driven they'll be to continually search for answers, explore, and keep on with a line of thinking, task, or assignment.

Belief and Encouragement

Here is where the Bible and the best practices we know in psychology and counseling give us the same advice—encouragement keeps you going.

When Abraham and Sarah despaired because they were childless, God sent them heavenly visitors who cheered them (Genesis 18) into being parents at an elderly age. When the shepherd-soldier David felt so alone in King Saul's court, God brought him a friend in Jonathan (1 Samuel 14-18), who believed in him even onto his father's throne. When Mary was anxious about being the mother of Jesus, she was encouraged by her cousin Elizabeth to love the great gift from God, which she did, we are shown, to the very end (Luke 1, John 19:25).

Whatever goals different students pursue, the biggest determining factor in their achievement is true encouragement, which a variety of studies over decades tell us.[11] Encouragement and belief not only empower children, but build their resiliency, which is like greasing the engine that keeps them racing toward a goal.

That doesn't mean constantly praising your child or repeating, "I know you can do it." There may be times your kids can't achieve something, and your "You can do it" refrain only makes them feel more a failure or stops them from trying again. They think, *I couldn't do it then, so I'm not going to try now.* The better way to encourage is to:

- **Tell your children you believe in their hard work and desire to achieve.** This focuses on the worth of always trying and keeping on, regardless of achievement.

- **Help your child identify, and then you praise, the things they do well and right.** This helps them know what skills they possess and can rely upon in the face of another challenge.

To gauge how you're doing in this area, check yourself just like you'd check the oil level in an engine. On a given day or week, note how many times you praise what your child's doing right, and how many times you criticize what's done wrong or badly. You might be surprised to find you're not offering any feedback to your kids. More likely, you'll find it's so easy to be critical and you've not given enough positive encouragement to build resilience. It takes deliberation and intention to purposefully point out what your kids are doing well; and research shows it takes five positive comments to balance out every critical or negative comment.[12]

Freedom to Fail

Losing a race, failing a test, or messing up a friendship aren't always bad things for your child. In fact, they can be good because failure and defeat are inevitable in life, and learning early on how to not repeat mistakes, bounce back from them, and overcome teaches persistence. Mounting research shows how early failure can fuel people with the perseverance to achieve great things.[13]

"In life, you're going to lose more often than you win, even if you're good at something," says author Jean Twenge. "You've got to get used to that to keep going."[14]

I've told many a parent this over the years—make room for your kids to fail while in elementary school, where they can learn from mistakes in a protective environment. The stakes aren't as high when you get more chances to succeed on the assignments in school or games in a season. Childhood can be like learning to fly a jumbo jet. You don't hop in the cockpit of a multibillion dollar machine and take off. You start in a simulator where you can crash without hurting anyone or anything. You learn from each mistake. You practice until doing the right things becomes habit. And then you soar. The practice, the doing over, the trying again and again builds a muscle of persistence.

What you can do for your kids in the meantime is to keep looking for and using the teachable moments to:

- **Identify where things went wrong and problem-solve.** This doesn't mean make judgments or say things like "You should have done this." Banish *shoulda, coulda, woulda* talk from this discussion. Instead, identify without blame how this or that might change the outcome. For instance, "Let's look at how knowing multiplication tables helps do this part of the math test faster." Or, "Let's practice kicking the soccer ball toward a target so in the heat of the game it becomes more natural to hit it into the goal." This trail of thinking keeps you working onward for improvement.

- **Reframe failure.** Remind your kids that making a mistake or messing up are just steps toward success. Thomas Edison failed thousands of times before creating the light bulb, though he said, "I have not failed. I've just found 10,000 ways that won't work."[15] Failure allows you to stop and take stock of where you are and what your goal is. It gives you a chance to mark any progress toward a goal, not necessarily the destined goal itself. It enables you to think more deeply.

- **Teach how to negotiate,** which will help your child keep going through challenges in life. Start by showing it does no good to argue over position—you can't always be first, best, or at the top. You can look beyond where you are ("This time didn't work, but next time can!"). You can also call out the benefits of where you are and how to use that position, not bicker for a better one. Next, separate the problem from people: ask children to describe in their own words what's going wrong, with no blame allowed. This teaches them how to think rationally. Third, ask your child to create or invent ways of mutual gain in a conflict. For instance, you don't have to win to be a winner, or you may not get a top grade on this assignment but you can ace the class. Fourth, get your children to think of best alternatives. What is it they really, really want? If they can't win the championship game, can they do their personal best and have a great season? If they don't win the lead in the play, how about being the best supporting actor or part of the stage team? Get them thinking in these ways of how to go onward and forward by asking themselves, *What's most important here? Is there a way to achieve what I most desire in another way?*

Value Effort over Ability

Valuing effort over ability is a biggie. More and more we're finding that success comes by how much you try and work toward something versus your natural ability. The Bible's told us this from the beginning, how people achieve great things because of their heart and willingness to serve, not their human ability. Moses, for example, had a speech impediment and led his people out of slavery. Abraham was old when he fathered a nation. Lazarus was *dead* but rose to reflect Jesus's glory. None of these guys could have done what they did on their own ability. But God made them able to do great things and keep going (especially with Lazarus!).

Knowing that effort makes more a difference than ability will help your kids keep going toward whatever their goal.

A fellow teacher, Jim Stigler (also a Guggenheim Fellow, now associate professor at the University of Chicago, and winner of young scientist awards from the American Psychological Association), discovered this in 1979.[16] Stigler, while still a graduate student at the University of Michigan, went to Japan to research teaching methods. One day he sat at the back of a crowded fourth grade classroom, where youngsters were assigned to draw a three-dimensional cube. The teacher selected one boy to demonstrate on the board in front of the class, and he clearly struggled.

"Is this the correct drawing?" the teacher asked.

"No," classmates said.

"Try another way," the teacher encouraged, and the boy did. After several attempts and more shouts of "no" from classmates, he finally drew a perfectly three-dimensional cube.

The entire class applauded, and the boy basked in the accomplishment.

He also went on to do well in math because he'd learned the value of effort and trying.

That incident alone made Stigler wonder if good grades are the result of being smart and having a strong ability, or if hard work and effort achieves the good grades and develops the ability. Further study confirmed his suspicions. In Asian cultures, effort and perseverance mattered more for success, where American parents valued high levels of ability more.[17] Consistently, when Asian students received a poor grade in math, they began to spend double time and work studying to improve. However, American students doing poorly in math, explained away any bad grades as "I'm just not good at math." The American students were more accepting of a disappointment and didn't try to challenge it.

This attitude is such a danger for American parents and students today, the study concluded. If children decide they don't have enough ability, they tend to stop trying, and when they adopt an attitude of defeat, they do tend to live up to that attitude.[18]

That's why we've got to be even more diligent to remind our kids that effort, trying, and persistence pay off, says Dr. Carol S. Dweck.[19] She insists that praising your kids' abilities doesn't help them as much as praising their efforts. She confirmed this with a team at Columbia University who studied the effect of praise on students in twenty New York schools. Eighty-five percent of parents in the study thought it important to tell their kids they were smart—and their kids still underperformed.

"But emphasizing effort gives the child a variable that they can control," Dweck said. "They come to see themselves as in control of their success, where emphasizing natural intelligence takes it out of the child's control…a no good recipe for…failure."[20]

For purposeful parents, set on helping their kids thrive with perseverance, that means helping your kids avoid a fixed mindset and develop a growth mindset.[21]

The *fixed* mindset believes your ability is what it is, static, based on your intelligence. You're either smart or not, you must prove your ability, and always demonstrate your intelligence and skill. That's a lot of pressure to live up to, and why fixed mindset kids begin to avoid challenges, give up easily, ignore constructive criticism, and feel threatened by the success of others.

The *growth* mindset shows more resilience, believing intelligence can be developed, and that your abilities grow as you do, learning and developing skills, understanding, comprehension, and perception. Children with a growth mindset respond to challenges with enthusiasm, persist in the face of difficulty, see effort as the path to mastery, learn from constructive criticism, and find lessons and inspiration from the success of others.

The key difference is where the fixed mindset fears being judged, the growth mindset focuses on how to improve.

Danny, a third grader I'd known since kindergarten, was a perfect example of a child led to have a fixed mindset. Sent to my office one day for being disruptive during math class, he suddenly burst into tears.

"It is all your fault!" he cried. "You told my mother that I was gifted and she told my grandmother. Now I don't even know how to do long division!"

It was true. Tests identified Danny as gifted in an era when gifted children were enrolled into special programs. Then a proud mama and grandma lauded that status repeatedly until Danny felt increasingly protective of being "gifted," so much that he concentrated more on defending his smarts than stretching them. He'd become afraid of new challenges and was giving up on them, long division in math being one. He needed encouragement again for his efforts not his intelligence, scores, or outcomes. Once he got that encouragement, his defensiveness, fears, and misbehavior went away.

When you develop that growth mindset with your kids, you'll find them more engaged and persistent in their schoolwork, goals at home, and hobbies or other pursuits. Carol Dweck and her research team at Columbia found it most effective to:[22]

- **Be specific.** Instead of saying, "Great job" or "You got an A," tell your child, "Your work this week to read all your assignments and turn in your finished homework is not only getting you good grades in this class, it's helping you develop good habits for all your other classes, even a job someday."

- **Call out the processes used rather than the person.** Rather than tell a child, "You are so smart!" comment on an observation such as, "I like the way you proofread your paper when you finished to check for errors" or "Good for sticking with that hard assignment, staying at your desk to keep concentrating on the problems until you got to the answers."

- **Praise what's within your child's control.** In general a child can't control their IQ score, level of physical attractiveness, or whether they're more naturally gifted in athleticism or art. But they can control effort, attitude, responsibility, commitment, discipline, focus, choices, compassion, generosity, respect, and love. So look for what they're doing that's working well and specifically praise those areas, such as, "You were so focused in the chess match" or "You were so generous today to your sister," rather than "You looked so pretty today" or "You were so much faster in the race than those other kids." Your child will begin to see there are things in their control to carry on, rather than give up because they don't think they have a chance.

Realistic Goals

Nothing makes a child want to give up faster than facing a goal that seems unimaginable and unattainable, or one set so low there's no satisfaction in achieving it. A study conducted over twenty-five years found that what works better in helping you keep on is setting goals that are specific, measureable, realistic, and timely.[23] To do that, help your kids:

- **Identify their desire, and their strengths and weaknesses** in how to achieve it. This helps them see where to spend their time and attention first and most.

- **Map the way.** Write out, chart, or draw an actual map of what must be accomplished to move from where they are to where they want to be, being sure to list specific steps in between. For example, to grow a garden as a 4-H project, help your child write down steps in the order needed: ready the soil, plant, tend, water, weed, fertilize, and harvest. Have him or her note the estimated times for each task and what's entailed; for instance, raking or tilling, getting the seeds or plant starts, plotting what goes where and use markers, covering with chicken wire or some protection from squirrels and birds, sprinkling at morning or night or both, and so on. Writing out these things as a route to the goal not only helps children see how far they have to go, but how far they've come, making their dream more real with each step.

- **Define the best work habits.** Even elementary school children can begin developing punctuality, organization, cleanliness, and tidiness. It's never too early to get your children thinking on how patterns, practices, rituals, and routines add up to something and create a result. Ask them what repeated, measureable things they can do in working toward their goal to problem-solve, be systematic and efficient, take initiative, follow up, and show gratitude.

- **Think about a Plan B from the start.** Sometimes the route to a goal is circuitous. There are pitfalls or places they get stuck and stopped. Help your kids identify other ways of achieving their goal in case their first approach doesn't work. Learning to look for adjustments helps kids expand their creativity. Each time they think on an alternative way of accomplishing something, they see there are many ways of doing a thing. They begin to value diversity, and think in deeper ways about compromise and negotiation, all of which add to the fuel of perseverance as well.

Connect Work to Achievement

In an age when nearly every desire can be met instantly, it's even more important to help your children see how things come by time, energy, and effort. Help them make the connection, especially when too often they see money coming from an ATM at the push of a button, or dinner arriving in a paper dish after cooking five minutes in the microwave.

You can show them instead the truer picture of how the food we eat results from someone planting, growing, and harvesting the produce, then cooking the recipes; or how clothes result not from a trip to the department store but someone designing the patterns, weaving the material, cutting the cloth, and sewing the clothes. To do that:

- **Give them vivid illustrations of how things are created, achieved, and made.** At every opportunity, visit farms and manufacturing or production plants (search online for tours in your area), and attend rehearsals of community plays and orchestras (many often allow free entrance). If your child is interested in painting or making a small motor, look for videos online that show processes and people doing the work. Check out books that show what it takes to make things too: *How Stuff Works* by Marshall Brain (Chartwell Books, 2010), *My First Book of How Things Are Made: Crayons, Jeans, Guitars, Peanut Butter, and More* by George Jones (Cartwheel Books, 1995), *The Random House Book of How Things Work* by Steve Parker (Random House, 1991), *The Way Things Work* by David Macaulay (Houghton Mifflin, 1988), *How Things Work* by Neil Ardley (Reader's Digest, 1995), and another *How Things Work* by Ian Graham (Facts on File, 1994). Examples can inspire you to keep going and give you ideas on, and sometimes role models for, how.

- **Let them experience for themselves how steps lead to progress.** Books are read and written one chapter at a time. You reach the finish line by putting one foot in front of the other. When your children hit the steps toward their goal that seem unpleasant or boring, remind them that they get closer to what they want by simply doing the next thing. All the time, energy, and effort moves them forward from where they are now. Urge them to chart their course on a piece of paper or note accomplishments on sticky notes that they post in a visible place like their bedside or bathroom mirror. Seeing the steps helps them value each act, hour, and the work in relation to what they want to achieve.

- **Get them thinking how the journey and every inch of progress, not just the destination and goal, have value.** People work and go to school all week to enjoy the weekend. We live all the days of the year to celebrate a few holidays. You can save certain clothes and shoes for Sunday church and special occasions, or the good china for milestone dinners. But the in-between, the journey usually is where we are longer than at the destination. Check in with your kids on this. Ask them: What do you love about the work or process right now? What's your favorite part? Do you love this journey, whether you make the goal or not? Enjoying and at least appreciating the journey can keep them on it.

PERSISTENCE LOOKS LIKE THIS

I love watching the Olympics and learning the backstories of the athletes, how they got to the games, the sacrifices they made, the work, the perseverance. It makes the heart swell to see not just the medal presented to a proud athlete standing on a podium, their national anthem sounding in the background, but to hear how they rose early, worked late, spent their last dollars, traveled extra miles, and fought through injuries, pain, ridicule, self-doubt, and other overwhelming challenges to achieve their dream. They give the very idea of perseverance a face, many faces. To see tears in their eyes, and then that tenacious twinkle, gets me every time.

Your children may never stand in an Olympic arena. They may not show blood, sweat, and tears in the same way as an Olympian. But as you cheer them on in their pursuits every day, you get the chance to see that same kind of twinkle of tenacity and persistence in their eyes.

As abstract an idea as persistence may be, it really does show up tangibly in your kids, says Paul Tough, the best-selling author of *How Children Succeed*.[24] One day you see them fight through exhaustion to cross the finish line in a footrace. Another day you hear them say, "I'm going to figure this out." Yet another, after doing badly on a test, you watch them nose into the homework…without be told.

What just happened? you might wonder. *Can it happen again?* What do you look for, and continue to encourage?

The evident qualities of persistence that lead to success have to do more with character than raw ability, says Tough. The great news is these qualities are actually skills that can be learned: self-control, conscientiousness, curiosity, and optimism.[25] Other psychologists add to the top of that skill set: grit, zest, confidence, and, I would add, a teachable spirit, and tolerance when frustrated.[26]

Grit

When the going gets really tough, grit is what surfaces, that *je ne sais quoi* or certain something-something often described as the sheer tenacity to press on through the most difficult struggle.

Angela Duckworth, a psychology professor at the University of Pennsylvania who coined the term *grit* in the context of academic achievement, describes it this way: "This quality of being able to sustain your passions, and also work really hard at them, over really disappointingly long periods of time, that's grit." And grit can matter more to academic achievement and being able to reach your goals in life than skills or smarts, she says.[27] Two effective ways to cultivate grit include:

- **Taking risks.** Begin with talk in ways of greeting life and the next challenge as an adventure. Welcome the next step, reach for it, don't just accept what's practical and within grasp. Change the way you talk about that goal. Instead of "Here's what to do next," speak like an explorer and pioneer: "How far could we get? What would happen if...?" A child with grit will chase after the goal, take a chance, and stretch for it with an attitude of expectation and readiness.

- **Entertaining rigor.** This is helping kids think for themselves in the midst of difficulty. Show your child how to tackle the tough things, like understanding abstract principles by making them concrete. For instance if your third grader's goal is to ace a math test that uses lots of multiplication, help her or him see how multiplication works. Use peanuts, cotton balls, marbles, or other household items for equations. Set your kids onto a practice of always looking for how to make the abstract concrete. Another way of encouraging rigor is to start your kids on strategizing about problems. Can they talk about their approaches and a backup to try when a first one fails? This keeps them thinking, tackling, and figuring out solutions.

Zest

That *carpe diem* sense to seize the day and live to the fullest really isn't something just planted. Your children learn it by practicing sensibilities like:

- **The day, this situation, that task, this moment is new.** Have them let go of what was by focusing on what is. You say, "That was then, this is now." Put into practice the idea that each moment is a new chance.

- **No complaining.** Make it a rule early on for no howling at situations, rather doing something about them. This instills the idea they can change things, they can make a difference.

- **Thinking *next time* instead of *what if.*** This creates the belief that nothing is over—maybe that situation, but not the next. This is focusing on possibilities.

- **Doing the things they love and loving the things they do.** Your child has to scoop the dog poop in the park as part of a school project to beautify it? No one loves that, so you have him or her focus not on the poop, but the park. Focus the child on loving the fact the park will be clean, not scooping up the mess itself. Keeping their focus fixed on what they love, and they can love what they're doing to keep them going.

Self-Control

Self-control is twice as important as intelligence in predicting achievement and that drive to keep on achieving, discovered authors Sandra Aamodt and Sam Wang in going over decades of research for their book *Welcome to Your Child's Brain.*[28] Self-control is what gives you social skills and discipline; it helps you focus, delay gratification, pay attention, and keep going.[29]

The best way to teach self-control is with practice, repetition, and reinforcement with praise of good choices to exercise restraint.

One of the landmark studies showing this used what is called the Marshmallow Test. Groups of children, ages three to seven years, were offered one treat now or two treats later. It took only a couple times of taking one treat now for the children to learn that by waiting and being self-controlled their reward could double. And what helped those kids learn self-control so fast was parents who influenced the choice to wait.[30]

"An only child living with parents who reliably promise and deliver small motivational treats is going to have more reason to wait for her marshmallow because they show consistency, their child learns self-control from experience and practice," says Celeste Kidd, who conducted the latest study. "But for a child accustomed to stolen possessions and broken promises, the only guaranteed treats are the ones you've already swallowed."[31]

Another way to practice self-control is by engaging in activities that your child loves and that require active effort and mental concentration, things like building with Legos, racing through a maze, martial arts, or yoga. As the challenges progressively increase, your children learn to focus, concentrate, and control their will and impulses to achieve skill.

Confidence

When you're confident you can do something, you usually can and do. Even the youngest children know this, as Stephen, a bright six-year-old, demonstrated one day. He was quickly reconstructing geometric designs with cubes, and proclaimed, "I know the formula to make the line. Do you know my trick?" He didn't wait for an answer, he was so sure: "Believing in myself!"

That, Stephen did. He knew his strengths and had a growing, healthy sense of self-regard. He drew confidence from what he could do, and that helped him keep building even when the geometric designs got more intricate and difficult.

This is the kind of confidence built from parents who encouraged rather than manipulated and indiscriminately praised. But a lot of parents get tripped up in exactly how to praise and encourage in ways that build healthy confidence. They've bought into the myth that it's good to constantly laud and call out everything a child does.

That does more harm than good. The self-esteem movement in the eighties spurred a generation of parents who heaped bundles of praise on their kids for every little thing: You're on the team? Great, you get a trophy! You showed up? Outstanding! Everyone clap! You're going to quit? Well, here's a reward for trying!

Indiscriminate encouragement and praise results in too many children with bookcases at home full of trophies, ribbons, and accolades for being a part of things while never really making contributions, progress, or achievement. These kids didn't learn confidence and perseverance. No, they learned entitlement and a paper-thin tolerance in the face of a frustration.[32]

To build a healthy confidence that enables your children to try, act, and achieve, you:

- **Praise real efforts**, how hard they work and where they realistically do well. This helps kids know and feel good about their true strengths. For example you don't tell your child, "Great game. You're a wonderful soccer player." That doesn't make them confident or good at the game. Rather, you praise the effort and specific strength, "You worked so hard for that win. All your practice to move the ball down the field really shows!"

- **Enable them to express their feelings**. In a child's logic, if her feelings are not worthwhile, she is not worthwhile. Be careful not to tell your children how to feel ("Stop being angry"). Instead ask them what they're feeling, give them permission to express feelings by the environment you create. This doesn't mean you give them permission to act out in anger, hurt themselves, you, or others. It does mean you make it safe for saying, "I'm angry," or scared. Then you help your child learn how to bridle and manage feelings, not stuff them. You talk openly about feelings and what to do with them. You show your child they can control what they feel, and as they do so, they develop the confidence to keep going even when they're daunted or frustrated.

- **Instill in them the belief that God made them able, and where they're not, he is**—he's got things in control. This allows your child to do what he or she can, and leave the rest to God. There's no overwhelming pressure, just conviction that enables their best efforts.

Tolerance When Frustrated

I remember when my son Tom was three and a half years of age and I took off the training wheels from his two-wheeler bicycle.

Michael, then two and a half years of age, watched with excitement.

Tom hopped on his two-wheeler and made those first wobbly pedals. There was the usual wobble and struggle for balance as I helped him steady himself. Then Tom was sailing down the sidewalk, all on his own.

It was so exciting. Michael wanted to be just like his big brother, sailing down the sidewalk on two wheels too. Instead, he still had training wheels on his bike.

"Mommy," he begged, "please take them off."

"But, honey," I explained, "you're not ready yet. You don't want to wear out your tires or keep falling because you're learning to get your balance."

When we did take off the training wheels, Tom was determined to catch up to and even get ahead of his brother. He pedaled as hard and fast as he could, and because he was still learning to get his balance he didn't quite know how to stop on the two-wheeler. So he leaned and sort of half fell to keep Michael from getting ahead of him. It was a hard fall, and such a picture of what happens when kids are learning something new.

Some kids can get right up from that fall—Tom did from sheer determination not to let his brother get the better of him. But some kids will fall and then let that stop them. They'll quit and walk away. We're no different. I've seen people throw up their arms in exasperation and walk away, leaving a problem unsolved because they can't wrestle with it another minute. This is so common in school, especially when children are learning math, for them to put down the pencil and say, "That's it. Enough! I can't do it."

But they can—and you can help them learn to have more tolerance in the face of frustration. The best things to do:

- **Show them how to calm down and focus.** Whether they're learning to ride a bike or master a math equation, when the going gets tough or they fall or fail, show them the technique of taking a deep breath, refocusing, and starting again.

- **Help them learn impulse control, patience, and delayed gratification.** The best thing is to identify where patience is needed. For the youngest of children this means calling out, "Patience," and, "Wait till I'm finished speaking or doing this." You might even make a chart listing where patience and impulse control are needed, things like NO INTERRUPTING and WAITING MY TURN. Every time your child shows patience and impulse control, give them a sticker. Praise how many stickers they get as you go—every time, in fact, your child looks at a book rather than interrupts your phone conversation, or chooses to play with Legos instead of melting down because you said *no* to watching TV.

- **Back off and fade.** This lets your children wrestle with their problems on their own. Just as a baby will fumble with building blocks, then stack them, your children can figure out things on their own when left to turn over a problem, set it aside, come back to it, and try new problem-solving approaches.

- **Sweeten with words.** Sparks of encouragement actually fuel your kids' pursuits. Call out what your children are doing well and where they're making strides. Help them identify that intrinsic feeling of conquering something. For example: "Look how you're riding without training wheels. See how far you just pedaled!" They will keep going when they feel they're doing something right and succeeding or making progress.

- **Laugh wherever and whenever possible.** Laughter helps you enjoy one another and a challenge. It lifts the tension, anxiety, anger, and frustration, enabling a refocus and new try. A caveat is to be careful to never denigrate yourself, your child, or other people. You can, when appropriate, make fun of the situation. A great example comes from literature where the French swashbuckler Cyrano de Bergerac, in the play by the same name, betters a bully. The bully has put down Cyrano with the pronouncement, "Your nose is very large."[33] Cyrano dazzles bystanders rather than raging at them. He admits, "Yes, very," then outdoes the way he was belittled with creativity, originality, and brilliance. "You could have said at least one hundred other things," he says and gives examples in categories such as curious ("What is that large container for? To hold your pens and ink?"), descriptive ('Tis a rock! A cape! A peak! No, a peninsula!"), dramatic ("When it bleeds, it must be like the Red Sea."), cavalier ("Is that a hook to hang your hat on?"), admiring ("What a fine sign for a perfume shop"), and so on. Cyrano uses wit and humor to shame the bully's actions, enjoys some laughs in the process, and comes out more winsome. He also finds a way to go forward from ridicule, not be stopped in frustration, stating in the end that he does not need all the fancy, expensive show displayed by his critic. Rather, "I shall adorn my soul."[34] The point is to enjoy a challenge and one another, to open up yourself to things and not be so fixed on something that there's no joy.

A Teachable Spirit

One school year, I counseled the parents of a brother and sister who had each just been diagnosed with dyslexia. Jon and Janie were given immediate reading and writing support in the resource center, and at our first check-in point, we marveled at Janie's dramatic progress.

But, why, we wondered, *hadn't Jon done so well?*

"Attitude," the teacher from the resource center said. "Janie is very forgiving of herself when she makes a mistake. But Jon gets angry and gives up."

I noticed Mom and Dad exchange knowing glances as the teacher said, "He's that way on the playground too."

Jon's stubbornness was not news. He could blow up and shut down in an instant, and this was going to keep him from achieving if they didn't do something fast.

Can you really change an attitude?

Contrary to what you may have heard, yes. We've all heard it said: "You can teach skills but you can't teach a good attitude." But you can—and you want to start with your children now in order to help them keep pursuing and achieving their goals.

- **Work on coping skills to process feelings** like anger, frustration, and fear. A lot of times children haven't yet learned to identify their feelings. Jon was acting in anger when he felt afraid or anxious. He needed his parents to give him the words: "Are you afraid this assignment will be difficult? Are you sad when that boy won't give you the basketball?" Then he needed ideas on how to process those feelings. "Remember when Mommy was mad because the water wouldn't go down the drain in the kitchen sink? What did she do?" You can suggest good coping skills—take a deep breath, count to ten, think of something good to say or do (ask for help, try again). The older your children are, the more time you can give them to offer positive solutions on their own, giving feedback like, "You might do this or that but what do you want to do?" This helps them engage with their situation and persist in figuring it out. You can also help them change their focus from feeling one way to something else. Show them how their face gets all screwed up, or brows are knitted and hands clenched (even around a pencil), or their heart beats faster when they're anxious. Then help them connect the dots to how when they're anxious their concentration and energy goes to being anxious instead of problem-solving. When children can identify what is happening, they can begin to change from spending energy on frustration, fear, or stress, to focusing on breaking apart the problem, trying something new, and trying again. Ways to tell your kids to try anew: "Instead of crumpling in frustration, sit up straight. Instead of whining about how hard this is, take a deep breath and tell yourself you'll try a new way. Instead of frowning, raise your eyebrows to open up yourself for new ideas. Tell yourself: *I can do it*—and you will."

- **Nurture focused listening skills.** Teach your children that they can't listen unless they look—and looking means focusing both eyes and mind. That means when you give an instruction or direction, they need to stop what they're doing and look at you, and you need to be sure you do the same (look at them for their attention instead of texting something on your smart phone or working on something at the computer, stove, washer, or whatever). If your child has difficulty remembering auditory directions, have her repeat what's said back to you. This reinforces the instruction and helps memory. Psychologists call this part of "executive function," the ability to hold information in your mind to use at a later time. Practice giving your four- or five-year-old three-step directions, since all through life, from school and church sermons to the boardroom of corporations, points are often made and best remembered in three points. So, for your children, try instructions such as, "Please go upstairs, get your blue sweater, and bring me baby's pink blanket." Make a habit in your family of stopping, looking, and listening. Help them carry directions in their head by focused listening and repeating back important instructions and information. Now go one step more—ask them to use all their senses to listen, not just ears but eyes and heart. Help them understand that words have meanings and even more with the manner in which they're said. Play games that teach more focused listening with both words and gestures. Toddlers love Simon Says, where one person says "Simon says turn right, turn left, back up," and the other must do it fast. Sometimes Simon can be tricky, saying "jump" but then squatting. This tests how to hear directions, watch, comprehend, interpret, and respond. For older kids, with three or more people, play Continuous Story. Sit together and one person starts a story with one sentence, then each person takes a turn adding a sentence to build and continue the story. This game teaches how to keep eye contact, focus, and hear in comprehensive and creative ways.

- **Foster openness** as opposed to defensiveness. This means creating an atmosphere where questions are always welcome, and curiosity is rewarded with engagement and exploration.

It also means not encouraging constant justification for things done or left undone.

- **Exercise forgiveness**, including self-forgiveness because this is what greases the wheel of endurance and remaining teachable. That means you apologize for your mistakes, and expect your children to do the same. Did you mess up in accusing your child of something she didn't do? Did your kids, in anger, call you disrespectful names? It's important to say, "I'm sorry." Teaching and modeling the importance of acknowledging wrongs, mistakes, and angry or hurtful words is an act of humility that keeps one able to learn and builds trust. The Bible is practical in advice to us on this point. "Do nothing out of selfish ambition or vain conceit," Philippians 2:3-5 says, "Rather, in humility value others above yourselves, not looking to your own interests but each of you to the interests of the others. In your relationships with one another, have the same mindset as Christ Jesus."

A STEP TOWARD STRONGER PERSEVERANCE
How to Keep a Teachable Spirit by The Book

The Proverbs give us lots of examples about how to nurture a teachable spirit by showing us practices of the wise versus the foolish. You can help yourself, and your kids, keep on by pursuing the qualities of the wise. Think of these things. Read the Proverbs and talk about them with your kids. Use them for an evening devotion time. Ask your children how they can practice each quality in a particular week. Let them know that no answers are wrong, and these are things to meditate on and pray about daily to keep on living strong.

THE WISE...	THE FOOLISH...	THE PROVERB...
Quietly accepts instruction and criticism	Ignores instruction	10:8; 23:12; and 25:12
Loves discipline	Hates instruction	12:1
Listens to advice	Thinks they need no instruction	12:15; 21:11; and 24:6
Profits from constructive rebuke	Self-destructs by refusing rebuke	15:31-32 and 29:1

- **Hold fast to the importance of understanding versus being right.** There's a difference. You may answer a question correctly but miss the point of the lesson. Teach your kids to think before they speak: Listen. Wait a few seconds. Think about what your words might mean or do to someone else before you speak them.

- **Encourage flexibility.** This means teaching kids to get away from the rigid idea of always having to be right or of being argumentative because something didn't go their way in their time. You want them to develop flexibility, be open to engage new ideas and ways of doing things. You want your kids to take some chances, learn how to think on their feet, roll with the punches, compromise in healthy ways, and stay open to the ideas and feelings of others. Flexibility enables them to receive, learn, and grow, and keep a spirit of adventure. If your child is bossy or stubborn in ways that stop them or trip them up or keep them (and everyone around them) frustrated, talk them through those places. Ask them questions and get them to ask themselves: How can this be done differently? What if we tried this or that? Get them thinking on the *what ifs*. You can spot where to work on flexibility with your kids in everyday things like what they always order when you go out to eat, or ask for in meals. If they're always requesting the same things, they might be developing some rigidity. Get them to try something new—this kind of experimentation can spill over into how they approach problem-solving.

- **Teach detachment.** Being able to look at situation objectively helps in almost any situation, from solving a work problem to navigating relationships. Ask your kids to imagine how someone else might solve the problem. This takes their feelings out of the equation and taps their creativity to problem-solve. It gets them thinking less on their own frustrations and struggles, and more on the challenge itself and how to persevere through it.

Optimism

Why do some people seem more inclined to give up or be pessimistic? Martin Seligman, a psychologist and educator, wanted to know. As he puts it, "I was accustomed to focusing on what was wrong with individuals and then on how to fix it."[35] But in the process of studying negativity and how to change it, he discovered the most surprising thing about positivity: optimism, just like helplessness, can be learned.

That means you can teach your kids the kind of optimism that keeps them going through life, helps them find positive meaning in experiences and fuels the belief in their ability to make a difference for the better.

True, there are born optimists, people naturally inclined to always see the positive. The Bible tells us faith, or optimism and belief in the face of doubt, is a gift (1 Corinthians 12:9), and we're each allotted a measure (Romans 12:3-8). Some people get a greater portion just as others are blessed with more of another sort of gift (1 Corinthians 12:27-31).

That doesn't mean you and your kids can't learn to find the positive in a way that keeps you going. Just as Seligman's studies show, the Bible's told us from the beginning that optimism is a choice. After escaping from slavery, Moses told the Israelites in the desert, "I have set before you life and death, blessing and curse. Therefore choose life, that you and your offspring may live" (Deuteronomy 30:19 ESV). One of his best students, Joshua, took this gauntlet to heart and chose belief in God's promises, belief that God would help him lead the people into the Promised Land—and God did (Joshua 1-5).

When Seligman studied how children could learn optimism or pessimism, he exposed them to shocks. The children who could not control the shocks learned helplessness and gave up trying to withstand the shocks. The children who learned how to control the shocks developed optimism and confidence that there were things they could do to get to another environment. "They were inoculated, if you will, against helplessness," Seligman said.[36]

The inoculation benefited their mental health too, protecting them against depression and anxiety, increasing their problem-solving ability. Optimism helps you process information, Seligman concluded. Positivity enables you to step back from a problem, evaluate it in a wider context, and understand change and how terrible times and circumstances will pass ("it will change or you will change, and you will move through it.")[37]

Two great ways you can cultivate a positive outlook in your kids:

- **Challenge pessimistic thoughts and comments.** If your eight-year-old declares she's "just no good at this," offer alternative ways of looking at the situation. Maybe she needed to practice or pay more attention. Maybe she needs to try another approach because there's a better way for her. This teaches your child to look again, reflect in new ways, try again.

- **Teach healthy self-talk.** In the face of a challenge, disappointment, or loss, remind your children their feelings and responses aren't caused by events themselves but the way they think about these events—their self-talk. Help them identify positive thinking from the negative. If they're old enough to write, have them jot down their thoughts and feelings when something goes wrong. Otherwise talk this through. They might respond first with negative thoughts: *Bad events will last forever (or a long time). Things will never change. Everything I do is undermined. This is all my fault—I can't do anything right.* Ask them to write positive thoughts next to every negative one: *Bad events are just temporary setbacks. God wants to help me. I can move beyond this situation, these circumstances. I can overcome with my effort and abilities and God's help.* Now, during times of practice or their efforts, have your children wear a loose-fitting rubber band on their wrist. Every time they're tempted to think a negative thought, have them snap the rubber band—to snap out of pessimistic thinking. That means replace every negative thought with a positive one. This teaches them how to stop the negative self-talk loop in their minds and builds more of a habit for "I can do it" self-talk—and that keeps them going.

WE'RE MADE TO KEEP ON AND ENDURE

In the middle of using all these tools, doing your best to fuel your kids with perseverance, be sure to fill up your tank too. Run on encouragement, your own purpose of doing a mighty thing, on inspiration straight from God, your heavenly father, that parenting is one of the hardest and most rewarding things you can do.

Granted, it's so easy to not remember the encouragement and purpose when, no matter how intentional you are, the day takes a turn for the worse. The hot-water heater quits, your kids want to quit school, and you want to quit parenting because everything seems hard. The challenges can be enough to make you feel like Mount Rushmore's been plopped right in your path, and those presidents aren't offering a peep of help.

This is where God reminds us over and over in the Bible that to those who endure and put their trust and hope in him to work out things, there are great rewards:

> *"In due season, we will reap if we do not give up,"* he says in Galatians 6:9 (ESV).

> *"Even youths grow tired and weary, and young men stumble and fall; but those who hope in the Lord will renew their strength,"* he says. *"They will soar on wings like eagles; they will run and not grow weary, they will walk and not be faint"* (Isaiah 40:30-31).

Going on keeps you stronger, God is saying. You'll find peace and abundant life because as a parent you have a great purpose—God's prepared you to do great things in this role (Ephesians 2:10). He's got your back, can keep you running on hope because you're made for this, and help enable you to cross whatever mountain stands before you because he knows you can—he knows you can!

It's such a beautiful picture, isn't it, crossing those mountains? A happy picture of joy and triumph, the kind of picture I envisioned as Michael Sr.

described reading with his son Mickey. Yes, that's what I said, an amazing picture of triumph those two, Michael Sr., with his cigarettes rolled in one T-shirt sleeve, and his laid-back demeanor, and little Mickey, who giving in to fear in reading class was getting into fights out of frustration on the playground.

Who could have imagined triumph, perseverance looked like this?

Probably not most of us. Not those who looked at the little train engine in the childhood story and imagined he could pull a long train of freight cars up a steep hill. Not a world that looked to God for a savior then beheld a baby crying in a manger. Not you, maybe, looking at your messy kids wanting to quit, or your tired face in the mirror so ready to stop.

But take heart. One of the most fascinating gifts persistence gives us is how it changes the picture. When we run on the fuel of persistence, everything lights up. The tired and worn, weak and messy, look beautiful, like miracles, like winners.

The poet Edna St. Vincent Millay said it so well:

> *My candle burns at both ends;*
> *It will not last the night;*
> *But ah, my foes, and oh, my friends—*
> *It gives a lovely light.*[38]

So keep going, you purposeful parent. Glow!

MY PURPOSEFUL PARENT CHECK-IN
How Am I Doing with Perseverance?

I'm seeing my children persevere more, and being my best to bring out their best, by:

- Giving them the keys to drive on: autonomy and independence, skills and mastery for can-do spirit, and purpose for direction.
- Boosting their personal power every day with motivation, zest, belief and encouragement, enough freedom to fail, a value of effort over ability, realistic goals, and help connecting the dots between work and achievement.
- Giving them tools to develop tolerance when frustrated.
- Grooming a teachable spirit in them, myself, and within our household.
- Nurturing optimism, hope, and faith.

Conclusion

PARENTING TAKES A TEAM

…because help is all around you

One beautiful fall afternoon, a frantic mother called my school to report her son Kevin never made it home on the school bus. A search began. Most everyone involved felt a dread in the pit of their stomachs. We'd all heard too many stories of the worst possible scenarios and the fear of this situation turning into one more crouched at our heels.

Then the search team discovered Kevin sauntering through his neighborhood with his friend Brian, both completely at ease.

It turned out Kevin had asked permission for Brian to ride the bus home with him. But the request was denied because our school required written permission from a parent, and there was none. Kevin decided to do what he wanted anyway. He and Brian took their time making their way home.

We were relieved Kevin was safe but knew the incident wasn't over. We needed to go through his choices with him to make sure this never happened again.

His mother knew too, only her take was completely different. The next morning she called to inform the school that the fault for the temporarily missing Kevin was ours—his teacher's, the administration's, the bus driver's, and everyone whose paths crossed Kevin's in a day. Everyone, that is, except hers and except his.

When we tried to talk about needing her help to get Kevin to follow the rules and processes designed to keep him safe, she insisted this wasn't the issue at all. Kevin's teacher and our administration grieved that call. We knew a day could come when a child's choices to break the rules could not be defended and could lead to the harm we all feared.

And I was especially reminded that when it comes to getting our kids where we want them to be, whether that's home or happy, it takes a team.

You can be the best parent. Your child can have the best teacher, be in the best school and part of the best church and community. But without all of us working together for that child's best, without the child working with us, and without our trust in a loving God to always stand by us and show us the way, our best efforts can fail. It's too easy in this world to get lost and go a perilous way.

The good news is where your strengths end, another's begin. Where you're tired, another is ready. Where you want to quit, there are others to hold you up, keep you going, and get your children where we all want them to be: joyful, productive, thriving, and walking with God. So on top of all the tools you now have for love, discipline, purpose and passion, character, responsibility, and perseverance, here's one more: the ability to pull it all together, to call upon and allow others to help—and here's how to activate the team it takes to raise thriving, joyful children.

PARENTING TAKES SCHOOLS

There's no question that children who love and navigate school well can do well in life. What's remarkable is that parents working *with* educators enable that success, not just the children or schools themselves. The difference parents make is dramatic too, according to the landmark study on this from the Equality of Educational Opportunity. Academically, in attitudes and performance, understanding and comprehension, communications and relationships, children do remarkably better when parents are involved in their schools and education.[1]

James Reed Campbell and his research team found just how remarkable when they studied how more than 10,000 "gifted" children in the United States, Greece, Japan, and China came to be so. The common thread they found was parents who cared enough to nurture, support, and enforce their children's efforts in school.[2] These parents were purposeful, intentional, and engaged, measured by how they:[3]

- **Listened and talked** with their children about what went on at school.

- **Knew from their intimate bond their children's concerns,** worries, and fears.

- **Shared their own reactions** to what their children did and experienced.

- **Checked in on home and schoolwork.**

- **Provided the structure and encouragement** for schoolwork and goals to be accomplished.

And because of these things, the children of such parents not only did well, but well above other students. Exceptionally well—well enough to be considered gifted.

So how to you practice involvement with your kids' schools or education so as to get the most out of them? There are several ways: help your kids love learning and school; team up with teachers; and reinforce good habits.

Help Your Kids Love Learning and School

First, whether you homeschool or send your child to a public or private school, you want your kids to engage with teachers in addition to you and with an educational system. This seems such a simple thing. Yet so many parents continue to struggle. Their kids orbit solely around themselves. That first day of school, these children cry, cling, and carry on; and even after many years in school, they still complain about the start of each new school year.

The way you deal with separation anxiety makes a big difference. Is your child by nature slow to warm up or is it a matter of boundaries and control?

Janet understood this perfectly. When her son Christopher was to start first grade, with longer school sessions every day, she knew she needed a plan. She'd already been through his fits entering both nursery school and kindergarten, which met for shorter shifts and every other day of the week. Chris had figured out how to get her to pull him from class or keep him home a day or two because he knew how to push her buttons. He'd complain he was going to suffer an allergy or asthma attack, at which Janet would jump into "keep him close and safe" mode.

After many false alarms, this smart mama could see what Christopher was doing. She knew too that he could manage his asthma attacks—and school.

She met with a doctor to list symptoms of oncoming asthma and allergy episodes, and helped Christopher identify the signs, avoid the triggers, and keep healthy. Then she equipped him and herself with things to fight their fear of the unknown. They went to school a few days before the start of first grade, met Christopher's teacher, talked through his health struggles, what to do in emergencies, and got a tour of the school and classroom. Janet enabled Christopher to help himself and she involved his teachers and the school. This sent a clear message to her son that going to school, or getting out of it, was not an option. It enabled everyone around Christopher to give him their best so he could be his best.

But too often there are parents like Sharon, whose son, Ryan, was entering kindergarten. With his curly blond hair and blue, blue eyes, Ryan looked like a little cherub but behaved the opposite. His cries of "I miss Mommy" echoed up and down the school hallways that whole first day of kindergarten, and the next. He could not, would not be soothed, distracted, engaged, or quieted.

When I called Sharon to talk about what to do, how we could work together to help Ryan make the transition from home to school and back, she was annoyed. The problem was the teacher, the school, the situation. As she ticked off who was to blame instead of honing in on what we could do together to make things better, she got angry.

Never mind, as we would learn later, that there were deeper issues going on, that Ryan was never left alone, not even with a babysitter on occasion, or that he never slept in his own bed, instead watched television with his dad on the couch until they fell asleep together, or that there were absolutely no boundaries in their lives, that Ryan was in control, demanding his parents by his side at all times, even to go to the bathroom and dress. Sharon was so entrenched in denial that there were any problems at home, the door to working with the schools, to learning and growing, was closed. Change was not on her agenda, so the school would have to handle the problems with Ryan alone.

While schools and teachers can fill many gaps in helping a child to thrive, they can do it better with your help. Without it, kids pay the price. Children like Ryan can learn that they cannot control their teachers or the classroom like Mom and Dad, but the process will be painful, taking many instances of choices and consequences. And how much smoother this lesson can be learned when parents and teachers work together. Some things you can do:

- **Get them to class on time.** Children won't like school if they're late for class and worried about what they've missed or feel they're an outsider because everyone else is already engaged in something they've yet to join. Getting them to school in time to get settled and engaged with their teacher and others creates belonging and confidence to learn.

- **Know when it's time for you to go.** Many parents are anxious about leaving their kids at school, and children sense that. When your kids start to cry or get clingy upon entering the classroom, the best thing to do is make a clean exit and leave. This seems so counterintuitive. You feel like you're abandoning your child, right? But by lingering, you keep your child sidelined from school. Your child is fixed on you so much there's no wiggle room for bonding with the teacher and classmates.

- **Get involved.** Know your children's teachers. Go to the open houses and conferences. Introduce yourself. This helps you keep the lines of communication open for any issues and opportunities. You'll learn the expectations your child will face about assignments and homework, and know how discipline is handled. The National Center for Education found that parent involvement with schools always improved children's engagement and learning because kids felt supported and encouraged, and involvement meant everything from attending conferences and concerts or other events, to fund-raising for the schools and volunteering in classrooms.[4]

- **Stay tuned in.** How do your kids feel about classes, teachers, other students, and events at school? You can always ask, but most kids don't like to be quizzed about "How was school?" or "What did you learn today?" The older they get, the less they may volunteer too. Instead, open them up with less testing-type questions, more pure curiosity: What snack did you get at school today? What book are you reading together as a class? Who made you laugh today and why? These questions will get at things you might never know otherwise and can help you and your child see what there is to celebrate about school.

Team Up with Teachers

Once your kids do make that transition to engage in school, you can influence how they'll do academically and in learning, especially in the areas of ability, discipline, confidence, and good work habits. In that study of 10,000 gifted children, Campbell found that parents could raise or lower a child's academic output in these areas by as much as 20 to 30 percent.[5]

They do so, he found, with all the day-to-day strategies, rituals and routines, plans, games, and recipes for success that they use to build a child's self-concepts, attitudes, and motivation to learn and achieve. Also in practicing the following ways of teaming up with your kids' teachers:

- **Communicate directly, respectfully, and productively.** It's so easy today to fire off an e-mail or text message to a teacher; but notes, whether electronic or penned on paper, can be misdirected and misunderstood. E-mails aren't always reliable. Handwritten notes may never make it past your kids' coat pocket. Things not expressed well, completely and clearly, can actually introduce more problems—frustration or anger, for instance—that are hard to clear away and get to the heart of resolving an issue. It's always better to talk on the phone or meet in person when there are things to discuss about your child.

- **Reinforce lessons taught.** Whatever topic your child is learning in school, deepen their learning by getting them to think, remember, make connections, and theorize beyond the classroom. If your kids are learning in science class about photosynthesis, talk about how plants grow in the park downtown or in your own backyard, tend herbs in a windowsill container, or read books about great gardens. There are endless ways of furthering and applying what's been taught in school, and what you add to classroom learning is priceless.

- **Check in and check up.** It's not helicoptering or hovering to make sure you're in sync with your kids' teachers on common goals for their growth and learning. Ask your kids about their assignments, tests, and quizzes. Encourage them in their efforts, and follow up to see how they did. Help them create timelines and charts that plot the work and pacing. Make time count, as discussed in more detail in the responsibility chapter, by establishing specific times and places for study.

- **Above all, commit to work together.** You can't go wrong in almost any situation to engage a teacher's experience, skills, and creativity by asking, "What can we do together to help my child?" This allows the teacher to engage you too. When parents and teachers work together, you send one clear message to your kids from the two greatest environments of home and school that encompass their world. I was reminded of this when Melissa, a bright second grader, ignored her teacher's instructions on a field trip to a nature center. Her class had been told not to pick flowers or take anything from the environment, but Melissa couldn't resist sneaking some stones into her pocket. Her teacher saw everything, confronted Melissa, made her return the rocks, and as a consequence write a note of apology to the nature center. Melissa started crying that night while writing that note. Her mom telephoned the teacher for the full story and then Melissa truly melted down, wailing in the background, "I'm bad! I'm bad! I wish I could die!" as Mom learned this was but one of many acts of disobedience lately. Alarmed, Mom took matters into her own hands. She kept Melissa home from school the next day for some special one-on-one time. The reaction seemed like a reward to Melissa, who seized the opportunity to beguile her mother into thinking her teacher didn't like her and was being hard on her. Only when Mom and teacher talked a few weeks later was Mom able to get a fuller picture: Melissa was consistently disobedient and trying to manipulate others to get her own way. At home, Mom would fold, see the answer as needing to coddle Melissa more, and that was feeding the beast. Instead Melissa needed Mom and teachers to help her better understand choices and consequences—and once everyone got on the same page of reinforcing the consequences, Melissa started to change. Teamwork does get the job done!

Reinforce Good Habits

You know now how order, routine, and ritual help children by giving them security and confidence to grow. The habits that will help them thrive, that you can influence the most in cooperation with the schools, include:

- **Instilling strong study skills** like committing to work before play, setting times and places for study, and following up on things from questions about schoolwork to outcomes of how it was done. One savvy teacher I know came up with the idea of letting students use their cell phones at the end of each school day to photograph the assignment board. The kids loved it. Their phones had to be kept in their backpacks until this one moment of the day, and using them to capture the assignment in a picture helped them, their parents, and the teacher be sure they had a record of exactly what needed to get done.

- **Clearing the clutter.** Combat what I call the Chaos of the Backpack. A child's school day begins and ends with the backpack in your home. That pack can be a place for clarity or clutter, the place where communication and assignments go back and forth between home and school or where papers are crammed between the leftovers from lunch or hats and scarves. Get your kids in the habit of loading and unloading their packs every night for the next day. Help them organize things with folders, pencil boxes, clips and rubber bands. The ways they learn to organize a task or a place will serve them in performing a job and keeping their own home someday.

- **Growing readers** because reading will help your child achieve and thrive more in every area of life: academically, vocationally, socially to connect ideas and with people, even recreationally for relaxation and as entertainment. The average elementary school teacher reads with your child individually fifteen minutes a week. You can double that time in one day. The goal is, by third grade, for a child to be reading to learn, not learning to read. Children who make a practice to read at home with their parents make significant gains in reading achievement compared to those who only practice at school.[6] Help kids comprehend more of what they read by doing things like writing down new words to them and looking up the definitions and meanings, circling verbs in directions, highlighting important information, and writing down questions about what they read (before, during, and after). These habits will help them all their lives, from putting together assemble-yourself furniture to reviewing contracts and agreements or work projects. Incidentally, since dyslexia is the most common challenge for children who fall behind in reading or complain about it, I always recommend testing for dyslexia early on. This complex condition affects the way the brain processes what's seen, heard, spoken, and other information; and common symptoms are trouble decoding words for early readers, and a lifetime problem of spelling correctly. You usually spot signs in the first three grades of school. And tackling how to manage it will help your kids. One of the best resources is the must-read book *Overcoming Dyslexia* by Sally Shaywitz, and co-director of the Yale Center for the Study of Learning and Attention. You'll find encouragement and practical ways for overcoming dyslexia's challenges.

PARENTING TAKES FRIENDS AND SOCIAL INTELLIGENCE

Growing friendships is one of the greatest signs of thriving. "No man is a failure who has friends," Clarence inscribes in the book he leaves for George Bailey in the final scene of the film *It's a Wonderful Life*.[7] Indeed, friends have saved George in his darkest hour after, all his life, he's saved them.

That is the power of a friend, both the Bible and psychologists agree.

"Two are better than one, because they have a good return for their labor," Ecclesiastes 4:9-12 says. "If either of them falls down, one can help the other up...if two lie down together, they will keep warm. But how can one keep warm alone? Though one may be overpowered, two can defend themselves. A cord of three strands is not quickly broken."

Friends give children resilience, joy, security, and confidence, study after study shows.[8] Children with friends achieve more academically and experience greater well-being, too. Friendships help prevent many of the woes we see afflicting too many children by the time they are teens—depression, suicide, bullying behavior, sad things.[9]

Your role in helping your kids make friends is essential. You give them the recipe for healthy friendships, introducing them to the ingredients of what psychologist Daniel Goleman calls "social intelligence," the way you connect with others and develop and negotiate relationships. "We are wired to connect," Goleman says, and in doing so, "We create one another."[10]

While you can't make others befriend your child, you can help your child be the friend others want. Children who tend to be most popular among their peers are good at interpersonal skills such as caring, sharing, and being helpful. They have strong verbal skills and self-control; most importantly, they exhibit empathy, perspective, taking and moral reasoning.[11]

So many of those ingredients are things you've learned from the principles and practices in this book. But there are a few other special ingredients you, as mom or dad, are best at giving that will foster friendship and social intelligence too.

Teach Respect

Do your kids push and shove in a crowd to get where they want to go or be first in line? Do they take toys from other kids or refuse to share playground equipment? How do they value the ideas, time, property, and feelings of others in a group?

Learning to take turns and play cooperatively with others is as essential a social skill for success in kindergarten as it will be years later in keeping a job or presenting a business project or starting a company.

Joshua's frustrated parents and teacher learned this as early as his first week in kindergarten. Joshua bullied other kids to make them play the games he wanted, or build with blocks as he decided. When he didn't get his way, he snatched toys from others or knocked down what they were building. He shouted over kids when they tried to protest and wouldn't play by anyone else's rules or ideas.

Sadly, he didn't make any friends this way, and because he wasn't confronted or stopped, he went through school friendless. By high school,

Joshua was a frustrated, angry loner. As a young man, he's lost job after job, always for the same reason: being uncooperative and unrelenting in his way of doing things. He's never learned to play or work well with others. What's sad is things could have been so different. He could have learned the codes of conduct that show respect and acknowledged two important truths—everyone is someone, and you don't have to win or be right to be a winner. You can teach your kids what Joshua never learned by upholding these practices:

- **Listening without interruption.**

- **Acknowledging feelings.** Let your children know they don't have to agree with what others say, but they must value other's right to say it. Help them to let others know they understand feelings. Making it a practice to identify feelings in your relationship with your child will help them practice it in turn: "I see you are sad" or "I'm sorry you are angry."

- **Always using the courtesies of civilization,** saying *please, thank you, excuse me,* and *I'm sorry.*

- **Being on time and fully present.** That means show up when and where you must, and when you do, pay attention. Don't let your body be somewhere while your mind, ears, and eyes go somewhere else (like a daydream, the cell phone, or a computer).

Teach the Art of Conversation

There is an art, as well as skill, to talking with someone, Ruth Feldman and her colleagues found in a study that showed kids learn both from their parents.[12] The children of parents who made it a practice to carry on conversations with them did well in life, too, Feldman found. They developed more social competence and better negotiation skills over time, things that helped them not only make friends but get opportunities and jobs.

With your kids, focus on listening, sharing, and discussing. One preschool teacher asked her students' parents to work with their kids on SLANT at mealtime conversations:

- **Sit up straight** to help yourself pay attention.

- **Listen** with your ears, eyes, body, and mind. Lean in and focus.

- **Ask** questions and engage!

- **Nod to acknowledge,** not necessarily agree, that you hear someone.

- **Track the speaker.** Repeat back what you thought you've heard to make sure it's right. Follow what's said. Comment on it and add or share your own ideas.

Open Your Heart and Home

This is the pot where all the ingredients for social intelligence and building friendships can cook. When you make time and space for others, they will want to be there.

Younger children need you to structure their time together. Whether you've set an official play date or just agreed to watch the neighbor kids, specify activities or games for them as a way of teaching them how to interact: "You can play dress-up with this box of things," or make cookies, get books from the library, build a fort in the backyard, put together puzzles, make up and put on a play or puppet show (making puppets out of socks or paper sacks) where everyone gets to play a part.

The older your children get, you probably don't have to give them as many ideas for activities. They may want to ride bikes together, play catch or a sport, swing on playground equipment, or just talk.

In the process you will learn, and help your children discover, their friendship style: Do they love being part of groups? Would one child rather spend more time with one friend then two or more? You'll also learn the names of your child's friends, their personalities and values, who is influencing or a leader or follower.

In the process, you help your child see how to open their hearts to love and forgive, and be loved and forgiven. This is part of feeding your child's very soul—and that is the greatest gift a parent gives a child.

PARENTING TAKES CHURCH

With all that life throws at us, parents especially need a safe place where we can share our troubles and anxieties—and what a comfort to know there are places beyond our homes for this. I discovered an important one when my (now-deceased) husband and I decided to attend a group for couples at our church in Darien, Connecticut.

I'll never forget the group's meetings. Everyone was candid in ways I hadn't expected. One man, who had enjoyed a very successful career, shared how later in life he took a chance on starting a company with a captivating new product that soon failed. He and his family lost everything, resulting in bankruptcy. Our group responded with prayer, encouragement, and practical help. When a woman shared the diagnosis she'd received of breast cancer, a steady stream of prayer warriors knelt at her bedside and delivered casseroles to feed her hungry sons through the two-year battle. There was joy too, when another person confessed overcoming cocaine addiction, and two members who had been widowed fell in love and got married.

We shared some of our most intimate experiences in that group, and I'd never experienced such transparency, authenticity, and genuine openness. There was no chitchat or gossip, no judgment. There were no pretenses or keeping up with the Joneses. Instead, masks came off, hearts were laid bare. Feelings, fears, and failures were openly shared.

I immediately felt at home, and, surprisingly, for all the sadness met that evening, I was encouraged. We all were. This was a safe place. No fault or failing would be used against anyone, just every problem confronted with grace and dealt with lovingkindness.

If a parent needs anything in helping their children grow and thrive it is mercy, support, and prayer—all the things that feed your soul, and all that this special church group gave G.K. and I.

These are the things the right church family can give you, too, and that you in turn can give to another parent sorely in need. More than ever, with so many single parents or homes where both parents work outside the home, you need this infrastructure both practically and spiritually. Human families can take hits and break up, but God's family endures forever.

This is yet one more area where the Bible's wisdom and the best practices in psychology and counseling agree—and it's a big area because it regards eternity and your very soul.

The Bible says the church is made for the very purpose of encouraging you and stimulating you to good works (see Hebrews 10:24-25). Surveys and research over the past twenty years show what the Bible's always said, that, indeed, people who regularly attend religious services have wider and more intimate friendships and social circles, stronger feelings of support, even greater health and well-being (from better immune systems to lower blood pressure and longevity).[13]

In other words, church does a body, and a parent, good by:

- **Giving you support through groups, particularly those for parents (single and couples), children, and teens.** Most of these groups offer prayers for specific needs and issues, guidance, communities of like-minded people, resources, practical help, and fun activities for joy and even stress relief.

- **Helping you know God's will and ways.** Bible studies, conferences and retreats will equip you with knowledge of Bible principles and people like you who have struggled, doubted, stumbled, and searched for answers. Scripture will encourage you, help you navigate everyday situations, and remind you of God's promises—leaving you with peace, perspective, and hope. Sunday school, children's church, and activities for youth will help you raise your children in love through classes, Bible stories, action rhymes, songs, memory verses, finger plays and activities, games, and crafts. You will get relief and support while your kids are learning too as many churches offer parents their own time, Time Outs, if you will, for renewal while their kids are in classes.

- **Providing fellowship** as you worship God together in a company of believers—people you can sing with, serve, and join in giving love to God. This buoys your spirit in ways all the world acknowledges because even the non-religious know and can recite the Twenty-third Psalm, where David proclaims, "[God], you...comfort me…. Surely your goodness and love will follow me all the days of my life."

- **Creating harmony for your life.** When Stacy Horn was twenty-six years of age, she was divorced, in financial difficulty, and miserable. She decided to do one thing that might bring her joy, so she auditioned for the Choral Society of Grace Church in New York. Over the thirty years she sang in the choir her life improved dramatically. She found harmony not only by singing in the choir but with her relationships, finances, physical fitness, and work.[14] Praising God, Horn says, "is the one thing that never fails to take me where disenchantment is non-existent and feeling good is guaranteed." The very act of singing in tough times, like whistling in the dark, gets you through the valleys, she says. It's an act of defiance against all that's hard and a proclamation of faith in all that's good and uplifting. So it is with living the Christian life. A national survey found that people pursuing basic Christian values pertaining to faith, family, community, and work reported being the most fulfilled and happy.[15]

- **Assuring you of belonging and your place in the world in ways you were designed to receive.** There are no Lone Ranger Christians, Rich Warren explains in his best-selling book *The Purpose Driven Life* because you were designed to be part of the church as a sheep is part of the flock, as a hand or foot is part of the physical body.[16] You are needed and essential. You bring something to the whole that no one else does. You complete the church just as the church completes you. "As I have loved you, so you must love one another," Jesus said. "By this everyone will know that you are my disciples" (John 13:34-35). The church family provides a laboratory for learning to love one another. In Christian fellowship, you meet with one another. You share meals, feelings, and experiences. You shoulder grief together and partake of one another's joy. There is communion and strength, and you will find the confidence you need to be the best parent, in turn creating belonging for your children.

PARENTING TAKES GOD

There will be times in parenting when you've done all you could, when you've applied every principle in these pages, taken every step within your power, and yet still feel at your wits' end with your kids.

Days of trouble will come, the Bible warns (see Ecclesiastes 12:1). But you are not left to live in those troublesome times alone or without help.

Turning to God is the best thing you can do before practicing a single principle, and after you've begun working them all into your life and your children's—because your kids may cause you worry. They may rebel. There may be times they break your heart. But God wrote the book on knowing all that. He's the most astonishingly loving father, and his kids have been causing worry in this world, going their own way as prodigals, and breaking his heart for centuries.

Still, he loves us.

Still, he waits.

Still, he has faith in us.

He will show us how to truly love and wait and have faith in our kids. He will be there for them and us, whether the going gets tough or is joyful. He will show us what it means to be patient for what the Bible promises: "Train up a child in the way he should go, and [even] when he is old he will not depart from it" (Proverbs 22:6 NKJV).

The training God's talking about incorporates all these principles. Just as working on my golf game over the years got me to a place of playing with grace, ease, and joy, so will taking the positive steps in this book get you and your children to living in grace and with joy.

The Proverbs put it this way: You'll reap abundance (28:19), find riches (10:4), ultimately follow a smoother path (15:19), and develop an open heart to give selflessly to others (21:25-26). It's that sowing and reaping principle, choices and consequences.

When you choose to partner with God in parenting, you will have practiced the best step of all. A step of faith and a step of love.

"A new command I give you," Jesus tells us in John 13:34, "love one another. As I have loved you, so you must love one another."

It's a principle and practice that changed the world and can change you and your kids. I'm reminded of this every time I see many a mom whisper in her child's ear, "How much do I love you?" and then the child laughs and spreads their arms wide, "This much," then leans in for a hug.

This is how it is with God and why you need him for every step you take as a purposeful parent—because how much does he love us to see us through?

This much, he says, and when he spreads his arms wide it saves the world and you and your child, and it's way more than a hug.

MY PRAYER FOR PURPOSE

*G*od, *I want to be the best parent I can be—proactive and guiding my child, not just reacting to situations and circumstances. I need you to help me.*

You promise that I can do all things through Christ who strengthens me (Philippians 4:13 NKJV). Help me hold on to this promise even when my child melts down, and I feel like melting down too. Help me to look again to your power as greater than my child's will or high energy, stubbornness, or even rebellion. Help me to remember, as you promise in Second Corinthians 12:9, that I can do all I need to do as a parent by relying on your strength and not my own.

Help me to continually take things to you in prayer—to talk to you about my hopes, fears, failures, and dreams. Especially, Lord, help me...

- *to hope:*

_____

_____

_____

_____

■ *with these fears:*

_____

_____

_____

_____

■ *where I fail:*

_____

_____

_____

_____

■ *with my dreams for:*

_____

_____

_____

That means I need your help in listening for you and your guidance, in spending time with you, in connecting with you in prayer, in reading your Word to know your will and ways, in being faithful to fellowship with other Christians. That means, Lord, I especially ask you to watch over my children in these areas:

_____

_____

_____

_____

God, I'm grateful for you and your willingness to love me, discipline me, shape my character, show me how to be responsible, ignite and unleash my purpose and passion, and help me persevere. You practice such lovingkindness with me in all these things. Help me to practice lovingkindness with my children. Show me how I can love like you. Show them how they can love like you too.

In your name, Jesus, I pray. Amen.

Appendix

YOUR SKILLS AND ABILITIES CHECKLIST

Some skills and abilities are so taken for granted that we forget what a gift they truly are, things like being calm under pressure or ever-friendly. This checklist can help you consider things in your children that you might not have thought of as abilities.

Accurate	Common-sense oriented
Adaptable	Competent
Ambitious	Competitive
Analytical	Confident
Articulate	Considerate
Assertive	Consistent
Calm	Coordinating
Careful	Cooperative
Cheerful	Courteous
Clear thinking	Creative

Deadline oriented

Dedicated

Dependable

Driven

Diplomatic

Discreet

Eager

Energetic

Fair

Flexible

Focused

Friendly

Good listener

Hardworking

Humorous

Industrious

Leader

Likeable

Motivated

Organized

Polite

Positive

Prioritizing

Problem solver

Punctual

Quick learner

Reliable

Resourceful

Respectful

Self-reliant

Sincere

Sociable

Strategic

Supportive

Takes initiative

Team player

Troubleshooter

Trustworthy

Understanding

Unflappable

NOTES

INTRODUCTION. PARENTING TAKES THREE

1. Genesis 2:15-24.

2. Exodus 17:12.

3. Genesis 7:1-3,8.

4. John 14:25-26.

5. Mark 6:7, Luke 10:1.

6. Mary Parke, "Are Married Parents Really Better for Children? What Research Says about the Effects of Family Structure on Child Well-Being," *Couples and Marriage Research and Policy*, May 2003, for the Center for Law and Social Policy (CLASP), also available online at www.clasp.org; accessed November 13, 2014.

7. Christine Facciolo, "More than 2.5 million grandparents take on role of parent," *The (Wilmington, Del.) News Journal*, April 12, 2012; http://usatoday30.usatoday.com/news/health/wellness/story/2012-04 -12/rise-of-grandparents-grandfamilies/54206854/1; accessed November 11, 2014.

8. Richard Fry & Jeffery Passel, "In Post-Recession Era, Young Adults Drive Continuing Rise in Multi-generational Living," *Pew Research Social and Demographic Trends,* July 17, 2014.

CHAPTER 1. LOVE: MORE THAN A HUG

1. The song "Nature Boy" by [E]den [A]hbez, published in 1947, recorded by Nat King Cole, released by Capitol Records, catalog number 15054, reaching the Billboard charts on April 16, 1948, where it stayed for fifteen weeks peaking at No. 1.

2. Beethoven's Symphony No. 9 was one of the first by a major composer to combine symphonic and choral elements, and the words are rooted in the poem and song "Gegenliebe" ("Returned Love"). The symphony was Beethoven's statement to the world that more brotherhood and love could change everything.

3. The Taj Mahal topped the list of the New 7 Wonders of the World (2001-2007), an initiative started in 2001 to choose Wonders of the World from a selection of 200 existing monuments. The popularity poll was led by Canadian-Swiss Bernard Weber and organized by the New 7 Wonders Foundation based in Zurich, Switzerland, with winners announced on July 7, 2007, in Lisbon. The Taj Mahal is the undisputed symbol of eternal love, a mausoleum built in India in 1631 by Mughan emperor Shah Jahan to honor the memory of his third wife, Mumtaz Mahal. When she died giving birth to their fourteenth child, he was so grief-stricken that he ordered the construction of the tomb immediately, putting the entire nation into mourning for two years. When it was finally completed, the Shah was rumored to have had the chief mason's right hand chopped off to ensure that the Taj Mahal would remain one of a kind.

4. "Edward VIII and Wallis Simpson," Bio., http://www.biography.com/people/groups/edward-viii-and-wallis-simpson; accessed November 11, 2014.

5. David McCasland, *Eric Liddell: Pure Gold, A New Biography of the Scottish Olympic Hero and Missionary to China* (Grand Rapids, MI: Discovery House Publishers, affiliated with RBC Ministries, 2001, Kindle edition). It was love for God and for racing that drove Eric Liddell to win the 1924 Olympic gold medal for the United Kingdom in the 400-meter race. Odds were against Liddell before he even made the United Kingdom's Olympic team. A younger sister in their missionary family criticized Liddell's pursuit of the Olympics instead of focusing on becoming a missionary to China. Then, when trials for the race he had trained for, the 100-meter, were to be held on a Sunday, and Liddell's religious conviction would not permit him to race on the Sabbath, his own coaches underestimated him. He could never endure and succeed in the longer race, they said. But Liddell, swapping events with a team member did just that, so he could compete. Liddell told his sister, "I believe God made me for a purpose. But He also made me fast, and when I run I feel His pleasure."

6. Dr. Ross Campbell, *How to Really Love Your Child* (Wheaton, IL: Victor Books, 1977).

7. Proceedings of the National Academy of Sciences Early Edition, "Maternal support in early childhood predicts larger hippocampal volumes at school age" by Joan L. Luby, Deanna M. Barch, Andy Belden, Michael S. Gaffrey, Rebecca Tillman, Casey Babb, Tomoyuki Nishino, Hideo Suzuki, and Kelly N. Botteron; edited by Marcus E. Raichle, Washington University in St. Louis, MO (January 4, 2012). Published online before print (January 30, 2012); http://www.pnas.org/content/109/8/2854.full.pdf+html; accessed November 11, 2014.

8. Nikolas Kristoff, "Cuddle Your Kid!" *The New York Times*, October 20, 2012; in a report drawing from the abstract "What Do Growing Childhood Socioeconomic Inequalities Mean for the Future of Inequalities in Adult Health?" by John Robert Warren, Minnesota Population Center, Department of Sociology, University of Minnesota (March 2012).

9. Jim Dryden, "Mom's love good for child's brain," Washington University in St. Louis Newsroom press release, January 30, 2012; http://news.wustl.edu/news/Pages/23329.aspx; accessed November 11, 2014.

10. "Mind Games" lyrics by John Lennon from the single released in 1973 on the 1969 album by the same title, *Mind Games,* from Apple Records in the United Kingdom. The song also is heard in the Beatles' *Let It Be* sessions, and was originally titled "Make Love Not War."

11. Susan Smalley, "The Power of Words," *The Huffington Post,* January 17, 2008.

12. William and Nancie Carmichael, *Lord, Love My Child* (Camp Sherman, OR: Deep River Books, 2012).

13. John Trent and Gary Smalley, *The Blessing* (Nashville: Thomas Nelson, 1986).

14. "Dethroning" is the term psychologist Alfred Adler used in 1927 to describe the diminished sense of place one child feels when another is brought into the home and given more attention. Mary Renck Jalongo, editor, *Enduring Bonds: The Significance of Interpersonal Relationships in Young Children's Lives,* part of the series Educating the Young: Advances in Theory and Research, Implications for Practice (Indiana, PA, University of Pennsylvania and New York: Springer-Science+Business Media, LLC, 2008), 76-77.

15. Sharon Jayson, "Mom's favoritism can affect kids, sibling rivalry as adults," *USA Today,* May 5, 2010; http://usatoday30.usatoday.com/news/health/2010-05-04-favorites04_CV_N.htm; accessed November 12, 2014.

16. The phrase or adage "Perception is reality" has been attributed in 1989 to Lee Atwater, chairman of the National Republican Committee, in the television documentary *Boogie Man: The Lee Atwater Story* from Stefan Forbes (director) and N. Walker (producer) for *Frontline,* PBS (Boston, MA: Inter Positive Media, November 8, 2011).

17. Jesus taught what has become known as the Golden Rule (recorded in the Gospel accounts of Matthew 7:12 and Luke 6:31), though a form appears in the Ten Commandments in the Old Testament (Leviticus 19:18 says, "love your neighbor as yourself"), and in the texts and literature of nearly every other religion and culture around the world. Citations are listed online in *World Scripture: A Comparative Anthology of Sacred Texts* by Dr. Andrew Wilson (editor) for the International Religious Foundation (1991) at http://www.unification.net/ws/theme015.htm; accessed November 12, 2014.

18. Active listening solutions based on combined ideas from Adele Faber and Elaine Mazlish in their books *How to Talk So Kids Will Listen and Listen So Kids Will Talk* (New York: Scribner, a division of Simon & Schuster, Inc., 1980, 1999, 2012) and *Siblings without Rivalry: How to Help Your Children Live Together So You Can Too* (New York: W.W. Norton & Company, Inc., 1987, 1998, 2012).

19. Gary Chapman, *The Other Side of Love: Handling Anger in a Godly Way* (Chicago: Moody Press, 1999), 11-13.

20. Diane Salvatore, "Can This Marriage Be Saved?" *The New York Times*, August 26, 2007; http://query.nytimes.com/gst/fullpage.html?res=9400E2D8113FF935A1575BC0A9619C8B63; accessed November 12, 2014.

21. Management of anger, considered a major stressor, addressed in "Exercise and stress: Get moving to manage stress," Mayo Clinic Staff, http://www.mayoclinic.com/health/exercise-and-stress/SR00036; accessed November 11, 2014.

22. Robert K.G. Temple, ed., Olivia Temple, trans., *Aesop: The Complete Fables*, "The Wasp and the Snake," (New York: Penguin Classics, 1998).

23. Kim Hubbard, "Touched by Diana," *People* magazine, February 2, 1998 also online at http://www.people.com/people/archive/article/0,,20124388,00.html; accessed November 12, 2014.

24. "Diana: Legacy of a Princess, A Royal Exhibition" aboard the Queen Mary (Sun Deck Gallery, Bow, Starboard Side) in Long Beach Harbor, CA, August 2012; http://www.queenmary.com/diana-collection.php; accessed November 11, 2014.

CHAPTER 2. DISCIPLINE: TEACH
THE CHILD YOU TREASURE

1. "Two Wolves, a Cherokee Legend," First People: Native American Indian Legends website; http://www.firstpeople.us/FP-Html-Legends/ TwoWolves-Cherokee.html; accessed November 12, 2014.

2. Diana Baumrind, "Childcare practices anteceding three patterns of preschool behavior," Genetic Psychology Monographs 75, no. 1 (1967), and *"Current Patterns of Parental Authority," Developmental Psychology Monograph 4,* no. 1 (1971).

3. Gershoff, E.T., "Parental corporal punishment and associated child behaviors and experiences: A meta-analytic and theoretical review," *Psychological Bulletin 128,* no. 4 (2002): 539-579.

4. Stanley Coppersmith, *The Antecedents of Self-Esteem: A Series of Books in Behavioral Science* (Mishawaka, MN: W.H. Freeman & Company, 1968).

5. Jane E. Brody, "Better Discipline? Train Parents, Then Children," *The New York Times,* December 3, 1991,; http://www.nytimes.com/ 1991/12/03/science/better-discipline-train-parents-then-children .html; accessed November 12, 2014.

6. Ibid.

7. Dr. Michael K. Meyerhoff and Dr. Burton L. White, "Making the Grade as Parents," *Psychology Today,* September 1986, 38ff.

8. Jeffrey Gitomer, *The Little Red Book of Selling* (Austin, TX: Bard Press, 2004).

9. Claire B. Kopp, *Baby Steps: A Guide to Your Child's Social, Physical, Mental and Emotional Development in the First Two Years* (New York: Owl Books, Holt Paperbacks, 2003; first published by W.H. Freeman & Company, 1994).

10. Daniel H. Pink, *Drive: The Surprising Truth about What Motivates Us* (New York: Riverhead Books, 2009).

11. Alan E. Kazdin, MD, *The Kazdin Method for Parenting the Defiant Child* (New York, First Mariner Books, Random House, 2009).

12. Ibid.

13. Rebecca R. Socolar, MD, "Spanking Children Is In Even Though It's Out," *The New York Times,* January 15, 1995), http://www.nytimes .com/1995/01/15/us/spanking-children-is-in-even-though-it-s-out.html; accessed November 12, 2014.

14. Dr. Irwin A. Hyman, "Education; Parents and Teachers Split on Spanking," *The New York Times,* August 16, 1989, http://www .nytimes.com/1989/08/16/us/education-parents-and-teachers-split-on -spanking.html; accessed November 12, 2014.

15. Rudolf Dreikurs, MD, with Vicki Soltz, RN, *Children: The Challenge: The Classic Work on Improving Parent-Child Relations* (New York: Plume/Penguin Books, 1990; Hawthorn Books, 1964.)

16. Dr. Lawrence Kutner, "Parental Differences on Discipline," *Times Daily*, September 28, 1989, quoting Dr. Darwin Dorr, Duke University, Durham, North Carolina; http://news.google.com/ newspapers?nid=1842&dat=19890928&id=BFQeAAAAIBAJ&sjid =EcgEAAAAIBAJ&pg=1980,5139000; accessed November 12, 2014.

17. Jane E. Brody, "Better Discipline? Train Parents, Then Children," *The New York Times*, December 3, 1991, http://www.nytimes.com/ 1991/12/ 03/science/better-discipline-train-parents-then-children.html; accessed November 12, 2014.

18. Naomi Mezey and Cornelia T. Pillard, "Against the New Maternalism," *Michigan Journal of Gender & Law 18,* no. 2 (2012).

19. H. Norman Wright, "Change is Difficult but Possible" in *How to Get Along with Almost Anyone: A Complete Guide to Building Positive Relationships with Family, Friends, Co-Workers* (Dallas, TX: Word, 1989; Thomas Nelson, 1991); also online (on page 3); http://www .ittechnology.co.uk/fcg/reflections/How%20to%20Get%20Along %20With%20%20Anyone.pdf; accessed November 13, 2014.

CHAPTER 3. PURPOSE AND PASSION: GIVE THEM THE WORLD

1. Rick Warren, *Raising Your Kids without Raising Your Blood Pressure: Study Guide* and accompanying A Three-Session Video-Based Study for Small Groups (Lake Forest, CA: Saddleback Church, 2011), 20.

2. Ken Robinson, and Lou Aronica, *The Element: How Finding Your Passion Changes Everything* (New York: Viking, 2008).

3. Ibid.

4. Ezra Meeker, *Trip through the Natchess Pass: Pioneer Reminiscences of Puget Sound* (Seattle, WA: Lowman and Hanford, 1905), 90-131 as rewritten from recollections, notes, and stories in his 1854 journal. Also online (page 15) of the excerpt; http://www.nachestrail.org/ media/pdf/6-MEEKER%201854%20Chapters%20of%20Trip %20Through%20Natchess%20Pass.pdf; accessed November 13, 2014.

5. James R. Campbell, *Raising Your Child to be Gifted: Successful Parents Speak!* (Cambridge, MA: Brookline Books/Lumen Editions, 1999).

6. Fr. Brian Cavanaugh, "Your Created Goodness: Developing and Improving a Positive Attitude and Healthy Self-Worth, A Concept for Spiritual Wellness"; *AppleSeeds*, October 2010, http://www.appleseeds .org/Your-Created-Goodness.htm; accessed November 13, 2014.

7. Online, you can use the free HumanMetrics Jung Typology Test™ for organizations and professionals to test personality: http://www .humanmetrics.com/cgi-win/jtypes2.asp; accessed November 13, 2014. The seventy-two question test takes only a few minutes to complete and scores are calculated automatically in seconds.

8. Mihaly Csikszentmihalyi, *Flow: The Psychology of Optimal Experience* (New York: HarperPerennial Modern Classics, 2008).

9. David McCasland, *Eric Liddell: Pure Gold, A New Biography of the Olympic Champion who Inspired Chariots of Fire.*

10. The National Association for Education in Young Children (NAEYC), in its "Call for Excellence in Early Childhood Education," based on years of research, shows how opportunities, experiences, education, and attention help uncover a child's natural gifts, talents, and abilities to emerge clearly before age eight. Summary online; http://www.naeyc .org/policy/excellence; accessed November 13, 2014.

11. Philip Galanes, "Sex? Yes. The City? Yes. But Things Have Changed: Allison Williams and Cynthia Nixon Talk About 'Girls' and 'Sex and the City,'" *The New York Times*, Fashion & Style, Table for Three (January 17, 2014); http://www.nytimes.com/2014/01/19/fashion/ Allison-Williams-Cynthia-Nixon-Girls-Sex-and-the-City.html?_r=0; accessed November 13, 2014.

12. "The Player: NFL Super Agent Drew Rosenhaus," interview with correspondent Scott Pelley (Robert Anderson and Nicole Young, producers) on *Sixty Minutes*, CBS News (September 12, 2012); http:// www.cbsnews.com/news/the-player-nfl-super-agent-drew -rosenhaus-16-09-2012/; accessed November 13, 2014.

13. G. Bruce Smith, "A Fantasia Experience: 65 Gifted Children Chosen to Attend Camp as Members of the Disney Young Musicians Symphony Orchestra," *Los Angeles Times,* July 26, 1992; http://articles .latimes.com/1992-07-26/entertainment/ca-5131_1_disney-young -musicians-symphony-orchestra; accessed November 13, 2014.

14. Benjamin S. Bloom, *Developing Talent in Young People* (New York: Ballantine Books, 1985).

15. Mike Wallace on *Sixty Minutes*, CBS News (November 24, 1991); http://www.youtube.com/watch?v=5oYAUjT2hqo; accessed November 13, 2014.

16. Brad Darrach, "Celebration of a Father: Barbra Streisand Resurrects Her Past in Her Hit Movie *Yentl,* and, at 41, Comes to Terms with Life and Loving," *People,* December 12, 1983, Volume 20, No. 24); http://www.people.com/people/archive/article/0,,20086553,00.html; accessed November 13, 2014.

17. Rick Warren, *Help Each Other with Your Faith: 40 Days of Love,* "You Can't Fully Understand," Daily Hope Radio Teaching Series (2/13/14); online audibly, free for download, at https://itunes.apple.com/us/podcast/daily-hope-rick-warren-podcast/id631094342?mt=2; accessed November 13, 2014.

18. Nicholas Wade, "Cloning and Stem Cell Work Earns Nobel," *The New York Times,* October 8, 2012, http://www.nytimes.com/2012/10/09/health/research/cloning-and-stem-cell-discoveries-earn-nobel-prize-in-medicine.html?_r=0; accessed November 13, 2014.

19. "Sir John B. Gurdon, The Novel Prize in Physiology or Medicine 2012, Autobiography, Education," Ganga Library, Inc.; http://www.gangalib.org/gurdon.php; accessed November 13, 2014.

20. Cindy Y. Rodriguez, "Caine's Arcade: 9-Year-Old Boy Builds His Own Cardboard Arcade," *The Huffington Post* (April 11, 2012); http://www.huffingtonpost.com/2012/04/11/caines-arcade-9-year-old-boy-cardboard-arcade-documentary_n_1414949.html; accessed November 13, 2014.

21. Caine's Arcade website, http://cainesarcade.com/; accessed November 13, 2014.

22. George H. Reavis, "The Animal School," originally written as curriculum for Cincinnati Public Schools where he was the assistant superintendent in the 1940s; offered to public domain via The Administration of the School Curriculum with References to Individual Differences; http://agsc.tamu.edu/384/AnimalSchool.pdf; accessed November 13, 2014. Also in illustrated picture book form (Peterborough, NH: Crystal Springs Books, 1999).

23. Tom Schulman, writer, Peter Weir, director, *The Dead Poets Society* (Touchstone Pictures, 1989).

24. Walt Whitman, "O Me! O Life!" in *Leaves of Grass* (New York: William E. Chapin, 1867 edition, reedited vastly from the 1860 edition).

25. John Strachan, *The Poems of John Keats: A Routledge Literary Sourcebook*, "Keats and Reality" from John Bayley (London: Routledge, an imprint of Taylor & Francis Group, 2003), 49. Also "The Vale of Soul-Making," a letter from poet John Keats to his brother and sister-in-law, George and Georgiana Keats (Sunday 14 February-Monday 3 May 1819); http://www.mrbauld.com/keatsva.html; accessed November 13, 2014.

26. Neal Halfon, Director of the University of California (Los Angeles: UCLA Center for Healthier Children, Families, and Communities).

27. "Childhood Obesity Facts" and "Health Effects of Childhood Obesity," U.S. Center for Disease Control and Prevention, National Center for Chronic Disease Prevention and Health Promotion, Division of Adolescent and School Health (October 20, 2008).

28. Dennis Cauchon, "Childhood pastimes are increasingly moving indoors," *USA Today,* July 12, 2005, http://usatoday30.usatoday .com/news/nation/2005-07-11-pastimes-childhood_x.htm; accessed November 13, 2014.

29. F. Thomas Juster, Hiromi Ono, Frank P. Stafford, "Changing Times of American Youth: 1981-2003, Child Development Supplement," Institute for Social Research (Ann Arbor, MI: University of Michigan, November 2004); http://ns.umich.edu/Releases/2004/Nov04/teen _time_report.pdf; accessed November 13, 2014.

30. Steven J. Holmes, *Young John Muir: An Environmental Biography* (Madison, WI: University of Wisconsin Press, 1999).

31. Steve Jobs in prepared text of commencement address he delivered at Stanford University on June 12, 2005, printed in the *Stanford Report* (June 14, 2005).

CHAPTER 4. CHARACTER: SHAPE THEIR SOULS

1. "Poll: Clinton's approval rating up in wake of impeachment," CNN .com (December 1998); http://www.cnn.com/ALLPOLITICS/ stories/1998/12/20/impeachment.poll/; accessed November 13, 2014. Russ Baker, "Portrait of a Political Pit Bull," Salon.com (December 22, 1998); http://www.russbaker.com/archives/pit%20bull%20all .htm; accessed November 13, 2014. Also, *Vanity Fair* editors, "Monica Lewinsky Writes about Her Affair with President Clinton, *Vanity Fair* magazine (May 6, 2014); http://www.vanityfair.com/online/ daily/2014/05/monica-lewinsky-speaks; accessed November 13, 2014.

2. Michael S. Josephson, founder and president of the Josephson and Edna Josephson Institute, Center for Youth Ethics and of Character Counts Coalition in "The 1996 Report on the Ethics of American Youth."

3. Ibid., "The 2012 Report Card on the Ethics of American Youth"; http://charactercounts.org/pdf/reportcard/2012/ReportCard-2012 -DataTables-HonestyIntegrityCheating.pdf; accessed November 13, 2014.

4. Ashley Fantz, Lindsey Knight, Kevin Wang, "A closer look: How many Newton-like school shootings since Sandy Hook," *CNN News,* June 19, 2014, http://www.cnn.com/2014/06/11/us/school-shootings-cnn -number/; accessed November 13, 2014. Also "Timeline of Worldwide School and Mass Shootings: Gun-related tragedies in the U.S. and around the world," Pearson Education Publishing; http://www .infoplease.com/ipa/A0777958.html; accessed November 13, 2014.

5. Mark Schwahn, writer, and Greg Prange, director, "With Tired Eyes, Tired Minds, Tired Souls, We Slept," One Tree Hill (Season Three, Episode 16, first aired March 1, 2006), The WB television network; http://en.wikipedia.org/wiki/With_Tired_Eyes,_Tired_Minds,_Tired_Souls,_We_Slept; accessed November 13, 2014.

6. Jiminy Cricket is the character created by Ward Kimball for the 1940 Walt Disney film *Pinocchio,* based on the unnamed cricket originally created by Carlo Collodi in *The Adventures of Pinocchio*, first serialized in a newspaper in Rome 1881-1882, then in book form in 1883, revised and reissued many times over the following ten years by various publishers.

7. Mark Wheeler, "Be happy: Your genes may thank you for it," UCLA Newsroom, July 29, 2013, University of California Los Angeles; summary online: http://newsroom.ucla.edu/releases/don-t-worry-be-happy-247644; accessed November 13, 2014.

8. Ibid.

9. "Research Shows that Spiritual Maturity Process Should Start at a Young Age," November 7, 2003, 2009, The Barna Group, Ltd., Ventura, CA; https://www.barna.org/barna-update/article/5-barna-update/130-research-shows-that-spiritual-maturity-process-should-start-at-a-young-age#.VEL0tPnF8no; accessed November 13, 2014.

10. Erik H. Erikson, *Childhood and Society* (New York: W.W. Norton & Company, 1950, 1963, 1985, 1993).

11. Ross Campbell, MD, *Relational Parenting* (Chicago: Moody Press, 2000).

12. Harper Lee, *To Kill a Mockingbird* (Philadelphia: J.P. Lippincott and Company, 1960; also New York: HarperCollins, 1988), Part 1, Chapter 3.

13. Martin L. Hoffman, and editors W. Kurtines and J. Gerwitz, "Empathy Social Cognition, and Moral Action in Moral Action," *Moral Behavior and Development: Advances in Theory, Research and Applications* (New York: John Wiley and Sons, 1984).

PURPOSEFUL PARENTING

14. Marian Radke-Yarrow and Carolyn Zahn-Waxler, *Roots, Motives and Patterns in Children's Prosocial Behavior* (New York: Plenum, 1984).

15. Daniel N. Stern, *The Interpersonal World of the Infant* (New York: Basic Books, 1987), 30.

16. Jessica Lahey, "Teaching Children Empathy," *The New York Times* (September 4, 2014); http://parenting.blogs.nytimes.com/2014/09/04/teaching-children-empathy/?_php=true&_type=blogs&_r=0; accessed November 13, 2014.

17. "Acquiring Wisdom" video featuring Charles Stanley, InTouch Ministries (Sunday, February 24, 2013); http://www.intouch.org/resources/sermon-outlines/Content.aspx?topic=Acquiring_Wisdom_Sermon_Outline; accessed November 13, 2014. And http://www.intouch.org/broadcast/video-archives/content/topic/acquiring_wisdom_video; accessed November 13, 2014.

18. "Toward a State of Esteem," The Final Report of the California Task Force to promote Self-Esteem and Personal and Social Responsibility (January 1990).

19. Jean Piaget, *The Origins of Intelligence in Children* (New York: International University Press, 1952).

20. Suniya S. Luthar and Shawn J. Latendresse, "Children of the Affluent: Challenges of Well-Being," *Current Directions in Psychological Science* (August 14, 2007); online at the U.S. National Library of Medicine and National Institutes of Health at http://www.ncbi.nlm.nih.gov/pmc/articles/PMC1948879/; accessed November 13, 2014.

21. D.J. Stayton, R. Hogan, and M.D. Ainsworth, "Infant obedience and maternal behavior: The origins of socialization reconsidered," *Child Development* 42 (1971): 1057-1069.

22. M.W. Berkowitz, and J.H. Grych, "Fostering Goodness: Teaching parents to facilitate children's moral development," *Journal of Moral Education* 27 (1998): 371-391.

23. Evelyn Holt Otten and the Indiana Department of Education, *Developing Character through Literature* (Bloomington, Indiana: ERIC Clearinghouse on Reading, English, and Communication and Indiana University, with The Family Learning Association, 2002).

24. "High Mileage Moms—The Report," Surface Transportation Policy Project (Washington, DC, 1996-2014).

25. Edward M. Hallowell, *The Childhood Roots of Adult Happiness* (New York: Ballantine Books, 2002).

26. Ibid.

27. J. Richard Udry of the University of North Carolina for the National Longitudinal Study of Adolescent Health, "The State of Our Nation's Youth," Horatio Alger Association, a nonprofit organization (Alexandria, VA: November 2001).

28. Betty Black, Department of Child and Family Studies, University of Wisconsin, Madison, "Social Status and Patterns of Communication and Unacquainted Preschool Children," *Developmental Psychology 26*, no. 3 (1990): 379-387.

29. Rick Warren, *Daily Hope with Rick Warren* devotional (June 5, 2013); www.rickwarren.org.

CHAPTER 5. RESPONSIBILITY: "I'VE GOT THIS"

1. Kate Bayless, "What Is Helicopter Parenting," *Parents* magazine (2013); http://www.parents.com/parenting/better-parenting/what-is-helicopter-parenting/; accessed November 14, 2014.

2. "Helicopter parent" was first used as a term in 1969 by Dr. Haim Ginott in his best-selling book *Between Parent & Teenager* (Macmillan, 1965, 1988, page 18) where a teen complains, "Mother hovers over me like a helicopter." The term became so commonly understood that it entered the Merriam-Webster Dictionary of Britannica Encyclopedia in 2011.

3. Eli J. Finkel and Gráinne M. Fitzsimmons, "When Helping Hurts," *The New York Times*, May 10, 2013, on the study "Helping or Hovering? The Effects of Helicopter Parenting on College Students' Well-Being" by Holly H. Shiffrin et. al. at the University of Mary Washington, and published in the *Journal of Child and Family Studies 23*, no. 3 (2014): 548-557.

4. Michele Borba, *Parents Do Make a Difference: How to Raise Kids with Solid Character, Strong Minds, and Caring Hearts* (Hoboken, NJ: Jossey-Bass, 1999), xv-xvii.

5. Commonly attributed to Benjamin Franklin.

6. Alan Alda interview with Michael Gazzaniga, one of the world's leading brain scientists; Jim McGaugh, of the University of California, Irvine; noted memory researcher Dan Schacter; Harvard Medical School's Bob Stickgold; and Helen Neville, of the University of Oregon, "The Man with Two Brains: Remembering What Matters," Scientific American *Frontiers*, PBS (December 2009); transcript online at http://www.pbs.org/saf/transcripts/transcript703.htm#1; accessed November 14, 2014.

7. Michael Rutter, *Fifteen Thousand Hours: Secondary School and Their Effects on Children* (Cambridge, MA: Harvard University Press, 1979, 1982).

8. George E. Vaillant, MD, *Triumphs of Experience: The Men of the Harvard Grant Study* (Cambridge, MA: Belknap Press, Harvard University, 2012).

9. Ibid.

CHAPTER 6. PERSEVERANCE: NEVER GIVE INP

1. Watty Piper (the pen name of Arnold Munk), *The Little Engine that Could* (New York: Platt & Munk, 1954). Munk acknowledged on the copyright page: "Retold by Watty Piper from *The Pony Engine* by Mabel C. Bragg, copyrighted 1930 by George H. Doran and Co." However, in a recent book, Roy E. Poltnik's *In Search of Watty Piper:*

The History of The Little Engine Story (New Review of Children's
Literature Librarianship, 18, 2012), pages 11-26, Bragg insisted "the
story belonged to the realm of literature." The story behind the origins
of this story is also printed online by Plotnik for the University of
Illinois at Chicago, at http://tigger.uic.edu/~plotnick/littleng.htm;
accessed November 14, 2014.

2. Daniel H. Pink, *Drive: The Surprising Truth about What Motivates Us*
    (New York: Penguin Group Inc., 2009), 189.

3. Edward L. Deci and Richard M. Ryan, "Facilitating Optimal
    Motivation and Psychological Well-Being Across Life's Domains,"
    Canadian Psychology 49, no. 1 (2008): 14; also online at the
    American Psychological Association website http://psycnet.apa.org/
    psycinfo/2008-03783-002; accessed November 14, 2014.

4. Daniel H. Pink, *Drive: The Surprising Truth about What Motivates Us,*
    106.

5. Ibid., 90-91.

6. Mihaly Csikszentmihalyi, *Beyond Boredom and Anxiety: Experiencing
    Flow in Work and Play*, Twenty-fifth Anniversary Edition (San
    Francisco: Jossey-Bass, 2000), XIX.

7. Ibid.

8. Daniel H. Pink, *Drive: The Surprising Truth about What Motivates Us.*

9. Robert Brooks and Sam Goldstein, *Raising Resilient Children: Fostering
    Strength, Hope, and Optimism in Your Child* (New York: McGraw-Hill,
    2001).

10. Michael J. Gelb, *How to Think Like Leonardo da Vinci: Seven Steps
    to Genius Every Day*, Part II, Curiostá (New York: Dell, a division of
    Random House, 1998).

11. Sara Truebridge, *Resilience Begins with Beliefs: Building on Student
    Strengths for Success in Schools* (New York: Teachers College Press,
    2014), 1-23, 68-69, 73-75.

12. Jack Zenger and Joseph Folkman, "The Ideal Praise-to-Criticism Ratio," *Harvard Business Review,* March 15, 2013, http://blogs.hbr .org/2013/03/the-ideal-praise-to-criticism/; accessed November 14, 2014.

13. Paul Tough, "What if the Secret to Success Is Failure?" *The New York Times Magazine,* September 14, 2011; http://www.nytimes.com/ 2011/09/18/magazine/what-if-the-secret-to-success-is-failure.html ?pagewanted=all&_r=0; accessed November 14, 2014.

14. Ashley Merryman, "Losing Is Good for You," *The New York Times,* September 24, 2013; http://www.nytimes.com/2013/09/25/opinion/ losing-is-good-for-you.html; accessed November 14, 2014.

15. Renee Jacques, "Sixteen Wildly Successful People Who Overcame Huge Obstacles to Get There," *The Huffington Post,* September 25, 2013, updated February 13, 2014; http://www.huffingtonpost .com/2013/09/25/successful-people-obstacles_n_3964459.html; accessed November 14, 2014.

16. James W. Stigler and Harold W. Stevenson, "How Asian Teachers Polish Each Lesson to Perfection," *American Educator,* Spring 1991, http://intlschool.org/storage/pdf-files-initial/stigler_asian-teachers.pdf; accessed November 14, 2014.

17. Carol S. Dweck, *Self-Theories: Their Role in Motivation, Personality, and Development* (Philadelphia: Psychology Press, 1999), 17.

18. Carol S. Dweck, *Mindset: The New Psychology of Success* (New York: Ballantine Books, 2006).

19. Ibid.

20. Po Bronson, "How Not to Talk to Your Kids: The inverse power of praise," *New York* magazine, August 3, 2007; http://nymag.com/news/ features/27840/; accessed November 15, 2014.

21. Carol S. Dweck, *Mindset: The New Psychology of Success.* (New York: Ballantine Books, 2006).

22. Ibid.

23. G.P. Latham, *Work Motivation: History, Theory, Research and Practice,* (Thousand Oaks, CA: Sage, 2006).

24. Paul Tough, *How Children Succeed: Grit, Curiosity, and the Hidden Power of Character* (New York: Houghton Mifflin Harcourt, 2012), 76.

25. Ibid.

26. Christopher Peterson and Martin Seligman, *Character Strengths and Virtues: A Handbook and Classification* (New York: American Psychological Association and Oxford University Press, 2004).

27. Tovia Smith, "Does Teaching Kids to Get 'Gritty' Help Them Get Ahead?," NPR, March 17, 2014; also online in audio and print http://www.npr.org/blogs/ed/2014/03/17/290089998/does-teaching-kids-to-get-gritty-help-them-get-ahead; accessed November 15, 2014.

28. Sandra Aamodt, and Sam Wang, *Welcome to Your Child's Brain: How the Mind Grows from Conception to College* (New York: Bloomsbury Publishers, 2012).

29. Paul Tough, *How Children Succeed: Grit, Curiosity, and the Hidden Power of Character,* 17.

30. Celeste Kidd, Holly Palmeri, and Richard N. Aslin, "Rational snacking: Young children's decision-making on the marshmallow task is moderated by beliefs about environmental reliability," *Elsevier 126,* no. 1 (2013): 109-114; http://www.sciencedirect.com/science/article/pii/S0010027712001849; accessed November 15, 2014.

31. Ibid.

32. Carol Craig, "A short history of self-esteem," The Centre Forum, Centre for Confidence and Well-Being, 2006; http://www.centreforconfidence.co.uk/pp/overview.php?p=c2lkPTYmdGlkPTAmaWQ9MTY0; accessed November 15, 2014.

33. Poet Edmond Rostand's play Cyrano de Bergerac, written and staged in 1897, Act I, Scenes i-iii.

34. Ibid.

35. Martin E.P. Seligman, PhD, *Learned Optimism: How to Change Your Mind and Your Life* (New York: First Vintage Books, Random House, 2006), Preface, iii.

36. Martin E.P. Seligman, *The Optimistic Child: A Proven Program to Safeguard Children Against Depression and Build Lifelong Resilience* (Boston: Houghton Mifflin Company, 2007).

37. Ibid.

38. Edna St. Vincent Millay, "First Fig," *A Few Figs from Thistles: Poems and Sonnets* (New York: Frank Shay, 1921), 9.

CONCLUSION. PARENTING TAKES A TEAM

1. James S. Coleman, *Equality of Education Opportunity: Data Sharing and Developmental Research,* Eunice Kennedy Shriver National Institute of Child Health and Human Development (NICHD), commissioned by the U.S. Department of Health, Education, and Welfare, 1966; www.icpsr.umich.edu/icpsrweb/ICPSR/studies/06389; accessed November 15, 2014.

2. James Reed Campbell, *Raising Kids to be Gifted* (Brookline Books, Cambridge MA, 1995), 19-24.

3. Ibid.

4. "Back to school: How parent involvement affects student achievement," The National Center for Education Statistics on Parent and Family Involvement in Education Survey for the 2007 National Household Education Surveys Program; http://www.centerforpubliceducation.org/Main-Menu/Public-education/Parent-Involvement/Parent-Involvement.html#sthash.iEwvgLx3.dpuf; accessed November 17, 2014.

5. James Reed Campbell, *Raising Kids to be Gifted,* 11.

6. Ibid.

7. Frances Goodrich, Albert Hackett, Jo Swerling, and Frank Capra in the film Capra directed and produced, *It's a Wonderful Life* (RKO Radio Pictures, 1946), based on the short story *The Greatest Gift* that Phillip Van Doren Stern wrote in 1939 and published privately in 1945.

8. Harry Stack Sullivan, *The Interpersonal Theory of Psychiatry* (New York: W.W. Norton & Company, 1997; reissued from the William Alanson White Psychiatric Foundation, 1953), showed, after a lifetime of research, the power of friendships in helping one develop well-being and health from childhood onward. His book was considered groundbreaking and definitive on the power of friendships for human development.

9. Roni Caryn Rabin, "Reading, Writing, 'Rithmetic and Relationships," *The New York Times,* December 20, 2010, also online at http://well .blogs.nytimes.com/2010/12/20/reading-writing-rithmetic-and -relationships/; accessed November 17, 2014.

10. Daniel Goleman, *Social Intelligence: The New Science of Human Relationships* (New York: Bantam Books, 2006), Prologue, 3-12.

11. M.K. Freitag, J. Belsky, K. Grossmann, K.E. Grossmann, and H. Scheurer-Englisch, "Continuity in parent-child relationships from infancy to middle childhood and relations with friendship competence," *Child Development 4* (1996): 1437-1454; also online at the U.S. National Library of Medicine and National Institute of Health at http://www.ncbi.nlm.nih.gov/pubmed/8890493; accessed November 17, 2014.

12. Ruth Feldman, E. Barnberger, and Y. Kanat-Maymon. "Parent-specific reciprocity from infancy to adolescence shapes children's social competence and diagnostic skills," *Attachment and Human Development* (London: Routledge, April 2, 2013), 407-423; also online at the U.S. National Library of Medicine and National Institutes of Health at http://www.ncbi.nlm.nih.gov/pubmed/23544455; accessed November 17, 2014.

13. Ellen L. Idler, "The Psychological and Physical Benefits of Spiritual/ Religious Practices," *Spirituality in Higher Education Newsletter 4,* no. 2 (2008):, 1. And Wallace, J.M. and T. Forman, "Religion's role in promoting health and reducing risk," *Health Education and Behavior* (Issue 25), 721-741.

14. Stacy Horn, *Imperfect Harmony: Finding Happiness Singing with Others* (New York: Algonquin Books, 2013).

15. Christopher G. Ellison and Linda K. George, "Religious Involvement, Social Ties, and Social Support in a Southeastern Community," *Journal for the Scientific Study of Religion 33* (1994): 46-61.

16. Rick Warren, *The Purpose Driven Life* (Grand Rapids, MI: Zondervan, 2002), 133-135.

ACKNOWLEDGMENTS

This book is the culmination of my fifty-year career spanning kindergarten through high school in ten nationally-acclaimed school districts as a teacher, team leader, counselor, and school psychologist. It's impossible to recognize and thank the steady stream of so many teachers, parents, administrators, and professors with whom I've worked and learned from throughout these years. But I want to try.

I hold dear the experiences and family histories that were shared as youngsters and parents poured out their hearts to me. The case studies used here, although scrambled to keep confidentiality, enlighten the pages of this book. I am forever grateful and indebted to all the outstanding educators, loving parents, and beautiful children who have shared their lives with me and collaborated to solve problems and assure children's social-emotional and academic success.

I am thankful to my pastor, Rick Warren of Saddleback Church, for preaching on "The Decade of Destiny" that inspired me to pray and surrender the past decade of my productive life to Jesus Christ. As a result, I prayed and heard God whisper, "The book." Immediately, I understood.

Since the 1980s, I've been personally driven by passion to discover how Bible instruction and principles deemed as best practices in psychology intersect and connect to form optimal child-rearing practices—this book is the result of all my questioning and discovery.

I thank my son, Michael Van Dyck, not only for his fervent prayers, but also for spearheading this goal into action by contacting my literary agent Shannon Marven of Dupree Miller and Associates. I am extremely grateful to Shannon for believing, recognizing the potential, and setting the path to follow.

I am so very appreciative of Jeanette Thomason for wisdom, clarity of thought, and perseverance.

I am forever grateful to Stephen Arteburn and New Life Radio for championing the cause in so many ways to bring *Purposeful Parenting* to life. I thank Dr. Jill Hubbard of the New Life Radio team for sharing her keen, heartfelt insights regarding raising her own children that she shared in the Foreword.

I am grateful to Lacy Lynch for her tenacity and perseverance to make things happen.

I am so appreciative of Ronda Ranalli for her clarity of purpose while remaining flexible and understanding, and I thank Mykela Krieg and her team for their creative work in designing a book cover with zest and appeal. My gratitude to all the many others at Destiny Image Publishers who worked to get this message into your heart and hands.

I am deeply grateful for Alan Wild who graciously gave of his time and expertise to launch *Purposeful Parenting*

ABOUT THE AUTHOR

JEAN BARNES is a veteran educator and pioneer in recognizing the importance of teacher-parent collaboration for the benefit of children. She's worked in preschools through high schools in ten school systems across the country nationally recognized as "outstanding," and been hailed for her work as a school psychologist, counselor, teacher, and team leader.

After retiring in 1999 from twenty years at Fairfield Public Schools in Connecticut she moved to Orange County, California. There she served the Capistrano Unified School District as a school psychologist.

She pioneered the groundbreaking Family Growth seminars that rouses parents and teachers to work together for the benefit of children. Her model program in 1983 earned a grant by the State of Connecticut, was published in *Promising Practice in Special Education and Students Services,* and led to professional development seminars for psychologists and counselors. The second model program she created, Love and Discipline (1990), and the third that she inspired and helped shaped, The Teacher-Parent Connection (1997), were presented upon request and are recommended by the National Association of School Psychologists.

With ten years in the classroom and forty years total as an educator and as a mom in a variety of roles (married, divorced and raising young children on her own, and then remarried and widowed and parenting adult children), Jean Barnes knows what works for parents and children to grow together. And her knowledge, experience, and effective practices are trusted by parents.

She earned her bachelor's degree from the University of Wisconsin at Madison, a masters from the University of Cincinnati, and a Certificate of Advanced Graduate Study in psychology from Fairfield University. Her doctoral studies in marriage and family therapy, as well as human development at the University of Connecticut, shaped many of her principles that help children thrive.